# SPECIAL NEEDS ADOPTIONS

T0347434

GARLAND REFERENCE LIBRARY OF SOCIAL SCIENCE
VOLUME 1151

# SPECIAL NEEDS ADOPTIONS
## PRACTICE ISSUES

RUTH G. MCROY

Routledge
Taylor & Francis Group

LONDON AND NEW YORK

First published 1999 by Garland Publishing, Inc.

Published 2014 by Routledge
2 Park Square, Milton Park, Abingdon, Oxfordshire OX14 4RN
711 Third Avenue, New York, NY 10017

First issued in paperback 2014
*Routledge is an imprint of the Taylor & Francis Group, an informa business*

Library of Congress Cataloging-in-Publication Data

McRoy, Ruth G.
      Special needs adoptions : practice issues / by Ruth G. McRoy.
         p.    cm. — (Garland reference library of social science ; v. 1151)
      Includes bibliographical references and index.
      ISBN 978-0-8153-2776-9 (hbk)
      ISBN 978-1-1380-0430-6 (pbk)

      1. Special needs adoption—United States.   2. Older child adoption—
United States.   3. Adoption agencies—United States.   4. Family social
work—United States.   I. Title.   II. Series.
HV875.55.M392   1999
362.73'4'0973—dc21                     98-30946
                                                    CIP

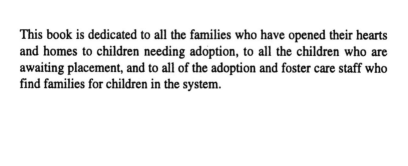

This book is dedicated to all the families who have opened their hearts and homes to children needing adoption, to all the children who are awaiting placement, and to all of the adoption and foster care staff who find families for children in the system.

# Contents

# Tables

# Preface

Although much has been written about outcomes of special needs adoptions, little examination has been undertaken on the unique practice issues associated with placing older special needs children in adoptive families. With the new federal mandate to double the number of children who are adopted or placed in permanent legal guardianships by the year 2002, it is more important than ever to study adoption outcomes from the perspective of public social service agency practice. This book presents the findings of a research project that was undertaken to identify practice issues that contributed to the following three types of adoption outcomes: intact placements (adoption finalized with no breakdown), disrupted placements (adoption breakdown before finalization of the adoption), and dissolved placements (adoption breakdown after finalization). Hopefully, the findings of this book will serve to call attention to the challenges of building families for the hundreds of thousands of children who are in foster care awaiting adoption.

We wish to acknowledge Pat Devin, Patsy Sanders-Buida, and Janis Brown for their initiation of this research project and for their dedication to achieving more positive outcomes in special needs adoptions in Texas. Their willingness to open files to outside assessments involves risk-taking, and we commend The Texas Department of Protective and Regulatory Services (TDPRS) for taking this risk in order to improve service delivery. Thanks also for their willingness to give permission to modify the report for publication.

Our gratitude also goes to the post-adoption service providers and adoption supervisors whom we interviewed. They provided excellent insights that aided in the development of our instruments and ongoing understanding of the issues involved in special needs adoptions.

Thanks to Cynthia Bargsley for her professionalism, help in obtaining cases, storing cases in her office, securing space for our staff to read cases, and being the frontline problem-solver. Another round of thanks goes to Janis Brown for her perseverance in obtaining cases for review from throughout the state. The TDPRS data management staff secured the original lists of potential cases and statistics for us, and we appreciate their time and effort. Chuck Gembenski, Jr., and the contracts division of TDPRS worked closely with us in the development of a workable contract, and we appreciate their perseverance.

Finally, thanks go to our research staff, whose intensive case readings, coding, data entry, analysis, and ongoing support made this study possible. Much gratitude for the hours of case reading and analysis goes to Susan Ayers-Lopez, Marilyn Gusukuma, Isaac Gusukuma, Victoria Johnson, Steve Onken, Chalandra Bryant, Cinda Christian, Lacey Sloan, Renee Escamilla, Judy Green, A. J. Ernst, Laura McDowell, and Patty Ducayet. We are deeply indebted to Patricia Brubaker, who volunteered countless hours to assist with this research project. Special thanks also to Dwight Brooks and Kelly Larson for computer consultation, to Sue Keskinen for data analysis, and to Marilyn Gusukuma for preparing the original report manuscript. Mollie Adams, Donna Newsome, Janine Saunders, Cassandra Moore, and Susan Ayers-Lopez have provided immeasurable help in proofing and editing the book manuscript. Deep appreciation goes to the following co-authors of several chapters in the book: Isaac Gusukuma and Steven Onken.

We also wish to acknowledge the very difficult nature of the tasks that caseworkers, supervisors, foster families, adoptive families, and post-adoption service providers are involved in daily. Over the past 10 years or so, many of the children coming into care have exhibited increasingly difficult behavioral problems, and we recognize how hard it is to keep up with all of the specialized knowledge needed to help families. We recognize that the availability of sufficient staff, funding, and service mandates can all influence effective child welfare service delivery.

We, as professional child welfare workers, academicians, and researchers are striving to understand the complicated dynamics in troubled birthfamilies and in special needs foster and adoptive families.

The observations and evaluations that are contained in this book are intended to help improve services to children and families. We, as researchers, do not hold all the answers, but we hope that an outside, objective look at practice and policy will serve as an impetus to enhance training opportunities for workers and families. A team approach between direct service practitioners, clinicians, supervisors, administrators, academicians, and researchers seems ideal to build knowledge continually, enhance child welfare practice, and improve the quality of life for the children in care.

# SPECIAL NEEDS ADOPTIONS

# CHAPTER 1

# Introduction

Placing children with special needs in adoptive families continues to be a challenge for child welfare professionals. The term "special needs adoptions" is generally associated with older children; sibling groups; children of color; and children with physical, emotional, or mental problems (Rosenthal, 1993). Frequently, the definition of a special need varies from state to state, and it depends upon the type of children the state has available for adoption (Pinderhughes, 1995) as well as the availability of families for those types of children.

Many of the children needing adoptive placement have been physically or sexually abused and/or neglected in their birthfamilies and are in out-of-home care in the nation's child welfare system. About 63% of children in the American foster care system are children of color. About 47% are African American, almost three times the percentage of African American children in the population at large (Washington, 1994).

The majority of the children placed in foster care come from birthfamilies who are poor. This does not mean that poverty causes neglect, but there is a higher likelihood that families with limited means will be reported for child neglect (DiLeonardi, 1993). Low-income families often live in dangerous environments characterized by lack of heat, exposure to lead paint, lack of proper sanitation, and overcrowded conditions. Other mediating factors such as psychological problems, poor parenting skills, and personal issues that result from coping with the stressors of poverty may impact the families. Parental alcohol or drug abuse, health problems, and social isolation may also be associated with the abuse and/or neglect (Pelton, 1989). These birthfamilies often do not have the resources to address the situational or personal factors that have led to child removal.

Once children are removed from their birthfamilies, the families are often offered educational or psychological services rather than the concrete and supportive services that many may desire to be able again to parent their children. These are families that clearly need help, but typically, the major service provided is child removal (Pelton, 1989).

While some children eventually return to their birthfamilies, others remain in foster care or some other form of substitute care. Once parental rights are terminated, many of these children are placed in adoptive families. Recruiting and selecting families to parent these children can be quite challenging, since many of these children, having been traumatized early in life, may have experienced painful separations from birthparents, siblings, and often several foster families while in care. Many express their anger, hurt, and loss through aggressive, acting-out behaviors. Disproportionately high rates of learning, behavioral, and personality problems have been found among this population (Brodzinsky, 1987). In an effort to find families for these children, many agencies consider "single, divorced, relatively uneducated, low income, disabled, parents over 40, parents already rearing large families, as well as two-career couples" (Sandmaier & Family Service of Burlington County, 1987, p. 5) as candidates for adoptive parenthood. Agencies are also now open to considering adoptions by foster parents and adoptions in which the family and child are of different ethnic backgrounds (transracial placements). These new practices represent significant shifts from the traditional placements of healthy white infants with two-parent, married couples (husband only working), who are usually less than 35 years of age. Despite these complexities in placements, the majority of special needs adoptions remain intact or stable.

Reports of disruption rates in special needs placements vary. The term "disruption" often is used to refer to all placements that result in the child's return to the agency, before or after consummation (Barth & Berry, 1988a; Glidden & Pursley, 1989; Hornby, 1986). Others distinguish between disruptions (occurring before finalization) and dissolutions (occurring after finalization) of the adoption (Festinger, 1990). In this book, both concepts will be utilized. Using data from four states and one New York county, the Urban Systems Research and Engineering (1985) estimated that the national rate of such problems ranged from 6% to 20%. Barth and Berry (1988a) reported a disruption rate of 10% in California; Rosenthal (1986) reported a rate of 12% in Oklahoma; and Partridge, Hornby, and McDonald (1986) calculated a rate of 8.6%. Rosenthal (1993) estimated that the national special needs adoption disruption rate is 10-15%.

Since for years successful special needs adoptions were considered next to impossible, at first glance these statistics may not seem too alarming. However, as we consider the many children and families whose lives have been adversely affected by failed adoptions, these disruption estimates are of major concern.

Most research to date has focused on child and family factors with limited attention to agency/worker factors leading to varying adoption outcomes. In an effort to improve child welfare service delivery to children in care and to families interested in adopting, this book presents the findings of a research project that took a very comprehensive examination of a large state agency's practices and child and family factors associated with outcomes in special needs adoptions. To contextualize the research, this introductory chapter presents a brief look at federal initiatives that have influenced special needs adoptions practice. Selected literature on adoption outcomes is reviewed in relation to the study presented in this book, and an overview of the subsequent chapters in the book is provided.

**BACKGROUND OF SPECIAL NEEDS ADOPTIONS**

Historically, the majority of prospective adoptive families has sought to adopt healthy, white infants. Children with "special needs" often grew up in foster care, as many believed these children were unadoptable. In 1961, there were approximately 166,000 children in out-of-home care (Newlin, 1997). However, later in the 1960s, the growing concern about "foster care drift" (children remaining in care for years) led to the advent of the permanency planning movement, in which agencies were encouraged either to reunify children with their families or to place them permanently through adoption (Nelson, 1985). Many states and parent advocacy groups launched campaigns to prove that families were indeed available for these children if legally freed for adoption (McKenzie, 1993).

In 1974, the passage of the Child Abuse Prevention and Treatment Act (P. L. 93-247) led to a significant increase in the identification of abused children, and consequently, there was a subsequent increase in the number of children entering foster care. By 1977, the number of children in out-of-home care had escalated to 502,000 (McKenzie, 1993). The first federal legislation specifically dealing with adoption (Hardy, 1984), Title II, was passed in 1978, and was designed to eliminate barriers to the adoption of special needs children. Public Law 96-266, the Adoption Opportunities Act of 1978, increased the federal role in funding adoption resources and established new post-adoption services and specialized minority adoption programs. For example, Public Law 96-266, the Adoption Opportunities Act of 1978, and Public Law 96-272, the Adoption Assistance and Child Welfare Act of 1980, were designed to increase federal funding and monitoring of foster care services. These initiatives mandated that reasonable efforts be made to preserve families, to reduce the child's time in foster care (through specific case plans, periodic case reviews, and disposition hearings), to find permanent adoptive homes for the child when needed, to provide for adoption subsidies and post-adoption services, and to establish minority adoption services and exchanges.

In previous years, since states would lose federal foster care match funding when a child went into a subsidized adoption, there was a disincentive to moving children out of foster care. The new legislation was designed to reduce new entrants into foster care and to prevent foster care drift. Case plans, tracking, and periodic case reviews were mandated to reduce the time children remained in care and to work toward family reunification. Intensive family preservation services were instituted in order to help reduce dependence on foster care and promote reunification with the family.

Additional federal initiatives were introduced in the 1980s, including the Adoption Opportunity Grants and the National Resource Center for Special Needs Adoptions to provide training for workers involved in special needs placements (Berry, 1994; McKenzie, 1993). As a result of all of these efforts, adoptive placements as well as family reunifications increased, and the number of children in foster care began to decrease. By 1986, there were about 280,000 children in the system, which was about 220,000 less than in 1977 (McKenzie, 1993).

In the late 1980s, however, foster care placements started to rise again as more infants and children of drug-addicted parents were removed from their birthfamilies due to abuse and neglect. The growing incidences of AIDS, teen parenthood, poverty, and violence also influenced the increase in children coming into care. According to statistics provided by the American Public Welfare Association, by

1992, approximately 429,000 children were in foster care (McKenzie, 1993).

Estimates in 1997 suggest that about 500,000 children were in care (Zumwalt, 1997), and approximately 100,000 will not be returning to their biological families. Barth (1997) suggests that this increase is due in large part to the low rate of discharging children from care, rather than the increase in foster care entrants.

Concomitant to the increase in the number of children in care, there has been a decrease in the number of foster families available to provide temporary care for these children. For example, in 1984, there were approximately 147,000 foster parents, but by 1990, the number had dropped to 100,000 (National Commission on Foster Family Care, 1991). The decline has been due in part to the growing economic necessity of dual earner households, the geographic mobility of families, and concerns about behavioral problems of children needing placement.

In response to some of these concerns, in 1993, the Family Preservation and Support Services Act (P. L. 103-66) was enacted by the federal government to require states to establish an integrated continuum of services for families at risk or in crisis, including reunification or permanency planning, pre-placement/preventive services, follow-up services, respite care, and parent skills training (Newlin, 1997).

In 1996, President Clinton announced a plan to double the number of children being placed in adoption or in permanent legal guardianships by the year 2002 (Child Welfare League of America, 1997). In order to accomplish this goal, Congress passed the Adoption and Safe Families Act of 1997. According to this act, the Department of Health and Human Services will set annual adoption targets for each state, and states will receive per child bonuses for placements made beyond their annual targets. Cash bonuses of $4,000 for each child adopted exceeding the previous year's number, and an additional $2,000 for each adoption of a child who is older or has some physical or emotional disability will be given by the federal government. Moreover, this federal legislation requires states to set up a permanent placement plan for a child after one year in care instead of the 18 months under current rules.

With the emphasis on decreasing the number of children in foster care and moving children more quickly toward permanence through adoption, greater attention must be placed on improving practice in special needs adoptions. Families must be found that are flexible enough to handle very difficult parenting challenges. Due to the varied degrees of childhood trauma experienced and older age at placement, special efforts are needed to recruit and train families to parent these children. Although the majority of special needs adoptions are stable, these placements are at much greater risk for problems than infant placements (Dickson, Heffron, & Parker, 1990).

It is possible that federal initiatives such as monetary incentives will serve to expedite adoptions, but unless current placement practices are examined, we may be creating a system in which children are placed too quickly, increasing the odds that the adoptions may disrupt or dissolve. This will be discussed further throughout the book.

## REVIEW OF SELECTED LITERATURE

### Adoption Disruptions and Dissolutions

A number of studies have examined factors associated with adoption disruptions and/or dissolutions of special needs placements. In a comprehensive review of research studies of adoption disruptions, Rosenthal (1993) noted that conflicting findings are evident on many factors presumed to be causing disruptions. For example, some studies suggest that factors such as child's gender, family income, educational level, ethnicity of adoptive parents, and specific behaviors of the child (such as sexual acting-out, stealing, and vandalism) may impact outcome. However, Rosenthal (1993) found the following factors to be more consistently associated with risk of disruption: "older child placements, inadequate background information or unrealistic parental expectations, rigidity in family functioning patterns, low levels of support from relatives or friends, history of physical and particularly sexual abuse prior to adoption, psychiatric hospitalization prior to adoption, acting-out, externalized behavioral problems and new placements rather than foster-adopt" (p. 82). Adoptions by foster parents, although for years discouraged in child welfare practice, have been found to increase the chances for an intact placement (Rosenthal, 1993).

Groze (1986) reviewed case records of 91 cases (13 dissolved) of special needs adoptions collected from a private, non-profit agency to assess child-related and family-related factors impacting outcome. He found that child's age was the best single predictor of disruption—the younger the child, the less chance for disruption. Presence of other children in the home, older age of the mother, and same-race placement were related to greater stability in adoptions. Second or subsequent placements for the child and higher income of the adoptive parents were related to more frequent disruption.

Barth and Berry (1988a) examined child, family, and agency factors that predicted disruptions. Factors such as older age of children, prior adoptive placement, non-foster parent adopters, special problems of the child, and higher education of the adoptive mother correctly predicted 70% of the disruptions. Unlike Groze, Barth found that child behaviors were better discriminators than age of child. Among the predictors of disruption that were associated with the characteristics of the adoptive family, other children in the home was the most important predictor of disruptions, and non-foster parent adoption was the next highest predictor. Other family predictors included fewer relatives in visiting distance, lack of contact with other foster or adoptive parents, higher education of adoptive mother, and lower frequency of church attendance. Impact of adoption on the family, comfort with adoption decision, and the development of positive personal interactions between parent and child also proved to be discriminating factors between disrupted and stable placements. Agency factors predicting disruption included whether information provided about the child was overly positive, greater stretch for adoptive parents in accepting a particular child, shorter waiting period from time of application to placement, and lack of information about the child (Barth & Berry, 1988a).

Westhues and Cohen (1990) collected family functioning data on 58 families before placement, which they followed up one year later. They found that couples with high expectations and whose reason for adoption was infertility were more likely to have disrupted adoptions. Moreover, adoption outcomes were more positive when fathers were involved in supporting the adoptive mother and were actively involved in parenting.

**Intact Adoptions**

Several studies of intact placements (e.g., Kadushin, 1970; Nelson, 1985; Rosenthal & Groze, 1992) have suggested that factors such as parental satisfaction, availability of adoption subsidies, accurate background information on children, availability of post-adoption and adoptive family preservation services, and specialized therapies are essential to successful placements (Rosenthal, 1993). Barth and Berry

(1988a) reported that other factors that might impact adoption stability include: (1) support network of adoptive families initiated before adoption and available throughout placement; (2) close attachment between adopted child and siblings; (3) increased attachment between child and adoptive parents over time; and (4) availability of subsidy for medical/therapeutic procedures. Groze (1996), in his four-year longitudinal study of 71 families with intact adoptions, found that these families were likely to use both formal and informal sources of social support, including professional service providers.

Other studies of special needs adoptions have focused on families that have adopted specific kinds of children, such as those with developmental disabilities (Glidden, 1991; Marx, 1990; Wimmer & Richardson, 1990); children with mental retardation (Glidden & Pursley, 1989; Glidden, Valliere, & Herbert, 1988); drug-exposed children (Barth, 1991a); children with handicaps (Rosenthal, Groze, & Aguilar, 1991); comparisons of single-parent to two-parent families (Groze & Rosenthal,1991a); comparisons of single, transracial, and Black adoptions (Shireman & Johnson, 1986); and problems experienced by adolescents in families that adopt older children (Ward & Lewko, 1988).

**Methodological Issues**

Although a few prospective, longitudinal studies have been conducted (e.g., Barth, Courtney, Berrick, & Albert, 1994; Groze, 1996), the majority of studies of adoption outcomes tend to be retrospective, cross-sectional analyses using purposive sampling procedures. Most include sample populations from a particular agency, counties within a particular state, or data collected from specific regions of the country. Sample sizes have ranged from more than 1,000 (Barth & Berry, 1988a; Rosenthal & Groze, 1992) to a small clinical sample of 15 (Ward & Lewko, 1987a).

Data collection strategies varied considerably in the studies of adoption outcomes reviewed in this chapter. Several utilized mailed questionnaires (Glidden, 1989; Groze, 1996; Rosenthal & Groze, 1992). Barth and Berry (1988a) reviewed basic demographic and placement data on a large sample of California special needs children. They also interviewed a subsample of caseworkers (including adoptive family workers, child workers, and case supervisors) and parents to obtain greater detail on circumstances of disruption. Festinger (1986) interviewed caseworkers using a combination of mailed questionnaires and follow-up interviews to clarify ambiguities. Telephone interviews were used to discuss disruption with caseworkers. Glidden (1991) used semi-structured interviews with parents of adopted children with developmental disabilities. Groze (1986) reviewed adoption records of a private, non-profit agency. Nelson (1985) conducted in-person interviews with adopted children's primary caretakers. Several researchers analyzed case records (Hornby, 1986; Kagan & Reid, 1986; Lawder, Poulin, & Andrews, 1986; Partridge et al. 1986) and Sack and Dale (1982) reviewed clinical data from adoptive families in private therapy.

Smith and Howard's (1991) exploratory case analysis of disrupted adoptions in Illinois served as a methodological model for the study reported in this book. These researchers systematically reviewed case records of 74 intact and 74 disrupted adoptions and recorded information on a survey form. They found that factors such as sexual abuse, sexual acting-out in the adoptive home, and strong attachment to the birthmother were risk factors for disruption. Foster parent adoptions were associated with greater adoption stability.

**OVERVIEW OF THIS BOOK**

This study utilizes Smith and Howard's (1991) case review methodology of closed adoption cases, and builds on the work of Barth and Berry (1988a) and Groze (1996) to identify family, child, and agency factors that may have influenced disrupted and dissolved, as well as intact, adoption outcomes. As mentioned earlier in this chapter, increasing numbers of children are entering the foster care system, and with the new legislation that will hasten the process of termination, more children will become available for adoption. Child welfare professionals will need to be well-prepared to handle their growing caseloads and to know what factors to consider in selecting families for children. It is with that purpose that this book was written.

The following chapters provide not only empirical data from a study of intact, disrupted, and dissolved adoptions, but also specific child welfare practice and training recommendations. This book focuses on the findings of an intensive qualitative examination of 80 state agency case files documenting children's experiences in the children's protective services system, foster care, and adoption. The case file analysis began with the child's first entry into the system, so data were available on the birthfamilies, foster placements, and on the adoptive placements. In addition, assessments were made of birthparent factors and other child background factors that may have impacted outcome, such as history of abuse, feelings of grief and loss, behavioral problems, parents' and child's expectations, relationship with siblings, and preparation for adoption. Interactional variables are explored, including match between child and family, transition planning, adoptive parent marital relationship, parent-child relationship, and worker/agency factors. Factors leading to stable, disrupted, and dissolved adoptions are compared and contrasted. Special attention is given to examining outcomes of foster parent adoptions, single-parent adoptions, sibling placements, and transracial adoptions. De-identified case vignettes and notes from case reviews are included throughout the book.

Related theoretical and practice issues are discussed throughout the book to improve understanding of special needs adoptive families. The research is primarily based on an analysis of worker documentation of case records. However, this book also provides the findings of in-depth interviews with state agency special needs adoption supervisors and post-adoption providers who have unique perspectives on the factors that may have led to the intact, disrupted, and dissolved placements. Recommendations for improving practice through better transition planning, matching children and families, and assessing families for potential abuse are discussed in detail. Training needs that emerged from the study are identified, and specific recommendations are provided for training foster and adoptive families and workers to increase the success of special needs adoptive placements.

## ORGANIZATION OF THE BOOK

This book is organized into four units, as follows: Overview of the Study, Placement Outcomes, Adoption Service Delivery Issues, and Implications for Training and Practice. The research design, instruments, sample selection process, and data analysis strategies are described in the following chapter. Background characteristics of children and families in the sample are presented in Chapter 3. Chapter 4 contains an overview of the similarities and differences between intact adoptions, those that disrupted prior to finalization, and those that dissolved after finalization. Chapter 5 introduces additional agency, adoptive family, and child factors that emerged in the intensive analysis of the process of placing children in special needs adoptions. Both positive agency placement practices and practices needing improvement were identified, and family and child interpersonal characteristics identified in the case analysis are discussed in terms of placement outcomes.

Unit 2 contains four chapters that address placement issues and outcomes. Each chapter in this unit begins with a synopsis of the research and practice literature on each placement issue. Chapter 6 presents the findings related to planned and unplanned foster parent adoptions. Chapter 7 focuses on outcomes for single-parent adoptions. As in previous studies the majority of single-parent adopters in this study were people of color. Chapter 8 addresses sibling placement issues. Although much of the existing literature examines the pros and cons of placing siblings together, this chapter highlights specific factors that can influence adoption outcomes in cases in which siblings are placed together or apart. Another very controversial topic, transracial adoption, is addressed in the following chapter. The majority of the transracial adoptions in this study involved White families adopting Hispanic children. Specific recommendations are given for workers to consider in making these placements.

Unit 3 examines several adoption service delivery issues that may affect adoption outcomes. Agency pressure to find placements for children sometimes leads workers to engage in poor placement practices, which can set the stage for adoption disruptions or dissolutions. Chapters 10 and 11 focus on two of these practices: mismatches between parents and children, and poor transition planning for children being moved from foster care into adoption.

Rushed placements may also sometimes lead workers to overlook "risk factors" of some potential adoptive parents for special needs children. In 15 of the 80 cases reviewed, adoptive parents allegedly abused children placed in their care. Chapter 12 examines these cases and offers practice suggestions for improved assessments of prospective adoptive families. Findings from in-depth interviews with state agency adoption supervisors are provided in Chapter 13, and insights of post-adoption providers are presented in Chapter 14. Their experiences in providing therapy to adoptive families are particularly important in finding ways to improve adoptions practice.

Unit 4 builds on the findings presented in earlier chapters and offers recommendations for training and practice in special needs adoptions. Critical training competencies for adoption workers, supervisors, post-placement providers, foster, and adoptive families are listed in Chapter 15; Chapter 16 summarizes some of the key findings that emerged from the study and offers suggestions for improved practice.

# Overview of the Study

# CHAPTER 2

# Research Design

For the purposes of improving service delivery and positive adoption outcomes for special needs children, the Texas Department of Protective and Regulatory Services (DPRS) initiated an evaluation study of the state agency adoption services program. Specifically, state agency staff sought to identify child, family, and agency factors that influenced adoptions with the following outcomes: intact, disrupted, and dissolved. Intact adoptions refer to placements that have been consummated (legally finalized) and in which the placed child is still in the adoptive home. Disrupted adoptions are placements in which the child has been removed from a pre-adoptive home before his or her adoption has been finalized (Groze, 1986). Dissolved adoptions are placements that break down after consummation. This chapter provides a description of the methodology and data collection procedures used in the research.

Unlike research studies that use an ideal elaborate stratified random sampling design, this research was dependent on two agency factors that limited the sample selection process: the availability of sufficient data in the state agency computer system to be able to identify a sample of cases that fit the criteria; and the subsequent availability of complete documentation on cases that met the criteria. Since this book utilizes public agency practice issues in special needs adoption as a major context in which to examine outcomes, the following discussion is provided not only to identify initial research design issues that are endemic to this type of investigation, but also to improve understanding about the context within which services were provided.

Initially, the researchers contracted to complete case readings on a randomly selected group of 40 intact and 40 dissolved placements. Specifically, the design called for a sample that could control for intervening variables, yet was comparable to samples identified in the literature review. For the purposes of this study, an ideal sample would include a randomly selected sample of cases in which: (1) the child was 3 years or older at time of placement; (2) the adoption was consummated between 1989 and 1990 (due to state legislation mandating disclosure of all case materials to prospective adoptive families, all families having access to the same type of adoption preparation Model Approach to Partnerships in Parenting [MAPP] and the availability of post-adoption counseling to all families); (3) the adoption dissolved no sooner than two years after consummation; (4) all adoptions were subsidized; (5) all adoptive parents were trained using MAPP; (6) the child had not experienced previous disruptions; and (7) there were no foster parent adoptions. The sample selection process for this type of research ideally would involve the selection of dissolved cases first, then matching with intact cases.

When this "ideal" sampling plan was presented to agency staff, the following concerns were raised: (1) full disclosure of background information to adoptive parents did not happen consistently until September 1989, and MAPP training was not implemented throughout Texas until 1991; (2) staff felt they might not be able to provide enough cases that fit all of the desired criteria, and/or have enough to choose a random sample; (3) as there have been dissolutions of infant placements, the staff requested that we also include younger children in the sample; and (4) the intact case list was the most readily accessible and would be available before the dissolved list; thus, due to time constraints, it was necessary to begin with the intact sample.

## INTACT CASES

A computerized list of closed cases drawn from the subsidy eligibility list was used to begin sample selection. All cases of currently intact adoptions that were consummated after 1989 were selected for inclusion in the original sample. To be included, all adoptions should have been consummated for at least one year. In the case of sibling placements where all siblings met the criteria for inclusion, the oldest child with complete case record information was selected as the "target child." The oldest child was selected so that the age range of the "target children" in the dissolved/disrupted sample most closely matched that of the intact sample.

Sixty-five cases of intact placements were selected that met the criteria, and staff requested that regional offices duplicate copies of the entire case records and forward them to the state office for review. Case records were to be drawn from all 12 regions of the state. Some delays were experienced in getting cases available for review and securing complete case records. Incomplete case records were eliminated from the sample. A total of 40 case records comprised the final sample of intact adoptions.

## DISSOLVED/DISRUPTED CASES

A sample of 50 cases identified as being dissolved, which met all of the eligibility criteria, was selected from a computer-generated list of 111 closed subsidy cases. (The closed subsidies indicate that the "target child" is no longer living with the adoptive parents.)

All 50 cases were to be ordered simultaneously; however, only the first 40 cases with complete case records that arrived in the state office were intended to be used in the sample. Upon closer examination of this sample of closed subsidy cases, several issues arose. Subsidy cases can be closed for a variety of reasons, such as: a consummated adoption has legally dissolved because the adoptive parents ask that the child be returned or because the state terminates the parental rights of the adoptive parents; an adoptive placement has disrupted; or the child has run away from home for an extended period of time or is living with friends or relatives of the adoptive family.

Several problems with sample eligibility for cases quickly emerged when the 50 cases arrived in the state office: (1) some of the records were of disrupted cases rather than dissolved; (2) in some cases, adoptions dissolved while the child and family were in another state, so complete records were not available; (3) recent dissolutions often had incomplete dictation because workers have 45 days to complete case record dictation; (4) many of the placements in the dissolved sample occurred before 1989; and (5) some of the identified cases were sibling groups placed in the same adoptive home.

The combination of the above issues made the generation of 40 eligible cases from the list of 111 closed subsidy cases impossible to accomplish in a timely fashion. In response, modifications were made to the sample eligibility criteria. Disrupted adoptions, as well as dissolved adoptions in which placement occurred between 1986 and 1988, were also included. Additionally, the children in both dissolved and disrupted adoptions had to have been in the home for a minimum of six months prior to the breakdown. Most current research in this area has combined disrupted and dissolved adoptions, so this sample is comparable with samples from current studies (e.g., Barth, 1988; Glidden & Pursley, 1989; Hornby, 1986). The time frame for the sample was extended back to adoptions that were consummated as early as 1985 because we were informed that these families should have received Training and Education in Adoption Methods (TEAM) training, which is similar to MAPP and would thus not pose a standardization issue.

Twenty-one eligible dissolved/disrupted cases were selected from the original 111 cases on the closed subsidy list. DPRS staff then obtained an additional 19 cases by contacting regional supervisors to request cases that, for unknown reasons, had not been identified on the closed subsidy list and other cases that tenured supervisors knew had dissolved. A total of 25 dissolved adoptions and 15 disrupted adoptions constituted the final sample of dissolved/disrupted adoptions.

Another potential standardization issue was identified during the sample selection process. The sharing of all background information with parents whose children were placed before September 1989 was not done consistently, as the law regulating complete disclosure did not take effect until then. To address this issue, a separate analysis was conducted of the 22 cases in which children had been placed for adoption before September 1989 to determine what background information was received about the target child, when that information was shared with the adoptive parents, and whether lack of information was identified as an issue in the case. It should be noted that in all of the cases in the sample, including this subgroup, the amount and type of information shared with the adoptive parents was difficult to determine from the case records. Often case narratives did not detail information sharing; terms such as "all information," "de-identified information," or "a summary of information" made it difficult to determine exactly what was shared.

Of the 22 cases in the group placed before September 1989, 8 cases were intact adoptions, 3 had disrupted, and 11 had dissolved. The amount of information sharing in each case was classified on a continuum ranging from "complete de-identified case history information" to "information was withheld." (To be coded "information was withheld," this had to be specifically stated in the record; this was not a coder judgment.) There did not appear to be a direct relationship between the amount of information shared and the outcome of the adoption. In 3 cases (2 intact and 1 dissolved), lack of information was identified by the research team and by the adoptive parents as a problematic issue. It should be noted, however, that other issues in these cases contributed to the families' problems as well, such as abusive adoptive parents, marital and financial problems of the adoptive parents, an abrupt transition from foster to adoptive placement, and adoptive parents coping with a large sibling group with many behavior problems.

## THE SAMPLE

The final sample consisted of 40 intact and 40 disrupted/dissolved (15 disrupted and 25 dissolved) cases. In the case of sibling placements where all siblings met the criteria for inclusion, the oldest child with complete case record information was generally selected as the target child. However, information in the case records was reviewed on all siblings placed with the target child.

### Data Collection Strategies

Following a similar procedure as Smith and Howard (1991) in their study of successful and disrupted adoptions, data were collected by a systematic review of case records. Detailed notes were taken regarding factors that possibly contributed to adoption outcomes. Cases were "staffed" and common themes were identified. After an extensive review of research on intact and dissolved adoptions, a detailed list of birthfamily, child, adoptive family, and agency issues was developed. From this list, a case review comment instrument was drafted and reviewed with staff. Open-ended questions were included in the data-collection instrument, and coders prepared lengthy narrative responses based on their review of the case records. This instrument was later pre-tested and further modified with a sample of non-eligible cases for the study.

Coders were trained in how to find data in the case narratives in order to answer the questions on the data-collection instrument. The coders also reviewed other agency manuals to become familiar with the numerous abbreviations that were found in the case records. Data were collected on the birthfamily, the child and his or her siblings, foster families, adoptive placements, and agency practices.

Case documents for review and assessment included children's protective service workers' narratives on the birthparents, service plans for birthparents, termination proceedings, foster placement records, sibling records, adoption home study narratives, placement records, post-placement summaries, copies of court records, and all other legal and medical documents pertaining to the case.

Some of the specific types of case data that were examined in each file are listed below.

- *Birthfamily Data.* Age at birth of child, number of other children, ethnicity, employment, income, educational background, reason for removal of child, relationship to adopted child, birthsiblings and other family members prior to removal, pre-placement, post-adoptive placement, health status, emotional stability, background, history of abuse, circumstances of child's birth, close relationships, relationship between birthparents, role of target child in birthfamily, family's living pattern, role of relatives, history of abuse, plan of service, visitation patterns, reaction to termination, strengths, and risk factors were among the factors assessed.

- *Target Child Data.* Numerous factors, including the following, were examined for each target child: age at placement, race, medical history, abuse history, relationship with birthfamily, visitation patterns, reasons for removal, agency efforts to place with extended family, child's perception of reasons for removal, child's feelings toward biological parents concerning removal, placement history, preparation for adoption, level of attachment to foster families, feelings about adoption, reaction to placement, post-placement considerations, post-placement contact with birthfamily, placement with siblings or contact with siblings, attachment to adoptive family, integration into adoptive family, mental health diagnoses, risk factors, strengths, treatment plan, and specific child behaviors and school issues.

- *Foster Care Placements.* Number of placements was identified. In addition, for each foster care placement, the following factors were assessed: foster parents' relationship/attachment to target child, abuse history, concerns or issues raised by foster parents, child's reaction at removal, and ongoing involvement of foster parents in child's life.

- *Adoptive Parents.* Age, educational level, ethnicity, medical history, abuse history, religious affiliation, alcohol/drug use, emotional stability, marital relationships, preparation for adoption, commitment to adoption, contact with birthfamily, type of child requested, background on other siblings in the home, reaction of adoptive family at time of placement, issues during placement phase, strengths, risk factors, willingness to seek help, type of information received on child before placement, support systems, concerns raised, and ongoing family risk factors were examined.

- *Agency Data.* Number of workers; quality of home study; preparation of family and child for adoption; services offered to birthfamily, foster family, and adoptive family and acknowledgment of the impact of grief, loss, separation, and abuse; quality and quantity of case documentation on each case, and evidence of addressing specific issues about the child with the family, were among the factors assessed. Many times the records included psychological reports on the child and information about the health history of the child from physicians' or hospital reports. The following types of information were also found in the record, though not as consistently: counselor/psychologist's recommendations for therapy or residential treatment; narratives written by foster mothers; letters from birthparents, birthsiblings, or foster parents to the child or the worker; and school reports and information on special education.

All of the preceding information in the file was read to gain as complete a picture of the child's situation and functioning as possible. This content analysis process made it possible to follow systematically the child's journey through the child welfare system from the point of initial investigation through the close of the case at consummation or, in open cases, to the end of the recorded narrative. Using this method, participant or worker recall issues could be avoided. Information included in the records from different workers and other professionals was cross-checked to provide a more accurate assessment of the child, birthparents, and adoptive families.

In addition, each case reader offered observations and an overall assessment of the following: the biological family's situation and agency response; the strengths of the adoptive family; stressors on the family; issues that seemed insurmountable; the assessment of other factors (worker/agency factors, adoptive parent factors, child factors) that may have led to the problems encountered by the family; and overall impressions, observations, and recommendations to the agency regarding the case. Data on the process of dissolution or disruption, impact on the child, reasons for dissolution or disruption, and current status of the child were also coded.

Each case record typically required at least 20 to 30 hours to read and record data on the data-collection instrument. Some dissolved cases involving sibling placements took between 40 and 50 hours each to review. In all, approximately 2,800 hours of case readings were conducted.

Two trained coders were assigned to read the same case and respond to questions on the case review instrument. Checks for interrater reliability revealed 80% agreement. Conventions were developed for specific low reliability questions such as the number of foster placements (whether to include emergency foster homes and brief hospital stays), thus reliability scores increased to 90%. As coders completed case readings and assessments, another staff person was assigned to review the case coding to be certain that all information was well-documented and accurate. Staff meetings were held on a weekly basis to review conventions and respond to new issues as they arose.

## LIMITATIONS OF THE STUDY

As noted by Smith and Howard (1991), data collection through the use of case records has some disadvantages that should be noted. Typically, case narratives are written by the primary protective services or adoption caseworker(s) assigned to the child's case. As such, all narratives are recorded from that person's perspective introducing a source of bias. Also, content of narratives and the amount of related information available may vary from region to region and by worker. Moreover, because of frequent worker turnover in many cases, there were often inconsistencies in writing styles and quality of narratives within the same case.

Some believe that case record analysis is flawed because the data is often biased. For example, Bush (1984) suggests that case records in child welfare settings "are written, *inter alia*, to deny the failure of interventions, to justify the refusal to serve 'bad clients,' and to justify the decision to extend hegemony over 'good' clients" (p. 1). Regardless of whether credence should be given to this assertion, the reality is that adoption decisions are typically based on these written case records, regardless of their validity. In order to improve practice, we must assess case documentations and give feedback to practitioners. For this reason, the case record analysis strategy was utilized.

Another limitation of this study is the lack of a completely random sample of dissolved/disrupted cases due to the small number of cases from the closed subsidy list that fit into the sample criteria. The remainder of the cases were requested from regional supervisors, and attempts were made to minimize selection bias by requesting more cases than were needed and choosing cases randomly from this group.

## DATA ANALYSIS

### Discrete Analysis

Discrete data analysis focused on descriptive statistics of the 80 cases. Key information available from the case reviews was identified. This information was factual in nature, requiring minimal coder interpretation. A codebook was developed as a means to record this key information gleaned in the case review instrument. Two revisions of the codebook were tested by having each research team member code one of the cases they had previously reviewed. Coding conventions were added in each revision of the codebook to reduce further the need for coder interpretation of case data. Coders were then assigned to code each of the cases. Overlapping items coded in the thematic coding described below were cross-checked with the discrete codes as a reliability check. Any discrepancies were resolved by a third senior staff member or the author.

### Thematic Analysis

Using Glaser and Strauss's (1967) constant comparative method, qualitative analysis techniques were used to review the narrative descriptions to better discern specific patterns and emerging themes. A thematic analysis coding system was developed and organized into five broad topical areas: (1) circumstances of child's removal from biological parents; (2) adoptive parent situation and issues; (3) child issues; (4) agency issues; and (5) implications for training. An assessment was also made for intact adoptions regarding whether the adoption, at the close of the record, could be characterized by a positive adjustment, at moderate risk for dissolution, or at serious risk for dissolution.

Within these broad areas, coders were asked to identify critical factors associated with adoption stability or dissolution in each case and to justify their codes. Cases were randomly assigned for thematic coding; however, assignment of cases was not given to the individual who had performed the review and note-taking of that particular case. This method of case assignment served as a reliability check. Any coding discrepancies between case reviewer and theme coder were resolved during weekly meetings of the research team.

Thematic analyses were conducted on the following issues: match between adoptive parent and child, sibling group placements, single-parent adoptions, transracial adoptions, foster parent adoptions, adoptions with abusive adoptive parents, and transition planning between foster and adoptive homes.

The final step in the thematic coding involved summarizing the coded data on a theme chart. Coders summarized their coding into three areas for each case: (1) adjustment category—positive, moderate risk, or serious risk; (2) applicable subcategories—single-parent adoption, transracial placement/adoption, foster adoption, minority/same-race placement/adoption, adoptive parents with emotional and/or psychological problems, abusive adoptive parents, adoptive parents with marital problems, adoptive parents with financial problems, adoptive parents with poor parenting of minor behavior problems, other major life stressors on adoptive parents that were independent of adoption, match between adoptive child and family, transition plan from foster to adoptive placement; and (3) adoption match categories— troubled target child placed in troubled adoptive family, troubled target child placed in adjusted adoptive family, adjusted target child placed in troubled adoptive family, and adjusted target child placed in adjusted adoptive family.

This book summarizes the findings associated with the adoptive family, child, and agency that influenced the varying adoption outcomes. The characteristics of the sample of the 80 cases reviewed in this research as a whole are presented in the following chapter. Chapter 4 provides a comparison between the intact, disrupted, and dissolved cases.

# CHAPTER 3

# Characteristics of the Sample
*with Isaac Gusukuma*

Demographic information was obtained through a review of protective service, foster care, and adoption files on 80 children and families in intact, dissolved, and disrupted adoptions. These data were coded and analyzed to assess similarities and differences in the characteristics of the three groups. Due to variations in the amount of detail provided in case recordings, there may be only limited data available on a few characteristics of the sample. Information on birthfathers of target children in the sample refers either to biological father, stepfather, or another person identified in the beginning of the CPS case record as the father figure in the child's life. This chapter specifically provides demographic characteristics of each group: intact, disrupted, and dissolved.

## INTACT ADOPTIONS

### Regions Represented

The 40 cases of intact adoptions were selected from almost every region in the state of Texas. Table 3.1 provides data on the specific number of intact cases reviewed from each region.

### GENERAL CHARACTERISTICS

The children in this sample were born between 1975 and 1989. Although one child in the intact sample was placed in adoption in 1985, the majority were placed between 1988 and 1991. Seventy-two and one half percent were placed between 1990 and 1991. All of the intact

**Table 3. 1 Intact Cases by Region**

| Region # | Region | Number of Cases |
|---|---|---|
| 1 (1)[1] | Panhandle | 5 |
| 3 (10) | El Paso | 1 |
| 4 (2) | Wichita Falls | 2 |
| 5 (3) | Dallas/Ft. Worth | 8 |
| 6 (7) | Austin/Central Texas | 5 |
| 7 (4) | Texarkana/Northeast Texas | 3 |
| 8 (8/11) | South Central Texas | 5 |
| 9 (8) | South Central Texas | 1 |
| 10 (5) | Tyler/Beaumont/East Texas | 2 |
| 11 (6) | Houston | 7 |
| 12 (9) | Midland/West Texas | 1 |
| Total | | 40 |

[1]To avoid confusion, region numbers in place at the time of data collection are used, and new region numbers are in parentheses.

adoptions were consummated between 1989 and 1993. Half were consummated in 1991. Full disclosure of background information to adoptive parents did not happen consistently until September 1989. Sixteen (40%) of the intact adoptions were fost-adoption placements (see Chapter 6) and five (12.5%) were out-of-state placements. Ten (25%) of the intact adoptions were transracial adoptions, in which the child's race was different from both of the adoptive parents. Four (10%) were single adoptive parent placements.

## CHARACTERISTICS OF BIRTHFAMILIES OF CHILDREN IN INTACT PLACEMENTS

### Age of Birthparents

At the time of the target children's removal, their birthmothers ranged in age from 16 to 47 and their birthfathers ranged in age from 18 to 57. Twenty-six (65%) of the birthmothers were in their 20s at the time of removal. Twelve (30%) of birthfathers were in their 20s, and 8 (20%) were in their 30s. Although much birthfather data was missing, there was evidence that 3 (7.5%) were in their 40s and 1 (2.5%) was in his 50s.

## Education, Income, and Occupation

According to the records, four stepfathers, 29 birthfathers and 4 other partners of the birthmothers were involved in the children's lives. The majority of the birthparents or parent figures had not completed high school. Four (10%) birthmothers and 2 (5%) birthfathers had completed elementary school, 10 (40%) birthmothers and 4 (10%) birthfathers had attended 6 to 9 years of school, and 18 (45%) birthmothers and 11 (27.5%) birthfathers had completed 10 to 12 years of school. One (2.5%) birthfather had completed about a year or so of either vocational school or college. Three (7.5%) fathers had had no formal education whatsoever.

Although the sources of income at the birth of the target children were often not recorded in many of the case records, evidence was found that 16 (41%) birthmothers were identified as unemployed, 4 (10%) were engaged in service or specialty occupations, and 2 (5%) were engaged in illegal activity. At the time of the birth of the target child, 16 (40%) birthfathers were employed in crafts, as machine operators, in services, as farm laborers, in protective service (such as security guards), or in handlers occupations. Two (5%) were involved in illegal activity, and 1 (2.5%) was unemployed. At the time of removal, 2 (5%) birthfathers were deceased, and only 7 (17.5%) birthfathers were identified as being unemployed. The majority had little or no identifiable source of income. At the time of removal of the target child, 21 (52.5%) of the birthmothers were unemployed, 4 (10%) were housewives, 2 (5%) were involved in illegal activity, 4 (10%) in service occupations. Seven (17.5%) birthmothers were on public assistance, and 4 (10%) had incomes below $3,000.

## History of Abuse

Although background information on over half of the birthfathers or father figures was unavailable in the case records, there was evidence that at least seven (17.5%) birthfathers had experienced abuse and neglect as children. Twenty-eight (70%) of the birthmothers had a history of abuse or neglect in their biological families.

**Use of Drugs**

The limited information in the case records on birthparent use of drugs revealed that 25 (62.5%) of the birthmothers and 14 (35%) of the birthfathers had a history of illegal drug usage.

**Reasons for Termination of Parental Rights**

The circumstances that led to the termination of parental rights in these cases primarily stemmed from neglect (12), physical abuse (8), abandonment (7), voluntary relinquishment (5), sexual abuse (4), or failure to follow the plan of service (4).

## CHARACTERISTICS OF ADOPTED CHILDREN IN INTACT PLACEMENTS

### Age, Gender, and Race

The children in this sample ranged in age at time of removal from less than 1 year to 10 years old. As noted in Table 3.2, the majority of children in intact adoptions were less than 7 years old at the time of removal, and over 60% were less than 4 years old. The average age at removal was 3.5 years. The children ranged in age from less than 1 year to 13 years at the time of placement (see Table 3.3). The average age at placement was 6.3 years. Time from removal to placement in the adoptive home ranged from immediate placement to 6.53 years. The average length of time in care before placement was 2.72 years.

**Table 3.2 Age at Removal**

| Child's Age | n | % |
|---|---|---|
| <1 year | 11 | 27.5 |
| 1-3 | 13 | 32.5 |
| 4-6 | 12 | 30.0 |
| 7-9 | 3 | 7.5 |
| 10 | 1 | 2.5 |
| *Total* | 40 | 100.0 |

In the sample of 40 intact adoptions, 18 (45%) of the adopted children were female and 22 (55%) were male. The majority were members of minority groups. Eighteen of the target children were White (45%), 8

**Table 3.3 Age at Placement**

| Child's Age | n | % |
|---|---|---|
| <1 year | 1 | 2.5 |
| 1-3 | 10 | 25.0 |
| 4-6 | 15 | 37.5 |
| 7-9 | 9 | 22.5 |
| 10-12 | 4 | 10.0 |
| 13 | 1 | 2.5 |
| *Total* | 40 | 100.0 |

(20%) were African American, 8 (20%) were Mexican American, 2 (5%) were Hispanic (other than Mexican American), 1 (2.5%) was Native American, and 3 (7.5%) were identified as multiethnic.

**Reasons for Removal**

In most cases, there were several reasons for removal from the birthparents. The majority, 31 (77.5%), of the cases involved child neglect. However, 14 (35%) of the children had been sexually abused, 12 (30%) had been physically abused, and 9 (22.5%) had also experienced abandonment. Other reasons for removal included voluntary relinquishment, sexual or physical abuse of siblings by family members, return of abusive stepfather to the home, a birthmother who refused to accept treatment for an active case of tuberculosis, and the emotional abuse of the target child.

**Experiences in Care**

Prior to the adoptive placement, 27 (67.5%) of the children had been in 1 to 2 foster placements. The average number of foster placements was 2.38. Five (12.5%) had been in 3 placements, 3 (7.5%) children in 4 placements, 2 (5%) children in 5 placements, and 3 (7.5%) had been in 6 foster placements before adoption. Three (7.5%) had been abused by foster parents while in foster care.

From the time of intake by the Child Protective Services Unit to the time of adoption, the number of caseworkers involved with each child ranged from 1 to 14. The average number of workers was 6. Almost one-third of the sample had between 8 to 14 workers. (The one child who had only one worker was placed in a foster adoption, and the foster care worker handled the adoption.) The total number of all placements for children in intact adoptions (excluding the final adoptive placement) ranged from 0 to 8. The average number of placements was 3.1.

There was evidence in case notes that 11 (27.5%) of the adopted children had good-bye visits with their birthparents and 11 (27.5%) had good-bye visits with their foster parents. It is possible that other children may have had unrecorded good-bye visits with their birthparents and/or foster parents.

### Number of Children with Siblings

Thirty-four (85%) of the children in intact placements had siblings. The majority of the children, 25 (62.5%), had from 1 to 3 siblings. However, 9 (22.5%) children had between 4 and 5 siblings. Twenty-five (73.5%) of the 34 children in intact adoptions had siblings placed with them for adoption. Although the number of siblings placed with the target child ranged from 1 to 6, the average was 2 siblings. Nineteen (47.5%) had 1 to 2 siblings placed with them while 4 (10%) had 3 to 4 siblings placed together, 1 (2.5%) was placed with 5 siblings, and 1 (2.5%) was placed with 6 siblings.

### Children with Disabilities and Medical Problems

Table 3.4 illustrates the types of disabilities of children in the intact sample:

**Table 3.4 Intact Adoptions: Disabilities**

| Disability | $n$ |
|---|---|
| Motor | 9 |
| Speech | 14 |
| Learning | 6 |
| Mental retardation | 8 |

### Child Behaviors

Using the Achenbach Child Behavior Checklist (Achenbach & Edelbrock, 1983) categories, coders were asked to code data found in case records pertaining to specific child behaviors before removal, in foster care, and during adoptive placement. The findings for intact adoptions are found in Table 3.5.

The records did not provide a lot of detail on behaviors prior to removal from the birthparent's home, which may account for the relatively few children with noted problematic behaviors at that time. Before adoptive placement, 13 (32.5%) of the children were involved in sexual acting-out and/or other acting-out behaviors. Seven children (17.5%) were both sexually acting-out and had other acting-out behaviors. There may have been an escalation of acting-out behaviors at that time due to the separation from birthfamilies, as well as the impact of moves between foster homes and the uncertainty of ever returning to the birthfamily or being adopted. For the most part, the instances of these behaviors decreased during adoptive or foster placement, which may account for the stability of those placements at this time. However, as problematic behaviors are continuing with some of these children, the recommendations section of this report identifies specific areas of concern and intervention needs.

## CHARACTERISTICS OF ADOPTIVE PARENTS IN INTACT ADOPTIONS

### Age and Race

The majority (64.9%) of the adoptive parents were White. Eight (20%) of the adoptive mothers were African American, and 5 (12.5%) adoptive mothers and 6 (16.2%) adoptive fathers were Mexican American. Only 2 (5%) adoptive mothers were Native American. Three of the African American adoptive mothers and 1 of the Mexican American adoptive fathers were single parents. Adoptive mothers ranged in age from 24 to 52 years at the time of placement. Their average age was 37.2 years. Adoptive fathers ranged in age from 27 to 54, and had an average age of 39.6 years. (Note: the base number of 40 was used for calculating adoptive mother percentages because data was available for the one adoptive mother who died during the placement phase of the child; however, the base number of 37 was used for adoptive fathers.)

**Table 3.5 Child Behaviors**

| Behavior | Prior to Removal | Before Ad. Placement | During Ad. Placement |
|---|---|---|---|
| Sexual acting-out | 3 | 10 | 4 |
| Eating problems | 0 | 7 | 2 |
| Acting-out | 1 | 10 | 6 |
| Depressed | 0 | 4 | 2 |
| Withdrawn | 2 | 3 | 1 |
| Impulsive | 0 | 4 | 0 |
| Cruelty | 0 | 1 | 0 |
| Physical aggression | 1 | 7 | 4 |
| Verbal aggression | 0 | 5 | 1 |
| Fire-setting | 1 | 1 | 0 |
| Bed-wetting | 1 | 8 | 3 |
| Hyperactivity | 1 | 4 | 2 |
| Self-abusive | 1 | 4 | 1 |
| Persistent disobedience | 0 | 7 | 3 |
| Vandalism | 0 | 1 | 0 |
| Arguing with siblings | 0 | 4 | 2 |
| Persistent non-compliance | 0 | 3 | 3 |
| Suicidal | 0 | 2 | 0 |
| Manipulative behavior | 0 | 7 | 3 |
| Homicidal tendencies | 0 | 1 | 0 |
| Threats/Use of weapon | 0 | 1 | 0 |
| Chronic/Severe lying | 0 | 7 | 5 |
| Stealing | 0 | 8 | 3 |
| Sabotaging relationships | 0 | 0 | 2 |
| Arguing with peers | 0 | 2 | 1 |

## Education, Income, and Occupation

Educational level of adoptive mothers ranged from elementary school through graduate school. One (2.5%) adoptive mother had completed only elementary school, and 11 (27.5%) had completed 10 to 12 years of school. The greater percentage of adoptive mothers had completed some college (45%), 5 (12.5%) of the adoptive mothers had completed college and 3 (7.5%) of the adoptive mothers had completed graduate school. Two (5%) adoptive fathers had completed only 6 to 9 years of school, and 11 (30%) had completed 10 to 12 years of school. Twelve (32%) of the adoptive fathers had completed some years of college, 6 (16%) had completed college, and 3 (8%) held graduate degrees. Sixty-one percent of the adoptive mothers earned less than $20,000 at the time of the adoption. Twenty-two percent earned between $20,000 and $40,000, and 1 (2.5%) earned over $50,000. Ten (25%) were housewives. About 30% were in either sales, technical, specialty, or managerial positions. Although 4 (11%) adoptive fathers earned less than $10,000 at the time of the adoption, 62% of the adoptive fathers in intact adoptions earned between $10,000 and $30,000 at the time of the adoption. Five (14%) of the adoptive fathers earned between $30,000 and $50,000, and 3 (8%) earned over $50,000. The majority (70%) of adoptive fathers tended to be employed in technical, sales, administrative support, transportation, or crafts positions. Ten (27%) were in either professional or executive level positions. Combined family income for adoptive parents in intact adoptions ranged from $14,000 to $118,000, and the average combined family income for this sample was $38,500.

**Religious Affiliation**

The majority (67.5%) of adoptive mothers and adoptive fathers (59%) were Protestant. Eight (20%) of the adoptive mothers and 8 (22%) adoptive fathers were Catholic. Two of the adoptive mothers (5%) and 2 (5%) of the adoptive fathers had no religious affiliation.

**Reasons for Adopting**

Nineteen (47.5%) adoptive mothers and 25 (67.6%) adoptive fathers chose to adopt because they wanted more children. Fourteen (35%) adoptive mothers and 5 (13.5%) adoptive fathers adopted because of infertility. Desire for a particular gender child (2.6%), sibling group (1.3%), particular child (6.5%), or relative placement (5.2%) were less common reasons given for adopting by both adoptive mothers and fathers.

**Previous Experience with Adoption and Parenting**

Fourteen (35%) of the adoptive mothers and 12 (32%) of the adoptive fathers had previous experience with adoption. Thirty-five (87%) of the adoptive mothers and 34 (92%) of the adoptive fathers had previous parenting experience.

## History of Abuse

Four (10%) of the adoptive mothers and 7 (18.9%) of the adoptive fathers reported a history of abuse in their family of origin.

## Commitment to Adoption

At the time of placement, 36 (90%) of the adoptive mothers and 32 (86%) of the adoptive fathers expressed a high commitment to the adoption. Four (10%) adoptive mothers and 4 (10%) adoptive fathers expressed a moderate commitment. Four (10%) adoptive mothers and 6 (16%) adoptive fathers decreased their level of commitment after placement.

## Contact with Worker After Consummation

After the adoption was consummated, 14 (35%) of the adoptive parents had additional contact with the worker.

## DISRUPTED ADOPTIONS

Fifteen cases of disrupted adoptions were reviewed in this study. Disrupted adoptions were defined as placements in which the target child was removed from the adoptive home prior to consummation of the adoption.

## Regions Represented

Case readings included disrupted cases from the following regions:

**Table 3.6 Disrupted Cases by Region**

| Region # | Region | Number of Cases |
|----------|--------|-----------------|
| 1 (1)[1] | Panhandle | 0 |
| 2 (1) | Panhandle | 2 |
| 3 (10) | El Paso | 2 |
| 4 (2) | Wichita Falls | 2 |
| 5 (3) | Dallas/Ft. Worth | 2 |

**Table 3.6 (continued)**

| Region # | Region | Number of Cases |
|----------|--------|-----------------|
| 6 (7) | Austin/Central Texas | 1 |
| 7 (4) | Texarkana/Northeast Texas | 2 |
| 8 (8/11) | South Central Texas | 1 |
| 9 (8) | South Central Texas | 0 |
| 10 (5) | Tyler/Beaumont/East Texas | 0 |
| 11 (6) | Houston | 3 |
| 12 (9) | Midland/West Texas | 0 |
| Total | | 15 |

[1]To avoid confusion, region numbers in place at the time of data collection are used, and new region numbers are in parentheses.

## GENERAL CHARACTERISTICS

Children in the sample of disrupted adoptions were born between 1978 and 1989, and were placed in their adoptive homes between 1987 and 1993. One-third of the children, 5 in this sample, were placed in 1991. Of the 15 disrupted adoptions, 2 (13.3%) were placed between 1987 and 1988, and 3 (20%) children were placed in 1989. Three (20%) were placed in 1992, and 2 (13.3%) children were placed in 1993. None of the children in the disrupted sample were placed in 1990. The placements varied for children in the disrupted sample: 2 (13.3%) were fost-adopt and 2 (13.3%) were out-of-state. Two (13.3%) were transracial adoptions, in which the child's race was different from both of the adoptive parents. Two (13.3%) were single-parent adoptions— one with a single adoptive mother and one with a single adoptive father. The adoptions in the sample disrupted between 1988 and 1993, with more (40%) disrupting in 1992 than in any other year.

## CHARACTERISTICS OF BIRTHPARENTS OF CHILDREN IN DISRUPTED ADOPTIONS

### Age of Birthparents

Birthmothers ranged in age at the time of the child's removal from 20 to 40 years, and birthfathers ranged in age from 21 to 60 years. Thirteen (86.7%) of the birthmothers and 7 (46.7%) of birthfathers were in their 20s. The remaining birthfathers were in their 30s, except for one 60-

year-old birthfather and one whose birth date was not listed in the record.

## Education, Income, and Occupation

Very limited information was available on the income, level of education, and occupation of birthparents in this sample. From the case record notations on occupation of birthmother at the birth of the target child, 6 (25%) were unemployed, 2 (13.3%) were engaged in illegal activity, 1 (6.7%) was a student, and 8 (53.3%) cases did not have information in the record. Three (20%) birthmothers were identified as being on public assistance. At the removal of the target child, about 50% of the birthmothers were unemployed, 1 (6.7%) was a clerical worker and 5 (33.3%) cases had no information in the record. At removal of the target child, 5 (33.3%) birthmothers were on public assistance. One (6.7%) had an annual income under $3,000, and other sources of income were not listed in the record.

Four (26.7%) birthmothers had completed from 6 to 9 years of school, 7 (46.7%) had completed 10 to 12 years, and 1 (6.7%) had finished college. (The birthmother who had completed college was murdered by her husband, and he relinquished rights to the children.)

According to the records, 3 stepfathers, 10 birthfathers, and 2 other partners were involved in the children's lives. Birthfather background information was especially sketchy. Information available on 3 birthfathers revealed that they were either equipment handlers, assemblers, or in professional specialty positions (such as a technical writer) at the birth of the target child. Their income was unknown at that time. At removal, 2 (13.3%) birthfathers were listed as unemployed, 5 (33.3%) were working at positions described above, and no data was available on the rest of the birthfathers. Birthfather income was unknown for 13 (86.7%) birthfathers. One earned less than $10,000 annually, and another earned between $10,000 and $20,000. One of the birthfathers had completed college, 3 had attended 10 to 12 years of school, and 1 had completed 6 to 9 years of school.

## History of Abuse

Fourteen (93%) birthmothers and two (13%) birthfathers were noted as having a history of abuse. This figure may actually be much higher for the fathers, but the data on fathers in general was very limited in the case records.

## Use of Drugs

Case records reported illegal drug use by 8 (53%) of the birthmothers, 10 (67%) of the birthfathers, and 2 (13%) father figures.

## Reasons for Termination

Primary reasons given for termination of parental rights were as follows: neglect (5), failure to follow plan of service (5), abandonment (2), physical abuse (1), sexual abuse (1), and voluntary relinquishment (1).

## CHARACTERISTICS OF ADOPTED CHILDREN IN DISRUPTED PLACEMENTS

### Age, Gender, and Race

The children in the sample of disrupted adoptions ranged in age from less than a year to 9 years at the time of removal from the birthfamilies. Their average age at was 4.5 years. At adoptive placement, their ages ranged from 3 to 12 years. Their average age at placement was 7.9. Time from removal to adoptive placement ranged from 1 to 8 years. Average time between removal and placement was 3.3 years. At the time of the adoption disruption, children ranged in age from 3.7 to 14.93 years. The average age at disruption was 9.07 years.

### Table 3.7 Age at Removal

| Child's Age | n | % |
|---|---|---|
| <1 year | 2 | 13 |
| 1-3 | 4 | 27 |
| 4-6 | 7 | 47 |
| 7-9 | 2 | 13 |
| Total | 15 | 100 |

### Table 3.8 Age at Placement

| Child's Age | n | % |
|---|---|---|
| 3 | 2 | 13 |
| 4-6 | 3 | 20 |
| 7-9 | 6 | 40 |
| 10-12 | 4 | 27 |
| Total | 15 | 100 |

There were 7 females and 8 males in disrupted adoptions. The majority were of minority parentage. Five (33.3%) of the children were White, 4 (26.7%) Black, 2 (13.3%) Mexican American, and 4 (26.7%) multiethnic. Two (13.3%) of the disrupted adoptions were transracial placements.

## Reason for Removal

As with the children in intact placements, several reasons for removal from their birthparents were typically given in each child's case records. Primary reasons for removal from birthfamily homes were abuse and neglect. Four (26.7%) children in disrupted adoptions had been sexually abused while living in their birth homes. Four (26.7%) children had been physically abused, 2 (13.3%) abandoned, and 5 (33%) had suffered neglect. Additional reasons were given for 6 (40%) of the children, including 3 birthparents who voluntarily relinquished their children, 1 target child who was emotionally abused, 1 target child who was dangerous to himself and others, and 1 whose birthparents were in jail.

## Experiences in Care

Children in this group had been in an average of 3.33 foster placements before adoptions. The actual number of placements ranged from 1 to 9 placements, and 11 (73.3%) had been in 2 to 3 placements. The total number of placements ranged from 1 to 11, an average of 3.9. Thirteen (86.7%) children in the disrupted sample had siblings, with 8 (53.3%) having siblings placed with them in the adoptive home. Ten (66.7%) had siblings placed for adoption in adoptive homes different than the target's adoptive home. The number of siblings placed with the target ranged from 1 to 4, with the average being 2.38. Three targets had 1 sibling placed in the adoptive home with them, 2 had 2 siblings placed with them, and 3 had 4 siblings placed with them. Two (13.3%) of the children in disrupted adoptions had been abused in foster care. Three (20%) were placed with abusive adoptive parents. The number of caseworkers ranged from 3 to 19, and the average number of caseworkers assigned to a case was 8.7. Good-bye visits with birthparents were mentioned in the records in 6 (40%) of the cases, 1 (8.7%) visited with foster parents, and 6 (40%) did not have a good-bye visit with anyone. Two (13.3%) cases had no information in the record on good-bye visits.

## Children with Disabilities and Medical Problems

Ten (67%) of the 15 children in disrupted adoptions had developmental disabilities. They included the following:

**Table 3.9 Disrupted Adoptions: Disabilities**

| Disability | *n* |
| --- | --- |
| Motor | 3 |
| Learning | 3 |
| Mental retardation | 2 |
| ADHD | 2 |

## Child Behaviors

A comparison of coded child behaviors identified in the case records as occurring prior to removal, before placement, and during placement in the adoptive family is provided in Table 3.10. Two-thirds of the sample of 15 disrupted adoptions were engaged in sexual acting-out behaviors while in substitute care before their adoptive placement, and 53% of these children were sexually acting-out during the adoptive placement.

**Table 3.10 Child Behaviors**

| Behavior | Prior to Removal | Before Ad. Placement | During Ad. Placement |
| --- | --- | --- | --- |
| Sexual acting-out | 1 | 10 | 8 |
| Eating problems | 1 | 2 | 2 |
| Acting-out | 0 | 9 | 8 |
| Depressed | 1 | 3 | 3 |
| Withdrawn | 1 | 2 | 0 |
| Impulsive | 0 | 2 | 1 |
| Cruelty | 1 | 1 | 0 |
| Physical aggression | 1 | 7 | 9 |
| Verbal aggression | 2 | 5 | 6 |
| Fire-setting | 1 | 1 | 1 |
| Bed-wetting | 1 | 4 | 3 |
| Hyperactivity | 1 | 2 | 2 |
| Self-abusive | 1 | 1 | 1 |
| Gang activity | 0 | 1 | 0 |
| Persistent disobedience | 1 | 5 | 6 |

**Table 3.10 (continued)**

| Behavior | Prior to Removal | Before Ad. Placement | During Ad. Placement |
|---|---|---|---|
| Vandalism | 0 | 2 | 3 |
| Arguing with siblings | 1 | 4 | 5 |
| Persistent non-compliance | 1 | 1 | 3 |
| Suicidal | 1 | 0 | 0 |
| Manipulative behavior | 0 | 1 | 3 |
| Running away | 0 | 0 | 2 |
| Homicidal tendencies | 0 | 0 | 1 |
| Threats/Use of weapon | 1 | 1 | 3 |
| Cult activities | 0 | 1 | 1 |
| Chronic/Severe lying | 0 | 2 | 4 |
| Stealing | 0 | 3 | 4 |
| Sabotaging relationships | 0 | 0 | 1 |
| Arguing with peers | 1 | 5 | 2 |

## CHARACTERISTICS OF ADOPTIVE PARENTS IN DISRUPTED ADOPTIONS

### Age and Race

Adoptive mothers ranged from 33 to 45 years of age and were an average age of 39.3 years at the time of placement. Adoptive fathers ranged in age from 29 to 46 years and were an average age of 37.6 years at the time of placement. Nine (64%) adoptive fathers were White, 3 (21.4%) were African American, and 2 (14.3%) were Mexican American. Seven (50%) adoptive mothers were White, 5 (35.7%) were Black, and 2 (14.3%) were Mexican American. One of the Black adoptive mothers and 1 of the White adoptive fathers (7.1%) were single parents.

### Education, Income, and Occupation

The majority (92.9%) of the adoptive mothers had completed high school. Only one had less than a 10th-grade education. Four ( 28.6%) had completed some college, 2 (14.3%) adoptive mothers had completed college, and 1 (7.1%) had completed graduate school. The majority of the adoptive fathers had completed high school (92.9%). Six (42.9%) had completed some college, and 1 (7.1%) had completed college. Three (28.6%) had completed graduate school.

At the time of the home study, 1 (7.1%) adoptive mother was retired, and 1 (7.1%) was a housewife. Seventy-one percent were employed in positions that were coded as administrative/managerial, technical, sales, administrative support, and clerical. The incomes of the working adoptive mothers (7 of 13) ranged from under $6,000 to $40,000. The majority of these mothers earned between $10,000 and $30,000. At the time of the home study, 5 (25.7%) adoptive fathers were in professional positions, and 3 (21.4%) were in sales. The remaining fathers were in technical, service, farm labor, and crafts. One (7.1%) was a student, 1 (7.1%) in the military, and 1 (7.1%) was a househusband. Income for adoptive fathers who worked ranged from $6,000 to $100,000. Two (14.3%) earned less than $10,000, and the majority (7 of 13) had incomes between $20,000 and $50,000. One (7.1%) had an income of over $50,000. Combined family income of this group ranged from $11,000 to $100,000, and the average annual income for families in disrupted adoptions was approximately $41,000.

## Religious Affiliation

Fifty-four percent of adoptive mothers and fathers were Protestant, and 3 (21%) adoptive mothers and 5 (36%) adoptive fathers were Catholic. Only 1 (7.1%) adoptive mother indicated no religious affiliation.

## Reason for Adopting

Adoptive mothers chose to adopt primarily because of infertility (64.3%). Two (14.3%) adopted because they wanted more children. Others adopted because they wanted specific children. Adoptive fathers' reasons for adopting were as follows: 64.3% wanted more children; 21.4% wanted a specific gender of child, and others wanted specific children.

## Request for a Specific Child

Almost half of the adoptive mothers and adoptive fathers who had disrupted adoptions had requested a specific child or sibling group.

## Fertility

Over half (57%) of the adoptive mothers were infertile, and 1 (7.1%) adoptive father had a medical problem that affected his fertility.

## Previous Parenting and Adoption Experience

Twelve (85.7%) adoptive mothers and 12 (85.7%) adoptive fathers had previous parenting experience. Four adoptive mothers (28.6%) and 5 (37.5%) adoptive fathers had previous experience with adoption.

## History of Abuse

Notes in the records indicated that 1 (7.1%) adoptive mother and 2 (14.3%) adoptive fathers had been abused in their families of origin.

## Commitment to Adoption

Fifty-seven percent of the adoptive mothers and 71% of the adoptive fathers expressed high commitment to the adoption. Fourteen percent of the adoptive mothers and fathers had a moderate commitment to the adoption. Slightly over half (57%) of the adoptive mothers and fathers decreased their commitment after placement. Five (35.7%) adoptive mothers and 5 (35.7%) adoptive fathers specifically stated that they would accept a sexually abused child, and 6 (42.9%) adoptive mothers and 6 (42.9%) adoptive fathers would accept a physically abused child or an emotionally abused child.

## Time Between Initial Discussion of Problems and Disruption

In 47% of the adoptions, the child was removed within 1 month of the initial discussion of problems with which the family could not cope. One (6.7%) adoption disrupted 2 months after the initial discussion, and 2 (13.3%) disrupted within 3 months, 2 (13.3%) within 4 months, and 2 (13.3%) within 7 months. The adoptive family initiated removal of the adopted child in 66.7% of the cases. In 26.7% of the cases, the worker initiated removal, and the target child initiated removal in 1 other case by running away from the adoptive home and asking to be removed.

## Location of Child After Disruption

At the close of the record, 6 (40%) of the target children in disrupted adoptions were in foster homes; 4 (26.7%) were in new adoptive homes, 4 (26.7%) were in residential treatment, and 1 (6.7%) was in a children's group home.

## DISSOLVED ADOPTIONS

### Regions Represented

Dissolved cases came from the following regions:

**Table 3.11 Dissolved Cases by Region**

| Region # | Region | Number of Cases |
|----------|--------|-----------------|
| 1 (1) | Panhandle | 1 |
| 2 (1) | Panhandle | 1 |
| 3 (10) | El Paso | 4 |
| 4 (2) | Wichita Falls | 5 |
| 5 (3) | Dallas/Ft. Worth | 2 |
| 6 (7) | Austin/Central Texas | 1 |
| 7 (4) | Texarkana/Northeast Texas | 3 |
| 8 (8/11) | South Central Texas | 4 |
| 9 (8) | South Texas | 0 |
| 10 (5) | Tyler/Beaumont/East Texas | 1 |
| 11 (6) | Houston | 3 |
| 12 (9) | Midland/West Texas | 0 |
| Total | | 25 |

## GENERAL CHARACTERISTICS

The children in this sample were born between 1974 and 1987 and were placed in their adoptive homes between 1985 and 1992. The majority had been placed between 1987 and 1989. The dissolved adoptions were consummated between 1986 and 1992. Eleven (44%) were consummated before September 1, 1989, and 14 (56%) after September 1, 1989. The adoption dissolutions occurred between 1988 and 1993. Almost half occurred in 1992. Four (16%) of the dissolved adoptions were foster adoption placements, 4 were single-parent placements, 1 (4%) was an out-of-state placement, and 4 (16%) were transracial adoptions.

## CHARACTERISTICS OF BIRTHPARENTS WITH CHILDREN IN DISSOLVED ADOPTIONS

At the birth of the target child, birthmothers in dissolved adoptions were categorized as having the following occupations: dishwasher (1), service (such as motel maid and waitress) (2), housewife (5), unemployed (5), student (1), professional specialty (such as production inspector) (1), illegal activity (1), and other (such as exotic dancer or tattoo artist) (9).

## Education, Income, and Occupation

Level of education for birthmothers ranged from middle school to 1 or 2 years of college. Six (24%) birthmothers had finished 6 to 9 years of school, 12 (48%) had had 10 to 12 years of school, and 2 (8%) had had some college. Birthfathers' educational levels ranged from elementary school to graduate school. One (4%) birthfather had attended only elementary school, and 4 (16%) had gone through middle school. Seven (28%) had completed 10 to 12 years of school, 1 (4%) had completed college, and 1 (4%) had completed graduate school. Data on the other 11 (44%) fathers were not found in the records.

Income levels at the time of the child's birth were often not available in the records. Data could only be found on 5 (20%) birthmothers who were either on public assistance or had incomes of less than $3,000. At the time of the child's removal from the birthmother, 11 (44%) of the birthmothers were unemployed, and 7 (28%) were in service (such as cook, motel maid, or elderly care), assembly, or farm labor occupations. At the time of removal, income data was unknown or missing on 13 (52%) birthmothers. Six (24%) had incomes less than $3,000, and 2 (8%) had incomes between $3,000 and $10,000. Three (12%) were on public assistance, and 1 (4%) birthmother was deceased.

According to the records, 5 (20%) stepfathers, 19 (76%) birthfathers, and 1 (4%) other partner were involved in the children's lives. Data on birthfathers or father figures was very limited in the case records. At the time of the child's birth, 12 (48%) birthfathers were employed in either technical, farm labor, crafts, assembly (oil field worker, general laborer), or handler (fence installer). Income levels were unknown. At the time of the child's removal, 6 (24%) fathers were unemployed, and 5 (20%) were employed in either managerial, specialty (logistics engineer), protective service (security guard), or craft positions. Income levels at the time of the child's removal were basically not available in the records. Two (8%) had incomes of less than $3,000, 1 (4%) between $3,000 and $10,000, and 1 (4%) was listed as being on public assistance. At the time the target child was placed, 3 birthfathers were listed as being unemployed, and 3 (12%)

were in crafts, assembly, or transportation positions. Income at placement was not contained in the records.

## History of Abuse

Eighteen (72%) birthmothers and 9 (36%) birthfathers or father figures of children in dissolved adoptions had experienced abuse or neglect in their childhood. Limited information in the records of 14 birthfathers made it impossible to assess their history of abuse.

## Use of Drugs

Eighteen (72%) of the birthmothers had a history of illegal drug use, and 12 of the birthfathers (the 12 on which information was available) had a history of drug usage. Six father figures had a history of drug usage, and 3 of these had biological fathers who also used drugs.

## Reasons for Termination of Parental Rights

Parental rights had been terminated in 8 (32%) cases as a result of physical abuse of the target child. Four (16%) children had been sexually abused, 6 (24%) neglected, 3 (12%) abandoned, and 3 (12%) birthparents had voluntarily relinquished rights to their child. Two (8%) parents' rights were terminated because of failure to follow their plan of service.

## CHARACTERISTICS OF CHILDREN IN DISSOLVED ADOPTIONS

### Gender, Age, and Race

There were 9 (36%) females and 16 (64%) males in the dissolved sample. Five (20%) of the children in dissolved adoptions were Black, 13 (52%) were White, 4 (16%) Mexican American, 1 (4%) Native American, and 2 (8%) were multiethnic. As noted in the tables below, the children in dissolved adoptions were removed between infancy and 12 years of age and were placed for adoption between 1 and 14 years of age. At the time of dissolution, the children ranged in age from 2 to 18 years. Their average age at removal was 5.2 years, and at placement, 8.4 years. Time from removal to placement in the adoptive home ranged from 8 months to 8 years. The average length of time in care before placement was 3.18 years. The average age at dissolution was 11.6 years.

**Table 3.12 Age at Removal**

| Child's Age | n | % |
|---|---|---|
| <1 | 4 | 16 |
| 1-3 | 6 | 24 |
| 4-6 | 8 | 32 |
| 7-9 | 4 | 16 |
| 10-12 | 3 | 12 |
| Total | 25 | 100 |

**Table 3.13 Age at Placement**

| Child's Age | n | % |
|---|---|---|
| 1-3 | 2 | 8 |
| 4-6 | 6 | 24 |
| 7-9 | 7 | 28 |
| 10-12 | 8 | 32 |
| 14 | 2 | 8 |
| Total | 25 | 100 |

**Reasons for Removal**

Most of the children had been removed from their birth homes as a result of physical abuse and neglect. Many had also been sexually abused and a few had been abandoned. Data were coded for each reason for removal as follows: 11 (44%) of the children in dissolved adoptions had been removed from their homes for physical abuse; 15 (60%) had experienced neglect; 8 (32%) had experienced sexual abuse; and 6 (24%) had been abandoned. Other reasons for removal included voluntary relinquishment, sexual abuse of a sibling by the birthfather, 1 target child who was considered dangerous to himself and others, 1 birthmother who had psychological problems, and 1 birthfather who was in a nursing home.

**Experience in Care**

Children in dissolved adoptions had been in an average of 2.5 foster placements. Eight (32%) had been in 1 foster placement, 8 (32%) in 2 foster placements, 7 (28%) in 3 to 4 placements, 1 (4%) in 6 placements, and 1 (4%) in 10 placements. These children spent an average of 3.18 years in foster care before placement. The number of years between removal and adoptive placement ranged from 1 to 8 years. The children in dissolved adoptions had been assigned an average of 10.5 caseworkers. The actual number of caseworkers ranged from 4 to 18. More than half (56%) of the children had had contact with 10 to 18 caseworkers. Three (12%) of the children in dissolved adoptions had experienced abuse in foster care, and 9 (36%) were placed in homes with abusive adoptive parents.

The total number of all placements for children in dissolved adoptions (excluding the final adoptive placement) ranged from 1 to 15 placements. The average number of placements was 4.3. These included foster placements as well as emergency shelter care and hospitalizations. According to case records, good-bye visits with birthparents occurred for 12 (48%) children, 3 (12%) had good-bye visits with foster parents, 6 (24%) had no good-byes, and 4 (16%) cases had no record of good-bye visits.

**Number of Children with Siblings**

Twenty-three (92%) of the children in dissolved placements had siblings. Thirteen (52%) had other siblings placed for adoption. Eight (31%) had 1, 4 (31%) had 2, and 1 (8%) had 4 siblings placed with the target child in the adoptive home.

**Children with Disabilities and Medical Problems**

Eighteen (72%) of the 25 cases of dissolved adoptions involved children with developmental disabilities. Specific disabilities and the frequency of occurrence is provided below:

**Table 3.14 Dissolved Adoptions: Disabilities**

| Disability | *n* |
|---|---|
| Motor | 2 |
| Learning | 7 |
| Mental retardation | 3 |
| Speech | 2 |
| ADHD | 4 |

**Children's Behaviors**

As noted in Table 3.15, children's behaviors in dissolved adoptions escalated after removal. Behaviors identified as occurring during placement seemed to increase and become more severe after consummation.

**Table 3.15 Child Behaviors**

| Behavior | Prior to Removal | Before Ad. Placement | During Ad. Placement | After Consummation |
|---|---|---|---|---|
| Sexual acting-out | 4 | 9 | 7 | 12 |
| Eating problems | 4 | 6 | 2 | 4 |
| Acting-out | 4 | 9 | 13 | 12 |
| Depressed | 5 | 10 | 8 | 10 |
| Hypochondria | 0 | 0 | 1 | 0 |
| Withdrawn | 2 | 3 | 1 | 4 |
| Drug abuse | 0 | 0 | 1 | 2 |
| Alcohol abuse | 0 | 0 | 0 | 1 |
| Impulsive | 3 | 4 | 5 | 7 |
| Cruelty | 2 | 4 | 4 | 6 |
| Physical aggression | 5 | 9 | 11 | 16 |
| Verbal aggression | 1 | 5 | 7 | 12 |
| Fire-setting | 0 | 1 | 1 | 2 |
| Bed-wetting | 2 | 9 | 5 | 4 |
| Hyperactivity | 3 | 6 | 9 | 10 |
| Self-abusive | 0 | 0 | 2 | 8 |
| Gang activity | 0 | 0 | 0 | 3 |
| Persistent disobedience | 3 | 5 | 6 | 10 |
| Vandalism | 1 | 2 | 2 | 5 |
| Arguing with siblings | 2 | 6 | 6 | 8 |
| Persistent non-compliance | 1 | 5 | 8 | 13 |
| Suicidal | 0 | 0 | 2 | 6 |
| Manipulative behavior | 2 | 6 | 7 | 10 |
| Running away | 1 | 1 | 1 | 8 |
| Homicidal tendencies | 1 | 0 | 1 | 6 |
| Threats/Use of weapon | 1 | 0 | 0 | 4 |
| Chronic/Severe lying | 1 | 7 | 7 | 11 |
| Stealing | 1 | 3 | 3 | 9 |
| Sabotaging relationships | 2 | 1 | 3 | 5 |
| Arguing with peers | 0 | 6 | 6 | 10 |

At the close of the record, these children were in the following locations:

**Table 3.16 Child Behaviors: Locations**

| Location | n |
|---|---|
| Foster home | 9 |
| New adoptive home | 2 |
| Residential treatment | 11 |
| Emancipated | 1 |
| Biological relatives | 1 |
| Adoptive father (living with AF while on parole) | 1 |
| Total | 25 |

## CHARACTERISTICS OF ADOPTIVE PARENTS IN DISSOLVED ADOPTIONS

### Age and Race

Adoptive mothers were born between 1940 and 1965. They ranged in age from 25 to 48 at the time of placement. Adoptive fathers in dissolved adoptions were born between 1935 and 1965 and ranged in age from 25 to 51 years old. The average age at placement of adoptive mothers was 37.4 years, and 38.6 years for adoptive fathers. Four (17.4%) of the adoptive fathers and 3 (13%) adoptive mothers were African American. Sixteen (69.6%) of the adoptive mothers and 16 (69.6%) of the adoptive fathers were White. There were 4 (17.4%) Mexican American adoptive mothers, 1 (4.3%) Mexican American adoptive father, and 1 (4.3%) Native American adoptive mother and adoptive father. One (4.3%) adoptive mother and 1 (4.3%) adoptive father were identified as multiethnic. One (4.3%) White adoptive mother and 1 (4.3%) Native American adoptive mother were single parents. One (4.3%) of the Black adoptive fathers and 1 (4.3%) of the White adoptive fathers was a single parent.

### Education, Income, and Occupation

Adoptive mothers' educational levels ranged from elementary school to graduate school. Six (26.1%) had completed college, and 4 (17.4%) of these had graduate degrees. One (4.3%) had attended only elementary school, 9 (39.1%) had attended or completed high school, and 6

(26.1%) had attended some college. Adoptive fathers' educational levels ranged from 10 to 12 years of high school to graduate school. Ten (43.5%) had completed 10 to 12 years of school, and 8 (34.8%) had completed some college. Five (21.7%) had completed college, and 4 (17.4%) of these had received graduate degrees.

At the time of the home study, 2 (9%) of the adoptive mothers were in the military, and 8 (34.3%) were unemployed. Others worked in managerial, specialty, sales, administrative support, and private household occupations. Their incomes ranged from under $3,000 to $36,000. Six (35.3%) of the 17 mothers with incomes earned less than $10,000, and 9 (52.9%) earned between $10,000 and $30,000. Only 2 (11.8%) adoptive mothers earned between $30,000 and $40,000.

The adoptive fathers held a variety of occupations, ranging from managerial to transportation. Four (17%) were in the military, with incomes ranging from below $3,000 to over $50,000. Three (13%) earned $50,000 or more. Fifty-nine percent earned between $10,000 and $30,000. The combined annual income ranged from $15,000 to $99,600, and the average income of families in dissolved adoptions was about $35,000.

**Reason for Adopting**

Six (26%) adoptive mothers adopted because of infertility, and 11 (47.8%) wanted more children. According to the records, 5 (22%) adoptive fathers adopted because of infertility, and nine (39%) adopted because they wanted more children.

**Fertility**

Eight (35%) of the adoptive mothers and 3 (13%) adoptive fathers were infertile. Five (22%) adoptive mothers and 2 (8.7%) adoptive fathers had other problems that affected their ability to have biological children.

**Request for Specific Child**

Eleven (48%) adoptive mothers and 10 (43%) adoptive fathers requested a sibling group, and 6 (26%) adoptive mothers and 8 (35%) adoptive fathers requested specific children. Eight (35%) adoptive mothers and 8 (35%) fathers would accept a sexually abused child, 9 (39%) adoptive mothers and 10 (43%) fathers said they would accept a physically abused child, and 11 (48%) adoptive mothers and 13 (57%) fathers said they would accept an emotionally abused child.

## Previous Parenting and Adoption Experience

Sixteen (69.6%) of the adoptive mothers and 16 (69.6%) of the adoptive fathers had previous parenting experience before the adoption. Four (17%) of the adoptive mothers and three (13%) adoptive fathers had previous experience with adoption.

## Religious Affiliation

Sixteen (69.6%) of the adoptive mothers and 18 (78.3%) of the adoptive fathers were Protestant. Four (17.4%) adoptive mothers and 2 (8.7%) adoptive fathers were Catholic. One (4.3%) adoptive father was Jewish.

## History of Abuse

Nine (39%) of the adoptive mothers and 3 (13%) adoptive fathers were identified as having a history of abuse in their families of origin.

## Commitment to Adoption

Twenty (87%) of the adoptive mothers and 18 (78.3%) of the fathers had a high commitment to the adoption, and 3 (13%) adoptive mothers and 3 (13%) adoptive fathers had a moderate commitment. After placement, 14 (60.9%) adoptive mothers and 12 (52.2%) adoptive fathers decreased their commitment to the placement.

## Time Between Initial Discussion and Dissolution

The time between initial discussion and dissolution ranged from 1 month to almost 2 years. Eight (32%) of the children were removed within the 1st month after discussion. Three (12%) were removed within the second month. Seven (28%) adoptions had dissolved within the first 2 months after discussion about problems had begun. Only 7 (28%) adoptions continued for more than 4 months after the first discussion of dissolution. Removal was initiated by adoptive families in 52% of the cases. In eight (32%) cases, the CPS or adoption worker initiated removal, and in 4 (16%) cases another party (unnamed in record) initiated removal.

## COMPARISON BETWEEN DISSOLVED AND DISRUPTED PLACEMENTS

Bivariate analyses were conducted to test the significance of the differences between dissolved and disrupted adoptions. No significant differences in the characteristics of the two groups were found on background of the children or birthfamilies. However, the only differences that approached statistical significance were found in adoptive mothers' commitment to adoption and child threats regarding use of weapons. Adoptive mothers in dissolved adoptions had a higher commitment to the adoption at placement than did mothers in disrupted adoptions ($p < .05$). This may have accounted for their proceeding with consummation of the adoption and continuing to try to work on problems during the placement.

Children in disrupted adoptions were more likely to have made threats about the use of weapons during the placement than children in dissolved adoptions ($p < .02$). Three of the disrupted adoptive families and none of the dissolved families had experienced these threats. This seems plausible, as families that may have experienced serious threats from the child during the placement would be more likely to choose not to finalize the placement than those who had not experienced such threats.

## COMPARISON TO DEMOGRAPHIC CHARACTERISTICS OF FAMILIES IN OTHER STUDIES

Due to the small sample size in this study, we chose to assess generalizability by comparing the sample characteristics to those in other studies, as well as to the general population of DPRS cases. A comparison between the demographic characteristics of families in this study and families in other studies reveals much similarity. In this section, comparisons will be made with samples in two other studies (Barth & Berry, 1988a; Smith & Howard, 1991). The Barth and Berry study was chosen for comparison because it has much acclaim by child welfare practitioners and includes a sample of intact, disrupted, and dissolved adoptions. By design, the study reported in this book is similar methodologically to the Smith and Howard (1991) study. However, the Smith and Howard study only compared intact and disrupted placements.

Although Barth and Berry's (1988a) study sample (832 stable adoptions, 78 disrupted, and 16 dissolved) was much larger than this study, many of the demographic characteristics of the adoptive parents were similar to this sample. For example, adoptive parents in Barth and Berry's (1988a) study had bimodal education levels of high school graduation and some college education. The average age of adoptive mothers in Barth and Berry's study was 38, and adoptive fathers 40, very similar to the parents in this study. The majority of the families in this study and Barth and Berry's (1988a) were White. Unlike Barth and Berry's study, by design, all families in this sample received subsidy. More than half received subsidy in Barth and Berry's study. The median adoptive family income in Barth and Berry's study was $24,000, and the median family income in this study was $32,000.

Also, by design, none of the children in this study had previous adoptions, while 3% of the foster parent adoptions and 14% of the non-foster parent adoptions in Barth's study involved children with previous adoptions. Also, similar to Barth's sample, the majority (57.5%) of the children were male. All of the children in Barth's study were over 3 years of age at placement. Sixty-seven (84%) of the children in this sample were over 3 years of age at placement. All but 8 (10%) children were placed in-state in this study, as compared to all the children in Barth's study. Ten (12.5%) of the adoptions were by single parents in this study, as compared to 15% in the Barth and Berry study. The 2 largest ethnic groups represented in both Barth and Berry's study and this study were Whites and African Americans. About 20% were Mexican American or Hispanic in this study, compared to about 14% in Barth and Berry's study.

The Smith and Howard study involved systematic case readings of a group of 74 disrupted cases and 74 intact placements. As in our study, the majority of the children were male and White. The next 2 major ethnic groups represented in the Barth and Berry study, Smith and Howard study, and our study were African Americans and Hispanics. Thirty-six percent of the intact adoptions in the Smith and Howard study and 40% of the intact placements in our study were foster parent placements. The average age at removal from birthfamilies in the Smith and Howard intact sample was 3.6 years, and the average age in our study was 3.56 years. The average age at removal from birthfamilies in our disrupted sample was 4.5 years, and in the Smith and Howard disrupted sample 4.6 years. The average age at placement in our study was 6.3 years for intact adoptions, and 7.9 for disrupted placements. In the Smith and Howard sample, the average age at placement was 7.3 years for intact and 8.4 years for disrupted adoptions. Despite some of the problems in the sample selection process in this study, the final sample is not significantly different in demographic characteristics from the samples used in the 2 comparison studies (Barth & Berry, 1988a; Smith & Howard, 1991).

## COMPARISON OF THE STUDY SAMPLE TO ALL DPRS CASES

In addition to checking the generalizability of our sample with other studies of special needs children and adoptive families, we compared the characteristics of the children and families selected in this study to the characteristics of all DPRS families that applied to adopt. The DPRS data presented in this section was prepared by the Forecasting and Program Statistics, Management Services Division, Department of Protective and Regulatory Services.

Table 3.17 compares selected characteristics of all DPRS families that applied to adopt during the same time period covered in this study and characteristics of all DPRS children who were adopted with those characteristics of the children and families in this sample. Our sample contained higher percentages of male children and lower percentages of females than in the overall DPRS sample. The majority of children in both the DPRS and the study groups were White, although there was a slightly higher percentage of African American and multiethnic children in the study group who were from dissolved and disrupted adoptive families. The DPRS sample has a higher percentage of children with one sibling in an adoptive placement than the study sample of children in intact and disrupted/dissolved adoptions. However, the study sample has a greater percentage of both intact and disrupted/dissolved adopted children who had no siblings in adoptive placements.

Children from both the intact and disrupted/dissolved adoptions in the study group appear to have experienced a significantly higher incidence of physical neglect and abuse and sexual abuse compared to cases in the DPRS population where information is available on the type of abuse experienced by the children. However, for the DPRS overall population, the large majority of data on the type of abuse experienced by the adopted child is missing.

The average age at placement and the length of time the child spent in the adoptive placement prior to consummation of the adoption was

**Table 3.17 A Comparison of 1984-1993 Selected DPRS Adoption Data with the Current Study Data**

| | DPRS Data | | Study Data | |
|---|---|---|---|---|
| | Total | Disrpt/Diss | Intact | Disrpt/Diss |
| Number of Children | 3,388 (100%) | 293 (8.7%) | 40 (100%) | 40 (100%) |
| **Sex** | | | | |
| Female | 1,714 (51.0%) | 142 (48.0%) | 18 (45.0%) | 16 (40.0%) |
| Male | 1,674 (49.0%) | 151 (52.0%) | 22 (55.0%) | 24 (60.0%) |
| **Ethnicity** | | | | |
| White | 1,709 (50.0%) | 172 (58.7%) | 18 (45%) | 17 (42.5%) |
| Black | 673 (19.9%) | 34 (11.6%) | 8 (20%) | 9 (22.5%) |
| Hispanic | 777 (22.9%) | 65 (22.2%) | 10 (2.5%) | 6 (15%) |
| Native American | 11 (0.3%) | 1 (0.3%) | 1 (2.5%) | 1 (2.5%) |
| Asian | 10 (0.3%) | — | — | 1 (2.5%) |
| Other | 208 (6.1%) | 21 (7.2%) | 3 (7.5%) | 6 (15%) |
| **Number of Siblings in Family in Adoptive Placement** | | | | |
| 1 | 1,712 (50.5%) | 160 (54.6%) | 12 (30%) | 11 (27.5%) |
| 2 | 422 (12.5%) | 30 (10.2%) | 7 (17.5%) | 6 (15%) |
| 3 | 157 (4.6%) | 12 (4.1%) | 2 (5%) | — |
| 4 | 49 (1.4%) | 5 (1.7%) | 2 (5%) | 4 (10%) |
| 5 | 22 (0.7%) | 2 (0.7%) | 1 (2.5%) | 4 (10%) |
| 6 | 4 (0.1%) | — | 1 (2.5%) | — |
| 7 | 1 (0.02%) | 1 (0.3) | — | — |
| 8 | 3 (0.08%) | — | — | — |
| No Siblings | 1,018 (30.1%) | 83 (28.4%) | 15 (37.5%) | 19 (47.5%) |
| **Types of Abuse** | | | | |
| Data Missing | 2,191 (64.7%) | 209 (71.3%) | — | — |
| Abandoned | 228 (6.7%) | 12 (4.1%) | 1 (2.5%) | 3 (7.5%) |
| Phys. Abuse | 246 (7.3%) | 13 (4.4%) | 9 (22.5%) | 17 (42.5%) |
| Sexual Abuse | 106 (3.1%) | 7 (2.4%) | 8 (20%) | 5 (12.5%) |
| Emot. Abuse | 161 (4.8%) | 11 (3.8%) | — | — |
| Phys. Neglect | 159 (4.7%) | 18 (6.1%) | 21 (52.5%) | 9 (22.5%) |
| Med. Neglect | 80 (2.4%) | 4 (1.4%) | — | — |
| Non-support | 163 (4.7%) | 15 (5.1%) | — | — |
| n/a | 54 (1.6%) | 4 (1.4%) | — | — |
| Other | — | — | 1 (2.5%) | 6 (15%) |

**Table 3.17 (continued)**

|  | DPRS Data |  | Study Data |  |
|---|---|---|---|---|
|  | Total | Disrpt/Diss | Intact | Disrpt/Diss |
| Average Age at Placement |  |  |  |  |
| In Years | 5.25 | 8.11 | 6.27 | 8.22 |
| Range (years) | .01-17.7 | .77-16.7 | .79-13.8 | .9-14.5 |
| Time from Adoptive Placement to Consummation |  |  |  |  |
| In months | 9.7 | 11.2 | 12.0 | 11.7 |
| Range (months) | 0-87 | .03-130.1 | .03-60.8 | 3.6-47.6 |
| Average Number of Placements |  |  |  |  |
| Placements | 3.1 | 3.3 | 3.1 | 4.1 |
| Range | 1-17 | 1-14 | 1-8 | 1-15 |
| Average Age of |  |  |  |  |
| Adoptive mother | — | 36.5 | 37.2 | 39.2 |
| Adoptive father | — | 38.3 | 39.6 | 37.6 |

similar for both the study group and the DPRS population. The average number of foster placements for children in intact adoptive families was the same for both groups. However, children from disrupted/dissolved adoptive families in the study population had a higher average number of foster placements prior to their adoptive placement than the general DPRS population of placed children.

Adoptive mothers in the disrupted/dissolved sample in the study group were on average slightly older (39.2 years) than the adoptive mothers in intact adoptions in the study group (37.2 years) and older than the adoptive mothers in disrupted or dissolved families (36.5 years) in the overall DPRS population. On the other hand, adoptive fathers in disrupted/dissolved adoptions in the study group were slightly younger (37.6 years) than the adoptive fathers in intact adoptive families in the study group (39.6 years) and those adoptive fathers in disrupted/dissolved families (38.3 years) in the DPRS population.

Data on the average annual family income for the general DPRS adoptive family population was not available for comparison with the study group. However, adoptive family information on the annual family income of 131 DPRS families that had disrupted or dissolved between 1984 and 1993 indicated that 47.2% (62 families) had an annual family income ranging from $34,000 to $63,000. This is very comparable to the entire study sample. As presented in earlier sections, intact families in the study group had an average combined annual income of $38,000. The dissolved and disrupted families in the study group had an average combined annual family income of $35,000 and $41,000.

## CONCLUSIONS

This chapter has provided a very detailed description of the birthfamilies, adoptive families, and target children who were part of the study sample. The demographic information on the birthfamilies suggests that most of the children were removed from very low-income, often unemployed, birthparents, many of whom have not completed high school. Parental rights were typically terminated as a result of neglect, or physical or sexual abuse. According to Pelton (1989), the most predominant characteristic of children in foster care is poverty. As mentioned in Chapter 1, many of these families do not have the resources to address the situational or personal factors that have led to child removal. Some of the parents have been engaged in illegal drug usage or other illegal activities. Once placed in the system, most of these children experience at least two, and often many more, placements before being adopted. The adoptive families in the sample had typically completed more education and had significantly more income than the children's birthfamilies.

The general characteristics of the adopted children and the adoptive families in the study group are similar to the DPRS population, and are also similar to the families and children in two well-known studies of disruption (Barth & Berry, 1988a; Smith & Howard, 1991). The comparison between characteristics of disrupted and dissolved placements yielded only two statistically significant differences. Adoptive mothers in dissolved adoptions had a higher commitment to the adoption at the time of placement than did mothers in disrupted adoptions. Adoptive families in disrupted adoptions were more likely to have experienced threats about the use of weapons than those in dissolved adoptions. The following chapter provides more detailed statistical comparisons between the intact, disrupted, and dissolved adoptions in this study.

# CHAPTER 4

# Intact, Disrupted, and Dissolved Adoptions: A Comparison

*(with Isaac Gusukuma)*

As mentioned in Chapter 3, the comparison between overall characteristics of the disrupted and dissolved cases yielded few significant differences between these two groups. Therefore, the two groups were combined to conduct bivariate analyses to determine factors that discriminated between the 40 disrupted/dissolved and 40 intact placements. This chapter presents the findings of these comparative analyses. Statistically significant differences were found between the two groups on the following factors: number of caseworkers involved with adopted child; number of foster parent adoptions; adoptive parents' commitment to adoption; and children's behaviors prior to removal, prior to adoptive placement, and during adoptive placement.

## NUMBER OF CASEWORKERS INVOLVED WITH ADOPTED CHILD

The number of case workers involved in a particular case from the time of initial investigation through consummation or dissolution was identified in each case record. Although the average length of time in care between first removal and adoptive placement did not differ significantly between the intact and disrupted/dissolved group, children in disrupted/dissolved adoptions had significantly more caseworkers involved in their cases. The average for intact placements was 6, and the average for disrupted/dissolved adoptions was 9.9 ($p < .01$). This difference could have been attributed to the more difficult nature of the disrupted/dissolved cases, and the fact that these children returned to the system after adoptive placement and were involved with more caseworkers than those who were in intact placements.

## FOSTER PARENT ADOPTIONS

Target children in intact adoptions were significantly more likely to have been adopted by their foster parents than those whose adoptions had disrupted/dissolved. Sixteen of the intact adoptions were foster parent adoptions, while only six of the dissolved/disrupted placements were foster parent adoptions (see Table 4.1).

## ADOPTIVE PARENTS' COMMITMENT TO THE ADOPTION

Adoptive mothers in intact adoptions were significantly more likely to have a high commitment to the adoption than adoptive mothers in dissolved/disrupted adoptions. Similarly, adoptive mothers and adoptive fathers in intact adoptions were significantly less likely to have changed (decreased) their commitment to the adoption than adoptive mothers and fathers in dissolved/disrupted adoptions (see Table 4.1)

**Table 4.1 Differences Between Intact and Disrupted/Dissolved Cases**

| Factor | Intact | | Disrupted/ Dissolved | |
|---|---|---|---|---|
|  | *n* | % | *n* | % |
| Number of caseworkers for child ($p < .01$) | 6 | | 9.9 | |
| Foster adopt ($p < .005$) | 16 | 40 | 6 | 15 |
| High AM commitment to the adoption ($p < .05$) | 36 | 90 | 28 | 75.7 |
| AM changed commitment ($p < .0001$) | 4 | 10 | 23 | 62.2 |
| AF changed commitment ($p < .05$) | 5 | 14 | 19 | 51.4 |

## CHILDREN'S BEHAVIORS

During the case reviews, coders used items on the Achenbach Child Behavior Checklist to code information found in case records on the behavior of children in disrupted/dissolved and intact adoptions. Behaviors were coded for three points in time: prior to removal from birthfamily, prior to placement with adoptive family, and during placement.

## Prior to Removal from Birthfamily

Often, the case records contained rather limited information on behaviors of children in their birthfamilies. In some instances, this information was not codeable, as there was no record of specific behaviors. Table 4.2 summarizes the information available on significant differences noted in child behaviors prior to removal from the birth home.

Prior to the final removal from the birthfamily, children in disrupted/dissolved adoptions were more likely to have been exhibiting aggressive, acting-out behaviors. Many of these behaviors may have resulted from the fact that they were often physically and sexually abused in the birthfamily. In addition, these children were older at the time of removal than the children in the intact sample (see Chapter 3).

Data on behaviors at time of removal were only available on 69 of the 80 cases, since either all workers did not obtain this information from birthmothers at the time of removal, or, if obtained, the information was not recorded in the case narratives.

**Table 4.2 Behaviors Prior to Removal**

| Children's Behaviors | Intact | | Disrupted/ Dissolved | |
|---|---|---|---|---|
| (n = 69) | n | % | n | % |
| Eating problems (p < .05) | 0 | 0 | 5 | 15.0 |
| Depressed (p < .004) | 0 | 0 | 6 | 19.0 |
| Impulsive (p < .05) | 0 | 0 | 3 | 9.7 |
| Cruelty (p < .05) | 0 | 0 | 3 | 9.7 |
| Physical aggression (p < .05) | 1 | 2.6 | 6 | 19.4 |
| Verbal aggression (p < .05) | 0 | 0 | 3 | 9.7 |
| Arguing with siblings (p < .05) | 0 | 0 | 3 | 9.7 |
| Persistent disobedience (p < .05) | 0 | 0 | 4 | 12.9 |

## Behaviors in Foster Care

As noted above, children in disrupted/dissolved adoptions were much more likely to have been involved in disobedient and aggressive behaviors prior to removal from their birth homes than were children in intact placements. While in foster care, the children were generally in an average of two to three foster homes. Reports of problematic behaviors such as self-abuse, manipulative behaviors, bed-wetting, persistent disobedience, stealing, fire-setting, vandalism, arguing with siblings, and verbal aggression, seemed to increase while the children were in care. This "increase" may have resulted from (1) negative acting-out behaviors being observed and recorded in the records for the first time; (2) the child's reaction to the losses experienced; and/or (3) being moved several times in foster care.

**Table 4.3 Behaviors in Foster Care**

| Children's Behaviors | Intact | | Disrupted/ Dissolved | |
|---|---|---|---|---|
| ($n = 79$) | $n$ | % | $n$ | % |
| Sexual acting-out ($p < .05$) | 10 | 25 | 19 | 47 |
| Physical aggression ($p < .05$) | 7 | 17.9 | 16 | 40 |
| Arguing with peers ($p < .010$) | 2 | 5 | 11 | 27 |

Interestingly, some factors that differentiated the two groups prior to removal became more common with both groups prior to the adoptive placement.

**Behaviors During Adoptive Placement**

The following table presents the findings of the analysis of children's behaviors during the adoptive placement:

**Table 4.4 Behaviors During Adoptive Placement**

| Children's Behaviors | Intact | | Disrupted/ Dissolved | |
|---|---|---|---|---|
| (n = 79) | $n$ | % | $n$ | % |
| Sexual acting-out ($p < .005$) | 4 | 10 | 15 | 37 |
| Acting-out ($p < .0005$) | 6 | 15 | 21 | 52 |
| Depressed ($p < .010$) | 2 | 5 | 11 | 27 |
| Impulsive ($p < .05$) | 0 | 0 | 6 | 15 |
| Cruelty ($p < .05$) | 0 | 0 | 4 | 10 |
| Physical aggression ($p < .0005$) | 4 | 10 | 20 | 50 |
| Verbal Aggression ($p < .0005$) | 1 | 2.6 | 13 | 32 |

**Table 4.4 (continued)**

| Children's Behaviors | Intact | | Disrupted/ Dissolved | |
|---|---|---|---|---|
| Arguing with Siblings ($p < .010$) | 2 | 5 | 11 | 27 |
| Arguing with Peers ($p < .05$) | 1 | 2.6 | 8 | 20 |
| Vandalism ($p < .05$) | 0 | 0 | 5 | 12.5 |
| Persistent Disobedience ($p < .05$) | 3 | 7.7 | 12 | 30 |
| Persistent non-compliance ($p < .05$) | 3 | 7.7 | 11 | 27.5 |
| Hyperactivity ($p < .01$) | 2 | 5 | 11 | 27.5 |
| Manipulative ($p < .05$) | 3 | 7.7 | 10 | 25 |

During the adoptive placement, adopted children in intact placements had significantly decreased their acting-out behaviors, while children in placements that eventually disrupted or dissolved had escalated these behaviors. Fifty percent of the children in disrupted/dissolved placements were involved in physical aggression and 52% in acting-out behaviors. Thirty-seven percent were sexually acting-out in comparison with 10% in intact adoptions. These behavioral differences may partially account for the differential outcomes of these placements.

## SIMILARITIES BETWEEN INTACT AND DISRUPTED/DISSOLVED SAMPLES

Also of interest are child, family, and agency variables that were expected to vary significantly by status of adoption, but did not. For example, intact adoptions had an average of 2.4 foster placements, and dissolved/disrupted adoptions had an average of 2.9. Children in intact adoptions had an average of 2.3 siblings, and children in dissolved adoptions had an average of 2.4 siblings. They also did not differ significantly in the number of siblings placed with the adopted child. Target children in intact adoptions had an average of 1.22 siblings placed with them, and target children in dissolved or disrupted adoptions had an average of .98 siblings placed with them.

As summarized in Table 4.5 below, similar numbers of children of color and White children were found in the two groups.

**Table 4.5 Ethnicity of Adopted Children**

| Race | Intact | Disrupted/ Dissolved | Total |
|---|---|---|---|
| African American | 8 | 9 | 17 |
| White | 18 | 18 | 35 |
| Mexican American | 8 | 6 | 14 |
| Hispanic | 2 | 0 | 2 |
| Native American | 1 | 1 | 2 |
| Multiethnic | 3 | 6 | 9 |
| Total | 40 | 40 | 80 |

Similarly, no significant differences were found in the ethnicity of the adoptive parents. Other similarities between the two samples are identified below.

## Regions

Cases in the sample came from every region of the state, and significant differences were not found between the number of cases reviewed from different regions.

## Out-of-State Placements

Eight of the adoptions were out-of-state placements. Five were intact, and three were disrupted/dissolved.

## Reason for Adopting

Fourteen of the adoptive mothers in intact adoptions and 15 of the adoptive mothers in dissolved/disrupted adoptions had given infertility as a reason for adopting. Similarly, 19 of the mothers in intact adoptions and 13 of the mothers in disrupted/dissolved adoptions were motivated to adopt because of their desire for more children.

## Characteristics of Birthparents

As described earlier in this chapter, no significant differences were found between the demographic characteristics of birthparents of children in dissolved/disrupted and intact adoptions, nor in the characteristics of adoptive parents who had either intact or dissolved/disrupted adoptions. The birthparent characteristics that were considered in the analysis included the following: income, education, occupation, history of abuse, and circumstances surrounding the termination of parental rights.

## Characteristics of Adoptive Parents

Adoptive parent characteristics that were similar in each group were the adoptive mother and father's income, education, and occupation. Factors that differed between parents in intact and dissolved/disrupted adoptions, and which approached statistical significance, were previous experience with adoption and with parenting, and a history of abuse. Each of these factors is discussed in more detail in subsequent chapters.

Thirty-five (87.5%) of the adoptive mothers in intact adoptions had previous parenting experience, and 28 (75.7%) of the adoptive mothers in dissolved/disrupted adoptions had parented before. Adoptive mothers in intact adoptions were more likely to have had previous experience with adoption. Fourteen (35%) of the adoptive mothers in intact adoptions and 8 (21.6%) of the mothers in dissolved/disrupted adoptions had previous experience with adoption.

Fifteen (44.1%) of the adoptive parents in disrupted/dissolved adoptions had abuse in their backgrounds, compared with 11 (30.6%) of the adoptive parents in intact adoptions. This is discussed further in the Chapter 12.

## CONCLUSIONS

The sample of cases selected in the intact and in the disrupted/dissolved sample were very similar with regard to a number of factors, including the following: number of foster placements; ethnicity of adopted children and parents; distribution across regions of the state; number of in-state and out-of-state placements; reasons for adopting; and characteristics of birthparents and adoptive parents, such as income, education, and occupation. Adoptive mothers in intact placements were more likely to have had previous parenting experience and experience with adoption. Significant differences between intact placements and disrupted/dissolved placements were found in incidences of foster parent adoptions and adoptive parent commitment, as well as in acting-out behaviors of children.

Children in disrupted/dissolved adoptions were more likely to have exhibited physically aggressive, disobedient behaviors prior to removal, while in foster care, and during the adoptive placement than children in intact placements. However, it should be noted that although significantly different from the children in disrupted and dissolved samples, acting-out behaviors of children in intact placements escalated after removal from their birthfamilies and prior to adoptive placement. These negative behaviors that occurred after removal may have been a response to the separation and loss, and tended to decrease once the child was in a secure adoptive placement.

Key differences were found in the commitment level of adoptive parents in intact versus disrupted/dissolved adoptions. Families that had high adoptive mother commitment to the child and to the adoption were more likely to have intact placements. Lack of commitment might lead to a greater likelihood of unstable placements. Adoptive mothers and adoptive fathers in disrupted/dissolved adoptions were more likely to have changed their commitment to the adoption than those in intact placements.

Foster parent adoptions were much more common in the intact sample. This will be discussed further in Chapter 6. The total number of siblings placed, either apart or together, did not vary significantly between the two groups. However, as will be noted in Chapter 8, other issues such as relationship with siblings, parental preparation for sibling placement, and behavior patterns of sibling groups resulting from birthfamily experiences contributed to different outcomes in sibling placements.

Each of the issues raised in this chapter will be discussed in much greater detail in subsequent chapters of this book. The following chapter identifies additional agency, adoptive family, and child factors that influenced adoption outcomes.

# CHAPTER 5

# Agency, Adoptive Family, and Child Factors in Special Needs Adoptions

Intensive case readings and thematic analyses yielded additional factors not yet presented, which may have led to the varying adoption outcomes in this study. Researchers reviewed each case and categorized emerging themes in terms of worker/agency factors, adoptive parent factors, and child factors. The findings are presented in this chapter. As noted in previous chapters, differential reporting and documentation could account for some variations in placement practices as delineated in case narratives.

## INTACT ADOPTIONS

Although this book focuses primarily on factors that have led to problematic outcomes in special needs adoptions, there were a number of strengths associated with agency practices, adoptive parents, and adopted children that served to stabilize the adoptions of many special needs children. These will be discussed below.

### Agency and Worker Factors

*Communication with adoptive family.* Evidence was found in seven (17.5%) case records of intact placements that workers had especially good communication with the adoptive families during the pre- and post-placement process. The workers seemed very committed to the adoptive families and worked closely with the families either to help obtain services or to supervise and assess services already in place.

*Good match.* As will be discussed in Chapter 10, there were 16 (40%) cases of good fit or match between the child and the adoptive parents. In these cases, the agency and/or worker did a good job in matching the needs of the child with the resources of the adoptive parents.

*Awareness of child's needs.* Coders noted seven (17.5%) cases in which workers were especially effective in assessing the child's needs, and in which they could communicate these needs to the adoptive family.

**Adoptive Parent Factors**

*Strong commitment.* Thirty-five (87.5%) of the adoptive families in the intact sample were identified as having a strong commitment to the adoption prior to the placement. Some of the words and phrases adoption workers used to describe this commitment in the files were "eager for a child/children," "strong desire for a child," "strong desire to be a parent," "dedication to parenting and to the child," and "strong advocate for the child in their home."

*Strong marriage.* Six (15%) of the intact married couples were described as having very stable, strong marriages. Other descriptive words used by adoption workers to characterize these marriages were "mature," "committed," and "tenured."

*Communication with child.* Nine (23%) families were assessed as having good communication skills with the adopted child and with others involved with the child. For example, in two cases parents were described as working hard to advocate for their adopted children in the schools.

*Openness to seek professional help.* Sixteen (40%) of the case records contained statements that suggested that the adoptive families were open to seeking help for their families through therapy. Some of the families were already receiving family therapy at the time of adoption or soon thereafter.

*Previous parenting experience.* The majority, 69 (89%), of the adoptive parents had had previous parenting experience. These experiences included parenting foster, adoptive, and biological children. Three of the 40 families had had no parenting experience at all. In two families the adoptive father had prior parenting experience and the adoptive mother had none.

Six (15%) of the adoptive families were involved in fost-adopt placements and had been parenting the target child, with the intent to adopt, for a significant period of time before the adoption. Ten (40%) of the intact adoptive families had been foster parents and chose to adopt the target child after serving as the child's foster parents for a period of time.

*Previous parenting experience with special needs children.* The families who had previous experience with special needs adoptions had the following commonalities in their familial characteristics: information-seeking, help-seeking, and strong support systems.

*Support system.* Eight (20%) of the families seemed to have strong systems in place for help and support. These included extended family, friends, and the church. The support was described as emotional, physical, and in one case, financial.

*Outside community involvement.* Four (10%) families were described as being very involved in church activities, clubs in the community, and neighborhood sports. In the case records, these families were identified as having high energy and being very active.

*Realistic expectations and flexibility.* Sixteen (40%) of the intact families seemed to be realistic and flexible in their approach to the adoptions. With realistic expectations, there is acceptance of the child and who the child is in all respects (i.e., emotional, psychological, physical, and in respect to abilities and achievement). With acceptance comes the flexibility to adjust to the child as the needs of the child change over time. Flexibility and realistic expectations have been identified in several studies as indicators of stable placements (Rosenthal, 1993).

*Positive personality characteristics.* In 17 (42%) cases, the following positive characteristics were used to describe these adoptive families: loving, caring, concerned, empathetic, and patient.

*Maturity/stability.* Adoptive parents were described as being stable or mature in 11 (28%) cases. According to two of the case narratives, the maturity of the adoptive parents may have resulted from life experiences, such as serious illness of one of the parents, or difficult marital issues that required therapy but had been resolved.

**Child Factors**

As discussed in Chapter 4, the children in the intact sample were slightly younger at the time of removal and placement and exhibited fewer acting-out behaviors than the children in the disrupted/dissolved sample. A few displayed assorted behaviors that can be attributed to the normal process of integration into the family. Six (15%) of the cases fit into this category, in which the children exhibited behaviors such as tantrums, self-absorption, being strong-willed, aggressiveness, and acting-out. These can be negative behaviors, but they are usually not long-term and may not necessarily require therapy to correct. Only 15 (26%) of the children in the intact sample had issues that needed to be addressed through therapy. These included non-communicative/ internalized sorrow, abandonment issues, non-identified trauma, sexual abuse issues, attachment issues, and loss issues. However, all of these were being handled relatively well during the placement.

## DISRUPTED/DISSOLVED ADOPTIONS

**Agency and Worker Factors**

*Failure to acknowledge importance of target child's separation issues.*
In 12 (30%) of the cases, the child was clearly dealing with issues of separation from birthparents, siblings, and foster parents; however, the case narratives did not provide evidence that these issues were being addressed with the child. In several cases, there was no discussion of how the child was dealing with the trauma of multiple placements or how the child was prepared for the termination of the birthfamily's parental rights.

Several records indicated that the children did not want to be adopted due to their loyalty to the birthfamily, yet the record did not reflect how these issues were addressed. In one case, the child was non-verbal and was unable to express his anger, grief, or understanding of the reasons for removal from the foster family. In another case, the target child cried when moved to another foster home, and the worker responded with, "What's wrong with you?" In this case, the worker's infrequent visits made it impossible to assist the child in dealing with the separation. During the placement, the child talked a lot about wanting to look up his birthmother and not wanting to be someone else's child. These statements signaled his confusion about the adoption and lack of opportunity to deal with his loss. In three other cases, the records suggested that the worker lacked sensitivity toward the child's feelings. For example, in one record, the worker specifically asked a 10-year-old child if he knew any reasons why the foster family would not want him, as they still had not decided to adopt him.

*Lack of thorough evaluation of adoptive parents prior to placement.* In 16 cases (40%), issues associated with the adoptive parents' feelings about adoption, experience with past abuse, and feelings about discipline and other important issues were not described in the home study narrative. Some files only contained one reference letter on the family. In several instances, reference letters mentioned some concerns about a prospective family or were just non-committal about the family, yet narrative accounts did not address how these were handled with the family.

As will be discussed further in Chapter 12, 14 of the adoptive mothers and 10 adoptive fathers had themselves been victims of child or spousal abuse. In 2 families, both the adoptive mother and adoptive father had been victims of abuse themselves. Moreover, 13 of the adoptive parents whose adoptions disrupted or dissolved allegedly abused a child in their care. For example, during the pre-adoptive assessment process, one prospective adoptive parent failed to answer 90% of the questions on a questionnaire used to assess parental attitudes about sexual patterns and tolerable sexual behavior. However, there was no indication in the agency worker's narrative that the adoptive parent's lack of clarity about the sexuality questions was ever discussed with him, prior to his being approved as an adoptive parent.

*Inadequate parental preparation, training, and support to deal with behaviors of the target child.* In nine (23%) cases, adoptive parents were not prepared to deal with the child's problems. For example, in one case the adoptive parents were told about the child's developmental delays before the adoption but were not told about the child's emotional problems, physical aggression, and sexual acting-out behaviors until after the adoption. The only recorded interventions (other than continued medication for ADHD) were made before placement and after dissolution. In another case, the child was engaged in sexual acting-out in the foster home but, according to the case narratives, little attention was given to preparing the adoptive family to have a realistic understanding and expectations of what may occur after the child was in the adoptive family. In several cases, although the record indicated that the family had access to all information on the adopted child before adopting, the adoptive mother claimed she was unaware of many of the child's previous behavior patterns and diagnosis as emotionally disturbed. Generally, the adoptive parents were in denial, and not attentive to what they were told or to what they had read.

In six (25%) cases, adoptive parents indicated that they did not know of the child's problems and did not receive support or assistance from the worker in resolving the problems. For example, in one case, the family, in desperation, requested that the worker spend the weekend with the family to get an understanding of the day-to-day problems they were having. The worker not only declined, but the record did not include any indication of specific help or referrals that were made for this family. In another case, the adoptive parents felt "abandoned" by the agency as they sought help for previously undisclosed and uninvestigated sexual abuse of the target child. This out-of-state family requested subsidy assistance for treatment. They contacted the regional and state offices, and even the governor's office, for help, but felt they did not receive satisfactory help.

Also, in several cases, problems arose after a family was allowed to adopt additional children while already parenting very difficult special needs children. Poor transition planning that occurred in 16 cases (40%), and poor matches in 32 cases (80%) were also worker/agency issues that led to disruptions and dissolutions. These specific issues are addressed in Chapters 10 and 11 in this book.

**Adoptive Parent Factors**

A variety of adoptive parent issues were identified as being related to the disruption or dissolution. These included the following.

*Adoptive parents' unrealistic expectations of the target.* In nine (23%) cases, adoptive parents had unrealistic expectations of the child's behavior or performance in school, often due to poor matches.

*Adoptive parent abuse of target child.* In 15 cases, adoptive parents abused the target child and/or another child in the home, which led to the disruption/dissolution. In four cases, the adopted child was sexually abused by the adoptive parents.

*Marital problems.* In 13 cases (33%), adoptive parents' marital problems contributed to the disruption/dissolution. These problems included poor communication, lack of equal commitment to the adoption, and unrealistic expectations of the impact that adopting a child would have on the marriage. In several cases, parents chose to adopt after raising children of their own and feeling that having other children in the home would bring them closer together. In one case, children were placed with parents that had minimal communication skills in their marriage, yet these parents were expected to cope with children who needed to communicate about sexual abuse trauma that they had experienced. Just as they ignored their marital difficulties, the parents ignored the children's problems by discontinuing therapy.

*Financial problems.* In 16 (40%) cases, adoptive parents developed financial problems, despite the availability of subsidies. In 1 case, the adoptive father declared bankruptcy of his business due to the high costs of residential treatment for the sibling group they had adopted. In 5 cases, one of the adoptive parents became unemployed during the course of the adoption, which led to severe financial problems. In 1 case of a single-parent adoption of 2 siblings, resources became extremely limited as soon as the mother lost her job. She applied for a subsidy to pay for the children's counseling, but did not begin to receive it for 3 months, and then only received subsidy for 2 months of counseling.

*Poor parenting skills.* In 11 (28%) cases, there was clear evidence that poor parenting skills contributed to the breakdown of the adoption. Families that had no previous parenting experience, and/or little experience with special needs children, and/or little ability to empathize with the situation of the child had tremendous difficulty parenting children who were placed in their care. Sometimes, problems stemmed from immature adoptive parents, lack of spousal support, history of abuse in the adoptive parent's background, or mismatch between child and parent. For example, an adoptive parent who had requested only a male infant received instead a sibling group of school-age sexually abused girls. The adoptive parent was unable to accept the children's acting-out behavior and had little empathy for the children's difficult past. The most obvious indicator of poor parenting skills involved parents who physically punished their children to try to get behavioral compliance. However, there were also reports in the record of cases in which parents used guilt or threats of adoption dissolution to try to change a child's behavior. For example, one adoptive mother told her acting-out child that "if you are not good, I will give you away." Some parents, despite having received MAPP training, were totally overwhelmed by the behaviors of the children in their care and did not know how to approach these problems.

In one case, an adoptive mother had been told by the agency worker that her sexually abused son would probably masturbate and engage in sexual acting-out behavior. However, she became very perplexed when this actually occurred, as her strong religious beliefs and traditional upbringing led her to believe that these behaviors were wrong and should be punished. Some of the parents refused therapy, since they felt they should be able to take care of family problems without outside help. Also, several families that did not feel comfortable with the fact that their child was on medication, weaned the child from medication that had been prescribed to control behaviors. In three cases, the adoptive parents appeared to use the target child as a scapegoat for all of the adoptive family's problems.

**Adopted Child Behaviors**

*Sexual acting-out.* A total of 19 (47%) target children had been sexually abused. Twelve children were sexually abused in the birthfamily, 3 in the foster home, and 4 in the adoptive home. The adopted child behavior that seemed to have the most impact on adoption disruptions and dissolutions was sexual acting-out. In almost half of the disrupted/dissolved sample, the target child was sexually acting-out. When this acting-out involved other children in the home, the target's adoption often disrupted or dissolved. In one case, the target child became pregnant by a birthson in the home. According to notes taken during the analysis of one case record, 4 male adopted siblings "exposed their genitals to their sisters and to children at school, wrote nasty notes to classmates, rubbed against sisters, and the adoptive mother observed one of the boys almost having sex with a puppy."

*Aggression.* In addition to sexual acting-out, the child's aggressiveness and acting-out behaviors in the adoptive home often led to disruptions/dissolutions. In one family, the target child was involved in lying, cheating, stealing, and very impulsive acting-out behavior. In at least two cases, the adoptive parents were physically threatened by the target.

In many of these cases of aggressive behavior and sexual acting-out, the child had not received therapy while in foster care and the behavior escalated in the adoptive placement.

*Developmental disabilities and delays.* As noted in Chapter 3, many of the target children had either been diagnosed or were suspected to have speech delays, learning problems, mental retardation,

ADHD, or other developmental disabilities or delays. This, of course, has a tremendous impact on the families that adopt these children, since the adoptive parents would need extra knowledge, resources, patience, acceptance, and expertise to guide the children appropriately throughout their lives. Also, many of these families had the added responsibility of other children in the home who also had developmental disabilities or delays. Some parents felt that they did not have adequate preparation for handling these types of problems or the associated stresses.

*Experiences in care.* In many cases, adopted children had experienced so many moves and separations, that they had difficulty settling into the adoptive family. For example, in one case, over a period of 4 years, a sibling group of sexually abused children had 12 caseworkers, had been moved 16 times from various foster homes to emergency shelters, and had been returned to the birthparents for periods of time ranging from 2 days to 3 to 4 months. There was no indication in the case record that issues of trust, autonomy, attachment, or self-esteem (in addition to the abuse) had been addressed. The adoptive family terminated therapy. The target child's adoption disrupted (but not that of his siblings); and afterward the child felt rejected by the birthfamily, foster parents, and adoptive parents, and by the biological siblings he tried to take care of and protect for much of the 10 years of his life.

In other cases, the children's negative experiences in foster care led to later problems. In one case, the foster mother of a 10-year-old child was extremely critical of the child, verbally badgered the child, and made very inappropriate comments to the child. For example, once when the child had inquired about seeing her biological mother again when she reached 18, the foster mother replied that the biological mother would probably be dead by then since she was an alcoholic. The child became very upset about the possibility of her mother's death. At other times, this foster mother had the child scrub the patio with a toothbrush as a punishment.

## CONCLUSIONS

The interaction of multiple factors associated with the adoptive parents, children, and agency led to varying outcomes of the adoptions in the study. For example, a poor transition plan, poor match, child's history of abuse, and lack of adoptive parents' previous parenting experience all led to the development of troubled adoptive parent-child relationships in many of these cases. Sexual acting-out in this study, as in the Smith and Howard (1991) study, was a factor in the majority of disrupted/dissolved placements.

The children in intact placements had generally been less traumatized, were younger, and displayed fewer externalized behaviors than the children in disrupted/dissolved placements. Adoptive parents in the intact group had more stable marriages, greater flexibility, more realistic expectations, more experience in parenting special needs children through foster care or adoption, and a greater commitment to the adoption and willingness to seek needed help. Children in disrupted/dissolved adoptions had been removed and placed at older ages, had been more severely traumatized, were exhibiting more troubling behaviors such as aggression and sexual acting-out, had experienced numerous losses, and were at greater risk at the time of the adoptive placements. The families who adopted these children seemed to be more marginal as well. Some had been abused themselves as children, had limited parenting experience, were less likely to seek help, had less realistic expectations of the child, and had less commitment to the adoption than the parents in the intact group.

The agency was more likely in the intact sample than in the disrupted/dissolved sample to have made good matches, to have engaged in good transition planning in moving the child into adoption, and to have exhibited an awareness of the child's and family's needs as well as a commitment to the family to find services as needed. Based upon the review of case records, these worker/agency strengths were identified as being exceptional in only a small portion of the intact sample. However, it is clear from these cases that better assessments as well as worker involvement may have made a difference in the outcomes.

# Placement Outcomes

# CHAPTER 6

# Foster Parent Adoptions

*(With Isaac Gusukuma and Steven Onken)*

Until the mid to late 1970s, foster parent adoptions were discouraged by adoption agencies. Most states had policies that emphasized that foster care was a temporary arrangement, and foster parents were warned not to become too attached to their foster children, as they would not be permitted to adopt them (Festinger, 1974). In fact, some agencies required parents to sign statements that stipulated that they would never try to adopt children in their care. According to Meezan and Shireman (1982), these policies resulted from the following concerns: (1) a need to maintain a pool of foster parents and preserve the integrity of foster care; (2) possible compromise of confidentiality of the adoption if the birthparents knew the location of the child's adoptive family, since they may have had contact while the child was in foster care (until recent years, open placements had been discouraged in adoption); (3) possible lack of appropriate agency efforts to match for compatibility between parent and child at the time of the foster placement; (4) the affect on other foster children in the home if the parents chose to adopt one child and not others; and (5) the potential for a decrease in family reunification efforts on the part of workers and the foster family, if a plan has been made for the foster parents to adopt.

As mentioned in Chapter 1, the emphasis since the 1970s on permanency planning for children as well as the growing number of "special needs" children needing placement led adoption agencies to reconsider the benefits of foster parent adoptions (Meezan & Shireman, 1982). In 1993 there were an estimated 460,000 children in foster care, which includes children in foster family homes, group homes, residential treatment, or institutional settings. By the latter part of this decade, it is predicted that over half a million children will be in foster care. Approximately 70% of these children live in foster family homes (Risley-Curtiss, 1996). The majority of these children are older, of minority background, and some have physical, emotional, or developmental disabilities.

In recent years, expanding the pool of possible adoptive family resources has become a major priority for adoption agencies and the nation (Risley-Curtiss, 1996). Policies have changed to facilitate the consideration of foster families as adoptive families, due in large part to the advocacy efforts of foster parent associations that have been fighting to preserve their rights as foster parents and to the realization that policies designed for the adoption of White healthy infants must be modified to reflect the growing need to gain permanency for older, waiting children of all races. Currently, in most states, legal and agency barriers to foster parent adoptions have been removed (Mica & Vosler, 1990), and many foster parents have been given preference in adoption placement decisions. In some states, foster parent preference increases in direct relation to the length of time in care. The Model Statute for Termination of Parental Rights, Model State Subsidized Adoption Act, and Model Adoption Act all include stipulations that advise giving foster parents preference when significant emotional ties have been established. The Model Adoption Act stipulates that factors such as length of time in care and the foster parent-child relationship should be considered in determining priority consideration for adopting (Proch, 1981). More recently, the Uniform Adoption Act provides for individuals who have served either as foster or de facto parents to be given standing to seek to adopt a child, given the child's needs (National Conference of Commissioners on Uniform State Laws, 1994).

Often, distinctions have been made between fost-adopt placements and unplanned foster parent adoptions (Barth & Berry, 1988a; Mica & Vosler, 1990). Fost-adopt placements refer to children who are *not* legally free for adoption, but who are placed in a home with the expectation that the foster parents will adopt if and when the birthparents' parental rights are terminated. These placements are often made in an effort to prevent multiple placements for children for whom adoption may likely be the outcome (Derdeyn, 1990). These adoptions, often referred to as "legal risk" adoptive placements, are controversial, since they present a sense of incongruity for foster parents and children because there are two goals in place: (1) family reunification; and (2) integration of the child into the foster family that could potentially become their adoptive family. However, these placements seem to be most appropriate when legal termination is very likely, that is, when birthparents have had their rights on other children terminated, when one parent has already relinquished and it is unlikely that the other parent will contest relinquishment, or when serious abuse of the child has occurred and reunification is highly unlikely (Barth & Berry, 1988a; Mica & Vosler, 1990).

In unplanned foster parent adoptions, no prior plan for adoption is made between the agency and the foster parents should the child become legally free. However, the close attachments that develop between foster parents and child may prompt families and workers to consider the possibility of adoption once parental rights have been terminated.

## STABILITY OF FOSTER ADOPTIONS

Very little, if any, distinction is made in the research literature between outcomes of fost-adopt (legal risk) and unplanned foster adoptions. Several studies have reported that foster parent adoptions (including both fost-adopts and unplanned foster adoptions) are more stable than non-foster parent adoptions (Barth & Berry, 1988a; Festinger, 1986; Nelson, 1985; Rosenthal, Schmidt, & Conner, 1988; Smith & Howard, 1991). For example, Smith and Howard (1991) reported that in their study 12% of adoptions by foster parents disrupted and 36% of adoptions by non-foster parents disrupted. Barth and Berry (1988a) suggested that the stability of foster parent adoptions might result from the family and child having a trial period to see if the adoption will work and, if not, the child may be replaced in another foster home. Although less stable for boys than for girls, Barth and Berry found that regardless of gender, these foster adoptions were more stable than non-foster family adoptions. They also noted that if children were adopted by foster parents less than a year after the foster placement, disruption rates were not significantly different from non-foster adoption placements; however, the longer the child is in the foster home, the greater the stability of the relationship, and the less likely it will be disrupted (Barth & Berry, 1988a). From their examination of adoptive placements of adolescents, Berry and Barth (1990) found that foster parent adoptions of teens appeared to be less likely to disrupt than adoptions by parents new to the teen. Interestingly, they found that these adoptions were more likely to disrupt if there were biological children in the home or other adopted children or pending adoptions in the home. No disruptions occurred in cases in which there were other foster children in the home (p. 217).

## ANALYSIS OF FOSTER PARENT ADOPTIONS

Content analysis of the 80 case records in this study revealed that 22 (27.5%) of the cases involved foster parent adoptions. The majority, 14 (64%), of the 22 foster parent adoptions were unplanned, and 8 (36%) were legal risk fost-adopts. Thirteen (7 unplanned foster adoptions and 6 fost-adopts) involved cases in which siblings were placed together. As in previous studies, foster parent adoptions were much more stable than non-foster parent adoptions. The majority, 16 (73%), of the 22 foster parent adoptions were still intact, 2 (9%) had disrupted, and 4 (18%) had dissolved. Characteristics of each of these placements will be described in this chapter.

### Intact Families: Unplanned Foster Parent Adoptions and Fost-adopts

Table 6.1 provides a synopsis of the similarities and differences in these placements. Ten (62.5%) of the 16 intact foster parent adoptions were unplanned foster adoptions, and 6 (37.5%) were fost-adopts (legal risk placements).

The 10 families that considered adoption after the foster child was legally free were more likely to be minority families, and to have adopted minority male children and children who were younger at removal than were the fost-adopt families. Four (40%) of the 10 children in unplanned foster parent adoptions were removed from their birthparents before the age of 4 months. Seven were inracial, and 3 were transracial foster placements of minority children with White families (one 6-week-old Black infant; one 8-week-old Mexican American infant; and one White/Hispanic 5-year-old). The majority (60%) of these unplanned foster adoptions were with minority families. Four of the families were White, 4 were Hispanic, and 2 were African American. Two of the children were placed in kinship foster care and 1 child was placed with a single foster parent. Four were placed almost directly from their birthfamilies into these foster homes. The 6 other children had been in other foster placements for the duration of between

**Table 6.1 Comparison of Characteristics of Intact Foster Parent Adoptions ($n = 16$)**

| Characteristic | Unplanned Foster Adoptions | Fost-adopt |
|---|---|---|
| Number | 10 (62%) | 6 (37.5%) |
| Reasons for removal | 7 neglected (mostly medical) and/or abandoned<br>1 physically abused<br>2 placed at birth (no abuse) | 2 sexually abused<br>4 abandoned/and/or neglected |
| Age at removal | 0-5 yrs. (avg. 1.51) | 0-7 yrs. (avg. 2.67) |
| Gender | 3 females<br>7 males | 4 females<br>2 males |
| Ethnicity of child | 5 Hispanic<br>1 Hispanic/White<br>1 African American/White<br>2 African American<br>1 White | 1 African American<br>5 White |
| Ethnicity of family | 4 Hispanic<br>2 African American<br>4 White | 1 African American<br>5 White |
| Number of prior placements | 4 placed almost directly<br>6 in care for 1 mo. to 2.5 years prior to placement | 3 in care between 5 months and 2 years<br>3 in only one other foster home |
| Age at placement | 1-6 (avg. 4.2) | 0-9 (avg. 4.3) |
| Single-parent placements | 1 | 1 |
| Transracial placements | 3 transracial (2 infants and one 5-year-old) | None |
| Time between placement and consummation | 10 months to 4 years | 10 months to 5 years |
| Cases involving sibling placements | 6 | 4 |

1 month and 1.5 years. Seven of the children had experienced neglect, and 1 had been physically abused, in their birthfamilies. Two were placed at birth and had experienced no abuse.

The majority of the adoptive parents had completed at least 10 to 12 years of school, and about one-third of the adoptive parents had college degrees. Seven of the 10 cases were categorized by coders as being a "good match" between child and adoptive family.

As noted in the table above, 5 of the 6 fost-adopters were White, and they were most likely to fost-adopt very young White children. The other fost-adopter was a single African American mother. None of the fost-adoptions were transracial placements. The children's average age at removal from their birthfamily was 2.67, although their ages ranged from birth to 7 years. Two had been sexually abused, and the 2 foster families with whom they were placed had received preparation in handling these issues. Four of the fost-adoptive parents had at least a high school education. No information was available in the records on the educational status of the other 2 families. Three of the children had been in only 1 other foster home before being placed in their fost-adopt homes. The 3 other children had been placed in other foster homes for 5 months, 19 months, and 2 years prior to the current placement. But even in these 3 situations, the children had only 1 other foster placement. Four of these fost-adopts involved sibling placements. Half of the cases were coded as a "good match" between child and adoptive family.

From the case records reviewed in our study, the following brief case assessments were developed of an intact fost-adopt and an unplanned foster parent adoption.

*Case Illustration 1 (Fost-adopt)*

> K., a five-year-old male child, was removed from his birthparents as a result of physical abuse. He and his sibling were placed in a fost-adopt home with an experienced, mature family already raising birth and adopted children. The foster family had previous experience with sexually abused children and was willing to take abused children under the age of twelve. K. had been in five foster placements before being placed in this home. The worker carefully assessed how the addition of K. would affect the other children in the home. Each agreed and communicated to the worker a good understanding of K.'s past and what issues it might bring up for them.

The foster family scheduled preplacement visits with two family members at a time, so that K. would not be overwhelmed. This family communicated with his previous foster parents to learn more about K.

Once placed in the fost-adopt home, K. was supervised at all times. Any concerns in this family were handled by joint decision-making in family meetings. The family was involved in using specific attachment techniques such as each family member reading bedtime stories and leaving K. with "good thoughts." Having a very strong marriage and an extremely positive relationship, the couple demonstrated trust and respect to family members and communicated well. They had consistent rules and viewed acting-out as healthy, enabling a child to express anger.

K. felt he was a member of the family before the adoption was consummated and felt he helped choose his family. The family expressed a willingness to participate in family therapy when and if needed.

## Case Illustration 2 (Unplanned foster adoption)

After four hospitalizations, L., a Hispanic male infant, was placed in foster care with a White couple in their mid-fifties. The birthmother had relinquished her rights because of her inability to care for a second child who had a diagnosis of cerebral palsy and possible mental retardation. The foster parents had already raised five children, but they became very attached to L. and asked the worker if they might be considered as possible adoptive parents for L. The agency encouraged this request as no other families had come forward for this child. The child was in the home 14 months before the adoption was consummated.

Despite the potential for problems, these intact foster parent adoptions seem to be very stable placements with well-prepared adoptive parents. Both the fost-adopt and unplanned foster adoption allowed the child to develop a relationship with adoptive family members before the adoption. These were also fairly ideal situations, because most of the children had not experienced multiple prior placements. The majority of the children were considered "low-risk," as most had been neglected, and *few* had experienced severe abuse or neglect prior to the placement. Most of these adoptions were considered "well-functioning" placements, as the adoptive parents had adopted very young children with *relatively few behavioral problems.* The children had typically been placed with their siblings. The families seemed very flexible, well-adjusted and very committed to the adoptions. Severe burns, cerebral palsy, possible retardation, and lack of a thyroid were among the major child problems that several families were facing.

As many of these families had prior experience as foster parents, they had realistic expectations of children with special needs. They may have had a stronger commitment to and understanding of what it takes to parent than non-foster parent adopters. These placements were also less risky situations than many of the non-foster adoptions. The children had been removed from their families at an earlier age and had been placed in fewer foster homes than had children of comparable ages who were eventually adopted by non-foster parents. The average age at removal for the 24 non-foster parent adoptions in the intact sample was 4.64 (compared to 1.51 and 2.67 for unplanned and fost-adopt), and the average age at placement was 7.62 for non-foster parent adoptions (compared to 4.4 and 4.3 for unplanned and fost-adopt).

**Disrupted/Dissolved Foster Adoptions**

Four (18%) of the 22 foster parent adoptions had dissolved and 2 (9%) had disrupted. One of the 2 disrupted and 3 of the 4 dissolved adoptions were unplanned foster adoptions. One disrupted and 1 dissolved placement were fost-adopts. Since the subsample size of disrupted/dissolved adoptions was so small, and no statistically significant differences were found in the number of foster placements and length of time prior to the adoption for either fost-adopts and unplanned foster parent adoptions in the 2 groups, the subsample was combined for further analysis. Table 6.2 provides a brief synopsis of these placements. As noted in the table, the average age at removal was 7.8 years, and average age at placement was 10.8. Before the final placement in the foster adoptive home, these children had been in from 1 to 6 placements (average 3 placements). All of the adoptive placements were inracial.

**Table 6.2 Characteristics of Disrupted/Dissolved Foster Parent Adoptions (*n* = 6)**

| Characteristic | Disrupted/Dissolved |
|---|---|
| Reasons for removal | 2 neglect |
| | 4 physical/sexual/ emotional abuse |
| Age at removal | 1.63-12.4 |
| | (avg. 7.8) |
| Gender | 3 females |
| | 3 males |
| Ethnicity of child | 2 Hispanic |
| | 4 White |
| Ethnicity of family | 2 Hispanic |
| | 4 White |
| Number of prior placements | 1-6 placements |
| | (avg. 3 placements) |
| Age at placement | 5-14 (avg. 10.8) |
| Single-parent placements | 1 |
| Time between placement and consummation (dissolved only) | 1 month to 2 years |
| Time between placement and disruption/dissolution | 4 months to 5 years |
| Cases involving sibling placements | 3 |

Although all the cases of disrupted/dissolved foster adoptions involved families with previous parenting experience, the following risk factors were present: (1) generally, the children were older at removal and placement (one exception); (2) the emotional stability of adoptive parents was an issue in each case; (3) there were different levels of commitment by each adoptive parent; (4) the adoptive parents were not required to seek family counseling; and (5) the children had experienced abuse and troubled backgrounds. In the case of the older child placements, the outcomes were primarily influenced by previous experiences, relationships in the adoptive home, attachment to previous caregivers, "poor match," and abuse by adoptive parents.

The following case examples illustrate the issues in these cases.

*Case Illustration 3*

N., a Hispanic nine-year-old female, and her 2 biological siblings, had been removed from their parents due to neglect. They were all very attached to their birthmother. The birthmother did not follow through with the service plan and parental rights were terminated. While in foster care, N. was sexually abused in one of her two foster homes.

N. and her siblings were placed with a fost-adopt family when N. was 12. Unfortunately, she and her siblings were placed in a home in which the fost-adopt father had difficulty expressing and managing anger. Occasionally, the father was physically abusive to the fost-adopt mother and to the children. The family was under severe financial stress and had difficulty handling the children's school problems, as they had high academic expectations for the children. N. was a chronic liar and the other siblings were extremely physically aggressive. About three months into the placement, N. accused the fost-adoptive father of sexual abuse. However, the accusation was not validated. In this fost-adopt family, the father was the primary caregiver. The children received counseling, but the fost-adopt parents failed to go in for their own counseling (which was recommended by the worker on three occasions during the placement phase). The adoption disrupted about 10 months later.

## Case Illustration 4

R., a White female was removed from her birthfather's home at the age of 12 as a result of physical, emotional, and sexual abuse by her birthfather. The birthmother had abandoned the child at birth. R. was very attached to the birthfather, for whom she had become the primary caregiver after he became very ill. R. had been in two other placements prior to this unplanned foster adoptive placement. Her foster adoptive mother was clinically depressed, and her foster adoptive father was not very involved in the family. The family was experiencing severe financial difficulties. R. was given a lot of responsibility in the home caring for several adopted siblings with disabilities. R. at one point attempted suicide. The adoption disrupted about eight months after placement.

These illustrations emphasize the need for the agency to evaluate carefully foster, as well as adoptive, families for emotional stability. Background information, including history of abuse within the foster family, must be considered. For example, in Case #3, upon closer examination, the agency learned that the fost-adopt father had been physically abused as a child by his own birthfather, and became physically abusive toward the fost-adopt child. The child had been neglected in her birth home, sexually abused in a previous foster home, and placed in a fost-adopt home with a physically abusive fost-adopt parent.

In five of the six cases of disrupted/dissolved placements, marital problems were exacerbated during the period of the child's placement. Also, in each of these cases, there was only one primary caregiver, and the other parent was less committed to the adoption. Better assessments of commitment of both parents to the adoption and marital relationships is essential. In addition, in several cases, foster adoption parents clearly needed counseling but were only encouraged, not required, to receive it. Family counseling might have strengthened the marital relationship and family relationships in many of these situations.

## Disrupted/Dissolved Foster Adoptions and Intact Foster Adoptions: A Comparison

Children in the disrupted/dissolved foster parent adoptions in this study were significantly older at the time of removal and placement; had been in more prior placements; and were more likely to have experienced physical, sexual, and emotional abuse than the children in the intact foster adoption sample. They had strong attachments to their birthfamilies, and in some cases, previous foster families. As Meezan and Shireman (1985a; 1985b) noted, the earlier children enter the system, the less likely they are to have formed close attachments and experienced multiple placements, and they may be more able to reattach in the new family. Moreover, parents sometimes find it much easier to relate to younger children. Children who have been in multiple placements and are older at initial placement are more likely to have issues of attachment, grief, and loss that can hinder their ability to form new, close attachments in foster or adoptive families (McRoy, 1994).

Although the adoptive parents in the disrupted/dissolved sample had previous parenting experience much like the parents in the intact sample, the emotional stability of the parents was an issue in each case. Clearly, if workers are to improve the likelihood of making better matches between parents and children, much more attention must be given in assessing foster parents' mental health, parenting skills, and commitment to the children. Attention must also be placed on the child's prior experiences, and the necessity of securing treatment for the child to address issues of loss, prior abuse, or neglect.

## CONCLUSIONS

Qualitative analysis of the case record data in this study yielded a number of important insights about foster parent adoptions. The foster parents in these cases that chose to adopt children in their care primarily seemed to have made the decision after having become very emotionally attached to the children. In a number of cases, the children themselves expressed an interest in having the foster parents adopt them. Some of the foster parents who adopted were infertile, and desired to parent children. Others had birthchildren who were grown and chose to raise more children through foster parenting and adoption. The adoption subsidy provided with most of the children made it possible to handle the additional financial responsibility.

As in previous studies, much stability was found in the foster parent adoptions. Of the 40 disrupted/dissolved placements reviewed in this study, only six (15%) involved foster parent adoptions. The majority (55%) of the 40 intact placements were foster parent adoptions. The stability of these placements may have been due to the longer period between initial placement and consummation; attachment between child and adoptive family; and adoption of very young children who had not been severely abused, neglected, or experienced numerous losses, moves, and traumatic situations. The workers may have made better assessments and matches in some of these placements, as most of the parents had had experience as foster parents and had worked with other children with special needs. In these cases, the family not only had access to the child's records, but also knew how the child behaved and knew what they could expect from the child. As a result of this trial period, the likelihood of a good fit or match between the child and family may have improved (Meezan & Shireman, 1982).

The foster parent adoptions that disrupted/dissolved seemed to have been affected by the same factors that contribute to adoption disruptions and dissolutions in general. Therefore, much of what has been identified as useful in preventing disruptions/dissolutions specifically also seems to apply to foster parent adoptions (i.e., careful screening of adoptive parents, fewer child placements, better matches, and ongoing therapy for child and family). Clearly, this suggests the need to utilize the same type of assessment, training, and preparation with foster parents as with adoptive parents. Additional worker training is needed in evaluating risk factors in each placement.

As mentioned earlier, foster parent adoptions are controversial, as they may actually be "adoptive placements by default," and provide infertile couples who might not ordinarily be approved for an infant with an opportunity to parent infants or very young children. The concern is that these placements are often made without consideration as to whether a specific foster family will make the best adoptive parents for a particular child (Gardiner, 1987; Mica & Vosler, 1990). This must be weighed against the fact that foster parent adoptions can sometimes prevent additional moves, transitions, losses, and broken attachments, which occur when children remain in foster care for a long time and must repeatedly move from one home to another. However, these study findings are similar to Barth and Berry's (1988a) in that the stability of foster adoption placements of children over the age of 12 is not significantly different than non-foster adoption placements. This suggests the need to place children early, reduce the number of moves, assess foster parents very carefully (much like adoptive parents), and consider "match" of child and family when making foster placements into adoptive placements. Therefore, if an unplanned foster adoption is in the best interest of the child, the foster parents, like adoptive parents, will have received the same scrutiny and consideration of "best fit" for a specific child.

Additional studies are needed that compare samples of intact foster parent adoptions and intact non-foster parent adoptions, to better identify the differences in each and how to take such differences into account when placing all children. For example, the level of involvement of the target child in selecting the permanent family seems to be much higher in foster parent than non-foster parent adoptions. Perhaps when workers are planning a fost-adopt placement, they need to engage the target child more actively (if age appropriate) in this decision-making process. Also, as previous parenting experience with children with special needs and prior relation with the child may be factors that lead to more stable placements, agencies should consider these as factors in selecting prospective adoptive parents. Moreover, future studies should compare family dynamics and communication in non-foster parent adoptions and in foster parent adoptions with children ages 12 and above, to learn more about the development of trust, attachment, and relationships in order to improve chances of adoption stability.

# CHAPTER 7

# Single-Parent Adoptions

With the growing number of children needing adoptive placements, agencies are seeking single parents, as well as two-parent families, for special needs children. Groze and Rosenthal (1991a) define single-parent adoptions as adoptions by unmarried persons. This definition does not include cases in which a divorce or death of a spouse results in a single-parent adoption (p. 67). To date, researchers have given only limited attention to outcomes of single-parent adoptions of special needs children.

Research studies that have compared characteristics of single-parent adopters and married couple adopters have reported differences between the two groups in gender, ethnicity, age of child adopted, educational level of parents, and family income. For example, Groze and Rosenthal (1991a) reported the findings of their retrospective study of these two types of adopters of special needs children. They found that the 122 single parents in their sample were more likely than two-parent families to adopt non-Whites, females, older children, and children with mental retardation. On the average, single adoptive mothers were significantly older than married adoptive mothers in their study, and the single mothers were more likely to have completed a high school education than mothers in two-parent families. As might be expected, single mothers in this study had significantly lower incomes than did two-parent families. The majority of the single mothers in their study were African American, in contrast with most of the two-parent adoptive families who were White (Groze & Rosenthal, 1991a). Similarly, other researchers have also reported that single adopters are more often members of populations of color (Branham, 1970; Feigelman & Silverman, 1977; Shireman & Johnson, 1976).

Similar to the Groze and Rosenthal (1991a) sample, Branham (1970), Shireman and Johnson (1976), and Feigelman and Silverman (1977) found that most single adoptive parents adopt children who are the same gender as themselves. However, Barth and Berry (1988a) found that single parents in their study were more likely to adopt boys. Although the majority of studies reporting statistics on adoption disruptions in single and two-parent families suggest no significant differences in disruptions between the two groups (Barth & Berry, 1988a; Berry & Barth, 1990; Boyne, Denby, Dettenring, & Wheeler, 1984; Festinger, 1986; Kagan & Reid, 1986; Rosenthal & Groze, 1992), two studies suggest that single parents have an increased risk for disruption (Boneh, 1979; Partridge, Hornby, & McDonald, 1986). It is important to note that these increased disruptions may be less a function of the type of adoption, but more a function of the severity of problems of a particular child and agency practices. Workers sometimes consider single parents as adoption resources for children who have some or all of the following characteristics: severe problems, older in age, of minority parentage, and those who have been available for adoption for some time and it is unlikely that a two-parent family will be found.

In this study, 9 (11%) of the 80 cases reviewed were adoptions by single parents. Only 3 (33%) of the single-parent placements were still intact at the time of the study. Two (22%) had disrupted, and 4 (44%) had dissolved. More detailed findings on single-parent placements by type of adoption outcome are reported below.

## INTACT ADOPTIONS

Two of the 3 intact single-parent adoptions were foster adoptions (see Chapter 6). At placement, the children were 1, $2^1/2$, and 12 years of age. Two of the children in these placements had experienced a history of abuse in their birthfamilies. All adoptions were consummated from 6 $^1/_2$ months to 3 years after the placement, and all involved male children placed with single adoptive mothers. One of the intact adoptions was an out-of-state placement.

In 2 of the 3 intact placements, the single adoptive mothers had previous parenting experience. One of the single adoptive mothers had adopted 3 other children and was raising 1 biological child prior to the target child's adoption. Another single mother was raising 2 adopted children prior to adopting the target child and his 4 biological siblings.

As in previous studies, the single adoptive parents were older than parents in two-parent adoptions. These single adoptive parents ranged in age from 32 to 53 years, with the average being 43. The average age of all adoptive mothers in the total intact sample was 37. Their educational levels ranged from high school completion to college degree.

All of the children placed in the intact single-parent homes were members of ethnic minority groups. Two of the children were African American males placed with African American single mothers. A Puerto Rican male was placed with an African American/White adoptive mother. Although these three cases are currently intact and normally would be considered successful adoptions, a review of the case record data on two of these intact cases reveals that in reality these cases are currently at risk for dissolution. The following notes extrapolated from agency records suggest possible problems emerging.

A 45-year-old single adoptive mother had been raising two adopted boys when she sought to adopt a sibling group of five. Four of the five siblings were placed in the home, three months before B., the oldest, a 12-year-old aggressive boy, was placed there. As this was an out-of-state placement, there were no post placement reports of direct worker contact in the record. B. remained in the home for two years before the adoption was consummated. During this period, the possibility of disruption came up several times, but the adoptive mother sought family counseling and individual counseling for B. The worker was kept updated by notes from the family therapist. B.'s memories of abuse while in his birth home, and his issues of loss of his prior foster family were very difficult for him to handle. The adoptive mother had experienced one adoption disruption in the past. According to the record, the adoptive mother's former spouse provided some help to her from time to time.

The other at-risk, yet intact, placement involved a $2^1/_2$-year-old who was described in the records as "a developmentally delayed male who attached indiscriminately and was very demanding" of his 32-year-old, college-educated, single adoptive mother. The adoptive mother had had no prior parenting experience and very limited financial resources. There was no documentation of worker visits to this family until 8 months after the placement. At that time, the worker noted that the adoptive mother was unemployed and was having trouble finding a job in her field. There was no indication that the worker provided guidance or assistance in helping her find a job. This adoption was consummated almost a year and a half the after placement, when the child was 4.

Both of these placements described above are clearly in need of post-adoption counseling and support if these adoptions are to remain intact. In the first case, the single adoptive mother is parenting seven children. Although they are involved in family therapy, this mother will probably need a lot of ongoing support over the years. The primary issues for the single mother in the second case were unemployment, limited financial resources, minimal post-placement support, and need for parent skills training. However, both adoptions remain intact and the parents seem very committed to the placements.

## DISRUPTED SINGLE-PARENT ADOPTIONS

There were two disrupted single-parent adoptions in this sample. One was a foster parent adoption by a single White adoptive father who adopted a White male child, and the other involved an African American single female who adopted an African American male child. The children in these cases were 7 and 10 years of age at the time of placement, and the adoptive parents were 38 and 39 years of age, respectively. Both chose to adopt because they felt the need to parent. One had prior parenting experiences, and the other had experience as a foster parent of special needs children. Transitions into the home and matching seemed to be major issues in these disrupted adoptions (see Chapters 10 and 11). The following case notes taken by the researcher illustrate some of these concerns.

> A single adoptive father was parenting, through a fost-adopt place-ment, a 10-year-old boy, J., when he began providing respite care for P., another 10-year-old boy, who had been residing in another foster home. After J.'s placement was consummated, the adoptive father considered adopting P. He met with P.'s caseworker and was told that P.'s background information was available whenever he wanted to read it. There was no indication in the case narrative whether the adoptive father actually read the child's background information. However, the adoptive father had been adamant with the worker that he did not want a child who was aggressive or destructive, both of which were characteristics of P., who had been sexually abused in his birth home and separated from his biological siblings throughout

most of his five prior foster placements. When the adoptive father decided to adopt P., he became the oldest child, as he was about two weeks older than J., the first adopted child living in the home. In the very early months of P.'s placement, the adoptive father sought therapy, but the focus was entirely on J. Sibling rivalry and P.'s destructive and acting-out behavior led to P.'s placement disrupting after he had been in the home four months.

According to the case documentation P. had expressed his desire to not be placed with a single adoptive parent, and the adoptive father really did not want to adopt a child with P.'s type of problem behaviors. It is unclear from the record why the adoptive father decided to pursue the placement; however, the placement seemed somewhat coerced and not carefully planned.

A 38-year-old single mother was parenting her 7-year-old biological son when she decided to adopt. The mother had no prior experience with special needs children and had said that she did not want a child with behavior problems. S., a 7-year-old boy, was placed in her home for adoption, within five days of meeting the mother and her son. S. had been sexually abused, was severely depressed, and had no record of receiving therapy prior to this adoptive placement. The adoptive mother considered therapy "punishment from God," and therefore refused to seek help once problems developed. S.'s adoption disrupted several months after placement.

There was no indication of extended family support for either of these adoptive parents. In the first case, the adoptive father appeared isolated and the records indicated that he had unresolved issues of childhood sexual abuse (see Chapter 12). Both of the single adoptive parents had previous parenting experience, but not with difficult, acting-out children. The adopted children had unresolved issues pertaining to the loss of their birthfamilies and previous experiences with sexual abuse.

## DISSOLVED SINGLE-PARENT ADOPTIONS

Four (40%) of the 10 single parent adoption cases in the sample had dissolved. The children in the cases were 5, 8, 10, and 12 years of age at placement. Two male children were adopted by single fathers, and 2 females were adopted by single mothers. Ages of the adoptive parents were 28, 32, 40, and 41. One of the children was White (placed with a White adoptive mother), one Mexican American (placed with a Native American/White adoptive mother), one White/Hispanic (placed with a White adoptive father), and one African American (placed with an African American adoptive father). None was a foster parent adoption, and only one was a sibling placement.

Three of the single adoptive parents had very little social or familial support, but they were receiving counseling. Three of the adoptive parents were parenting other children at the time of the adoption. The following case notes taken by the researcher illustrate these dissolved cases.

> A 28-year-old, single adoptive father with no previous parenting experience adopted an eight-year-old male child, M. The child was dealing with issues of loss, separation, and grief regarding his birthmother and siblings, who had been killed in a fire. M. became physically aggressive, homicidal, and suicidal. The adoptive father maintained his commitment to the child, but had become very fearful of the child. After the dissolution, the child was placed in residential treatment.

> A single female in her mid-forties was caring for an adult sister with Down's syndrome, when she adopted B., an 11-year-old girl who had been sexually abused. Soon after the consummation of B.'s adoption, the adoptive mother adopted another girl, N., age 10. B. recalled that problems began in her adoptive home, once N.'s adoption papers were signed. The adoptive mother became physically abusive to B. and the adult sister. This adoptive mother eventually committed herself to a psychiatric hospital, and the adoption dissolved.

In these cases, one of the children was dealing with serious issues of loss, and the other had been sexually abused. The former was placed with a parent with no previous parenting experience, and the latter child was placed with a mother who was emotionally disturbed. Better assessments were needed of the strengths and limitations of adoptive parents before placing children. In addition, much more worker contact is needed after placement to identify problems and situations of risk before it is too late. Much more attention must be given to the resources and parenting abilities of any parent, but especially for single adoptive parents who may have few, if any, resources or supports.

and parenting abilities of any parent, but especially for single adoptive parents who may have few, if any, resources or supports.

Pre-placement periods were very short in these dissolved cases of older child placements. One was placed 4 days after the initial meeting, and another was placed 5 days after the 1st meeting. The longest pre-placement period was 15 days. Two of the adoptions were consummated within 7 months, and 1 in 9 months. Two of the single adoptive parents whose adoptions dissolved continued to be very committed and still have contact with the target adopted child. (One adopted child has currently returned from residential treatment to the adoptive parent's home.)

## CONCLUSIONS

In this study, the majority of the single-parent placements had disrupted or dissolved, and although three were intact, two of the three were "at risk." The interaction of child, family, and agency factors influenced these outcomes. In these cases, adoptive parent factors included few or no support systems, financial problems, adoption of too many children, parental mental health issues, lack of preparation to handle acting-out disturbed children, and adoption of children with characteristics with which the parent was not comfortable. In one case, the adoptive mother was opposed to seeking therapy, and in another, the adoptive mother's abusiveness and emotional disturbance led to dissolution.

In common with previous studies of single-parent placements, the majority (70%) of the single-parent adopters were persons of color, and 80% of the target children were children of color. The majority (70%) of the single-parent adopters had adopted boys. However, the adoptive parent's gender, ethnicity, or level of education did not appear to have a significant effect on the adoption outcome. Ages of the adopted child and the adopted parents, as well as the gender of the adopted child, were not primary factors in these cases. However, the fact that the placed child was the same age or older as a child already in the home set the stage for some sibling rivalry in two of the families. Most of the children placed in the disrupted and dissolved single-parent homes were dealing with significant issues of loss as well as abuse, and exhibited aggressive, acting-out behaviors.

The problematic outcomes in this study should not suggest that single parents cannot be good resources for special needs children. However, it is important for workers to assess carefully the strengths and limitations of each prospective family. Three of the single parents in this study were engaged in seemingly successful adoptive placements when they decided to adopt again. The subsequent placements led to adjustment problems in the family, one disruption, and one dissolution.

Considering the fit or match between the child and prospective family is essential (see Chapter 10). To improve practice in special needs adoptions, agencies need to examine closely the assessment process for all adoptive parents; the impact of having families "stretch" to consider adopting more children or children who have characteristics that adoptive parents feel they cannot handle; and procedures and requirements for post-placement problem identification and intervention. Family attitudes toward seeking therapeutic intervention should also be assessed for all families seeking to adopt, as many families of special needs children will need therapy for the child and family. Longer pre-placement periods, and longer periods of close, post-placement supervision are needed to provide support to these families.

# CHAPTER 8

# Sibling Placements

When children are removed from their birthfamilies, they not only experience the loss of their birthparents, but they also may grieve deeply the loss of siblings (Hegar, 1988). This grieving and stress associated with the loss may be, in actuality, even greater than grieving parental loss. These sibling relationships, in many families, have provided emotional support and buffered the effects of a very conflictual family situation. In some instances, an older biological child has often served as a substitute parent for younger children, and through frequent interaction and support, the relationship deepens. Thus, children who have come from very dysfunctional birthfamilies may have stronger attachment to siblings than to their parents.

However, clinical evidence of problematic sibling relationships provides some support for the deliberate separation of siblings in subsequent placements. In some sibling relationships, the following may occur: (1) one child's emotional needs become so great that he or she needs the sole attention of the adoptive family; and (2) it becomes necessary to break dysfunctional relationship patterns such as constant scapegoating, violent sibling jealousy, or situations in which a parentified child is unable to give up the role. Other factors that influence the decision to separate or keep siblings together are: (1) the existing relationship between the children; (2) the size of the sibling group; and (3) availability of adoptive families with resources for handling more than one child (Ward, 1984). Hegar (1986) found that sibling separation was more likely to occur in cases of large sibling groups, older children, children entering care at different times, and children experiencing developmental disabilities.

Conflicting findings have been reported concerning gender differences in sibling placement decision-making. For example, Aldridge and Cautley (1976) found that: (1) girls were more likely than boys to be placed with siblings; (2) children with a history of fewer foster placements were more likely to be placed together than children with more previous placements; and (3) less emotionally disturbed children were more likely to be placed together. However, Staff and Fein (1992) noted, in their study of a private foster care program, that boys were more likely to be placed together than girls. These researchers also examined the impact of age and race on sibling placement disruptions in private foster care. In their sample, fewer White sibling groups were placed together, and of those that were, White sibling groups had significantly higher disruption rates than Black, Hispanic, or mixed race children. These researchers also noted that sibling groups consisting of teenage siblings were much more likely to disrupt than groups without teenagers. In their study, siblings who were initially placed together were less likely to have a disrupted foster placement than children who were placed separately (Staff & Fein, 1992).

Additionally, divergent findings have been reported on outcomes of sibling placements in adoption. For example, Boyne, Denby, Dettenring, and Wheeler (1984) reported that sibling placements are more likely to disrupt, while Rosenthal, Schmidt, and Conner (1988) found no differences in disruption rates between sibling placements and non-sibling placements. Festinger (1986) observed that children placed without siblings had a significantly higher rate of disruption than those placed as part of a sibling group. The higher rate of disruption may have occurred either because these children had greater problem severity and therefore were placed separately, or because the separation from siblings was so problematic that the children had trouble adjusting in the adoptive home (p. 25). Groze (1996) reported no strong differences between behaviors of siblings placed together and those placed apart in his sample of intact adoptions.

Some studies have suggested that adoptive family structure may impact outcomes of sibling placements. Kadushin and Seidl (1971) reported that sibling placements in homes that already had one or more children were more likely to disrupt than those with only the placed siblings. Lahti (1982), however, concluded that the age of the other children in the home is the key factor. According to Lahti, there is increased risk for disruption when sibling groups are placed in families with other children who are about the same age. Similarly, Barth and Berry (1988a) found no disrupted adoptions in sibling placements in homes with no other children.

The choice to place siblings together must be based on a very careful assessment of sibling relationships, the potential interaction effect which could occur when the child or siblings are placed in an adoptive family; and the child's or siblings' requests regarding their desire to be placed together (Ward, 1984). The structure of the adoptive family is also a factor to be considered. When separations are necessary, it is essential to try to minimize the impact of the loss by facilitating visitation and contact between siblings.

In this study intensive qualitative analysis of all records was conducted to identify all cases in which sibling placements had occurred. As mentioned in Chapter 2, in each case one child (the oldest in a sibling group) was identified as the target child and information was collected on siblings' relationships with the target child.

Forty-six (57.5%) of the reviewed case records involved sibling placements. Within this group, 25 (54.3%) of the target children placed with siblings were currently in intact placements, 8 (17.4%) children had been in placements that disrupted, and 13 (28.3%) had been in placements that had dissolved. Thirteen (28%) of the sibling placements were foster parent adoptions. The number of siblings placed with the target child ranged from 1 to 6.

Of the 46 families that had adopted sibling groups, the majority, 27 (59%), were currently parenting or had parented biological children. Eighteen (67%) were parenting biological children at the time of the adoption. Ten of the 18 (56%) placements had either dissolved or disrupted. A myriad of factors were found to influence placement outcomes when siblings were placed together. They are identified below in the following analysis of sibling placements in intact, disrupted, and dissolved placements in this study.

## SIBLING PLACEMENT ISSUES IN INTACT ADOPTIONS

Twenty-five (62.5%) of the 40 intact adoptions involved target children placed with 1 or more siblings. Fourteen (56%) of the 25 children in intact sibling placements were members of ethnic minority groups. Four were African American, 6 were Mexican American, 2 were Hispanic (non-Mexican American), 2 were racially mixed (Mexican American/White) and 11 were White. Seven were transracial placements of primarily Mexican American and Hispanic children with White families. One African American child had been transracially adopted by a White family. Fourteen (56%) of the 25 target children were female, and 11 (44%) were male.

Reasons for removal varied in this sample. Nine of the target children had been sexually abused, and 4 of these had also been physically abused. In 4 cases, neglect and abandonment had occurred. Neglect was one of the reasons for removal in 23 of the 25 cases. In 5 of those cases, neglect was the sole reason for removal. In 4 of the cases, neglect was coupled with abandonment. Four of the total neglected children had been sexually abused, 1 had been physically abused, and 4 had been both sexually and physically abused.

Thirteen (52%) of the adoptive families parented never had biological children, and 4 (16%) families had biological children who were no longer in the home at the time of the adoption. The ages of the adoptive mothers in this group at the time of placement ranged from 24 to 52 years, with an average age of 37.3 years. The ages of the adoptive fathers ranged from 28 to 49 years, with an average age of 38.9 years.

Although the age at removal of the target children in the intact sample ranged from infancy to 9 years of age, more than half were less than 4 years of age at removal. Average age at time of removal was 3.69 (see Table 8.1, below).

**Table 8.1 Age at Removal (Intact Sibling Placements)**

| Age | n |
|-----|-----|
| <1 year | 4 |
| 1-3 | 11 |
| 4-6 | 8 |
| 7-9 | 2 |
| Total | 25 |

At the time of placement, target children in intact sibling placements ranged from ages 2 to 13, with an average age of 6.87 years (see Table 8.2, below). Fifteen (60%) were younger than 7 at the time of placement. Length of time between removal and placement ranged from 1 to 7 years.

**Table 8.2 Age at Time of Placement (Intact Sibling Placements)**

| Age | n |
| --- | --- |
| 2-3 | 4 |
| 4-6 | 11 |
| 7-9 | 7 |
| 10-12 | 2 |
| 13 | 1 |
| *Total* | 25 |

The largest sibling group placed together consisted of 6 children placed with the target child. There also were 2 sibling groups of 4. Twelve of the target children had only 1 other sibling placed with them. Seven had 2 siblings placed together, and 2 had 3 siblings placed together. In one case, the adoption of 2 of the siblings disrupted, but the identified target child remained in the adoptive family.

Qualitative analysis of these sibling placements revealed the following factors that may have influenced the current intact status of these cases: (1) the majority of the children were less than 4 years of age at the time of removal, and less than 6 at the time of placement; (2) 13 (52%) of the children had not experienced any physical or sexual abuse, and most may have had less severe psychological damage in birthfamilies; (3) prior contact or knowledge of the children seemed to be a factor in several of the intact sibling placements; and (4) 10 (40%) of the intact sibling placements were foster parent adoptions, in which the parents and children had been able to develop a relationship before the adoption. Other examples of previous contact are illustrated in the case descriptions below.

Although three physically and sexually abused female siblings were placed together with an adoptive family, both the adopted children and adoptive family had received very good preparation for the adoption. The adoptive mother had spent three months tutoring the three girls before the placement. The children had an opportunity to develop a relationship with the adoptive mother, and the mother was able to learn more about the children and assess her family's ability to assume responsibility for the siblings.

A White, female, ten-year-old child and her eight-year-old sister were placed with a family parenting two other special needs adopted children. Prior to the placement, the adoptive parents had been baby-sitters for the target adopted child and had developed a relationship.

A sibling group of six (including a set of three-year-old twin girls), who had been neglected in their biological family, were placed in a relative foster adoptive family who were parenting three other children. The birthmother had requested a relative placement, and the adoption seemed to be working very well. However, the limited financial resources of the adoptive family may lead to future problems.

In other intact cases, it appeared that good matches between adoptive parents and children, willingness to seek therapy, committed adoptive parents, and good marital communication led to positive outcomes in the placements. In one case, a large sibling group of very needy children was placed out-of-state with a family already parenting several special needs children. However, social workers' ongoing encouragement and support seemed to make the difference in preventing disruption.

Although the majority of the sibling placements remained intact, many of the families had experienced very difficult issues stemming from the multiple placements. Notes from one case are provided below.

T., a parentified 14 year-old girl, was placed with her nine- and five-year-old brothers. The adoptive parents were successful in lessening the nine-year-old brother's dependence on his sister and allowing the child to speak for himself and not through his older sister. Unfortunately, other factors prevented the two boys from attaching in this home, and their adoptions disrupted although T.'s adoption is still intact.

At the time of the study, several intact families were experiencing major life stressors and were at risk for disruption. These stressors included: separation of adoptive parents resulting in a single mother parenting seven children; the responsibility of parenting sexual acting-out children; a severely disabled child; and parenting of several foster children and two acting-out adopted siblings.

## SIBLING PLACEMENT ISSUES IN DISRUPTED ADOPTIONS

Eight (53.3%) of the 15 disrupted adoptions in the sample involved sibling placements. As in the intact sample, the majority of the children were racial minorities. Three of the target children were White, 2 were Mexican American, 2 were African American, and 1 was multiethnic. Two of the placements were transracial. Five of the 7 target children were males, and 3 were females. Three were removed from their birthfamily as a result of neglect, 1 due to sexual abuse and neglect, 1 due to neglect and sexual abuse of siblings, 1 due to physical abuse and neglect, 1 due to physical and emotional abuse, and 1 due to murder of birthmother by birthfather. Their ages at removal ranged from less than a year to 9 years of age. The average age at removal was 4.8 (see Table 8.3, below). Four (50%) of the families in this group were raising biological children at the time of the adoption.

**Table 8.3 Child's Age at Removal (Disrupted Sibling Placements)**

| Age | n |
| --- | --- |
| <1 year | 1 |
| 1-3 | 3 |
| 4-6 | 2 |
| 7-9 | 2 |
| *Total* | 8 |

The target children's ages at placement ranged from 3 to 12 years, and the average age was 8.55 (see Table 8.4). At the time of disruption, they ranged in age from 6 to 15, with an average age of 10.1 years (see Table 8.5, below). They had been in the adoptive placement between 2 and 8 years. The largest sibling group consisted of 4 children. The 3 target children who each had 4 siblings were placed with their siblings, and all of these adoptions disrupted. One child had 3 siblings, 2 of which were placed with the target child. One target child had 2 siblings, both of which were placed with the target child. Three children had only 1 sibling, and that sibling was placed with the target child. Of the 8 disrupted sibling placements, only 1 was a foster parent adoption. At the time of placement, the ages of the adoptive mothers in this disrupted group ranged from 36 to 45 years, with an average of 41.1 years. At placement, adoptive fathers' ages ranged from 33 to 46 years, with an average of 39.6 years.

**Table 8.4 Child's Age at Time of Placement**

| Age | n |
|---|---|
| 3 | 1 |
| 4-6 | 2 |
| 7-9 | 2 |
| 10-12 | 3 |
| Total | 8 |

**Table 8.5 Child's Age at Time of Disruption**

| Age | n |
|---|---|
| 6-7 | 3 |
| 9 | 1 |
| 11-12 | 3 |
| 14 | 1 |
| Total | 8 |

Poor matches between adopted children and parents led to several disrupted adoptions. The following notes were taken from their case records:

> Five sexually and physically abused siblings were placed out of state with a two-parent family who already had adopted four sexually abused girls. Previously, the sibling group had been separated during a foster placement after returning to a pattern of sexual abuse learned in the birthfamily's home. Upon reunification in the adoptive home, they resumed their pattern of sexual acting-out. The adoption of two male children disrupted, and the family kept the three female children.

> Adoptive parents who were desperate for an infant adopted two school-age children. After the placement, it became apparent that the adoptive parents had marital problems, and the adoptive mother began abusing the children.

> An older, inexperienced couple decided to adopt because they thought their marriage might improve if they had children in the home. The adoptive mother felt that adopting children would give the

parents more time together. Their adoption of a sibling group of four disrupted one month after placement.

A family with financial problems, who were already parenting four biological children, was selected to adopt two siblings. Their biological children became very jealous of the time the adoptive mother spent with the adopted children. Also in this family situation, the target child who was accustomed to being the oldest of his siblings became a younger child in the new adoptive family. The target child had a difficult time adjusting to this role reversal.

When a sibling group of five was placed in a foster adoptive placement with parents in their mid-sixties, the stress of five very troubled children became too much for the family. The adoptive father became physically abusive, and the adoption disrupted.

Social workers' notes, found in the case records of two of these troubled family situations, recommended that the families receive counseling as soon as problems began to surface. However, both families refused, stating that they could handle their own problems. Evidently, they were allowed to refuse therapy, as there was no indication of further worker involvement until the disruption.

## SIBLING PLACEMENT ISSUES IN DISSOLVED ADOPTIONS

Thirteen (52%) of the 25 dissolved adoptions in the sample involved sibling placements. Target children in this subgroup included 6 females and 7 males. The majority of the dissolved sibling placements involved White children. Eight (61.5%) were White, and there was 1 (7.7%) Native American, 2 (15.4%) Mexican Americans, 1 (7.7%) multiethnic child, and 1 (7.7%) African American. Two of the adoptions were transracial (1 Mexican American child/White adoptive parents and 1 multiethnic child/White adoptive parents).

The primary reasons for removal from birthfamilies of three of these target children were physical abuse and neglect. Two were removed after experiencing sexual and physical abuse and neglect, 1 was sexually and physically abused, 1 was sexually abused and neglected, 1 was sexually abused, 2 were neglected and abandoned, 1 was neglected, 1 was abandoned, and 1 voluntarily relinquished. The children's age at removal ranged from 2 to 10 years of age, and the

average age of children at removal was 6.35 (see Table 8.6, below).
Four (31%) of the families had never parented biological children, and
3 (23%) others had no other biological children in the home at the time
of the adoption. Six (46%) of the families were parenting biological
children at the time of the adoptive placement.

**Table 8.6 Child's Age at Removal (Dissolved Sibling Adoptions)**

| Age | *n* |
|-----|-----|
| 1-3 | 2 |
| 4-6 | 7 |
| 7-9 | 3 |
| 10 | 1 |
| Total | 13 |

Age of the children at placement ranged from 4 to 14 years (see
Table 8.7, below). The target children ranged in age from 6 to 16 at the
time of dissolution, with the majority being between 11 and 14 years of
age. The average age at the time of dissolution was 12.8 years (see
Table 8.8, below). At the time of dissolution, the target children had
been in the adoptive placement for between 8 months and 7 years, with
the majority having been in placement for 1 to 3 years.

Target children had between 1 and 6 biological siblings. Four
target children had 1 to 2 siblings, 1 had 3 siblings, 3 had 4 siblings, 2
had 5 siblings, and 1 had 6 siblings. The number of the adopted child's
siblings placed with the target child ranged from 1 to 4. Eight of the
target children had 1 sibling placed with them in the adoptive home, 4
had 2 siblings placed with them, and 1 had 4 placed.

In the 6 cases in which the target child had no more than 2 siblings,
all were placed together. In another case, a target child was placed with
4 siblings. Five of the 6 target children who had 3 to 6 siblings had only
1 sibling placed with them, and the 6th had 2 of his 4 siblings placed
with him. Only 2 (15.4%) of these adoptions were foster adoptions. The
remaining 11 (84.6%) adoptive families had had no previous contact
with the children before the adoption. The average age of the adoptive
mothers in this group at the time of placement ranged from 30 to 48,
with an average age of 38.7 years. The adoptive fathers ranged in age
from 33 to 51 years with an average age of 42.1 years.

**Table 8.7 Child's Age at Time of Placement**

| Age | n |
|---|---|
| 4-6 | 2 |
| 7-9 | 4 |
| 10-11 | 6 |
| 14 | 1 |
| Total | 13 |

**Table 8.8 Child's Age at Dissolution**

| Age | n |
|---|---|
| 6 | 1 |
| 10-12 | 5 |
| 13-15 | 6 |
| 16 | 1 |
| Total | 13 |

A review of the dissolved adoptions involving sibling placements reveals a number of factors that may have led to the dissolutions. The children in the dissolved sample were older at the time of removal from their birthfamilies than in the other adoption outcomes, they had been more severely abused than the children in intact placements, and in some family settings, had experienced sexual abuse in the new adoptive placement.

For example:

> T., an 11-year-old sexually abused parentified girl, who had never received any therapy for abuse prior to the adoption, was placed with her older brother in an adoptive family raising two teenage birthsons. A few days after consummation, T. was raped by the adoptive parents' older birthson. Upon investigation the family learned that T. had been sexually active with both birthchildren in the home. T. later gave birth to a child fathered by the older birthson.

> S., a severely sexually abused eight and one-half year-old girl, was placed in adoption with her male sibling, who had sexually abused S. while in the birthfamily. The adoption dissolved after S. reported further sexual abuse by her biological brother and the adoptive

parents' son. The adoptive parents blamed S. for the problems. The girl was 11 $^1/_2$ years old at the time of the dissolution.

In the next case, the worker, despite professional advice to the contrary, supported a single mother in her quest to adopt a very troubled sibling group.

R. was placed with a White, 40-year-old single woman who wanted to have a family. The adoptive mother had requested to adopt a sibling group of two between the ages of 7 and 12, but did not express a gender preference. She was very happy to receive 11-year-old R. The adoptive mother was aware that R. had been sexually abused in previous settings and that she had three siblings, also abused, who were still in foster care.

A year later, the agency contacted this single adoptive mother to determine her interest in adopting two of R.'s three older siblings. The siblings' foster mother and psychologist said that it was not in the best interest of R. to be placed with her siblings. However, the state agency insisted that their policy was to place siblings together. About fifteen months after R.'s placement, two of her brothers were placed in the same adoptive home. At a later time, the adoptive mother contacted the agency and insisted that the oldest sibling be placed in the home as well. He was placed despite worker and therapist reservations. This oldest sibling, a fifteen-year-old boy, did not want to be adopted as he was attached to his caseworker in a group home. Once all the siblings were together, R. became aggressive, sexually acted out, needed constant supervision, threatened the adoptive mother and dog, and became involved in gang activity. The stress of these three siblings and R., who were all acting out, in addition to the financial burden on the single parent, led to the dissolution.

Poor placement decision-making seemed to account for several of these troubled adoptions. Also, in another case, the adoptive mother had a possible multiple personality disorder, and the parents had serious marital problems. Other examples are provided below.

A family that requested a sibling group with at least one boy adopted a sibling group with three girls. The adoptive mother had no previous parenting experience. According to the records, during the early phase of the placement, the target child, O., was called a "bitch" by the adoptive mother. O. was often scapegoated by the adoptive mother. All three girls were very fearful of the adoptive mother, and O. became the protector of her siblings in the adoptive home as she had been in her birth home.

A sibling group consisting of three boys and a girl was placed in a family raising three biological children. One of the adopted boys molested the family's biological daughter, and all three boys were engaged in sexual acting-out behavior with one another. The oldest adopted male sibling, seven, threatened the adoptive mother. The three boys were removed while their younger sister remained in the adoptive home after the dissolution.

From the following case notes, it appears as if adoptive parent abusive behavior led to the dissolution in this sibling placement.

A 10-year-old boy was placed with his younger 4-year-old brother in a home with an abusive adoptive mother and passive adoptive father. In this case, the younger brother was favored in the adoptive home, and the adoptive mother beat the older sibling severely just prior to removal.

In other cases, the worker's lack of contact with the family appeared to be one of the key reasons for the failure to identify problems earlier on in the adoption. In several cases, the children were very closely attached to their birthsiblings, as well as their birthmothers, and found it hard to attach to another family. In two cases, the children felt responsible and guilty for making the outcry of abuse that had led to their removal from their birthfamilies. Both engaged in self-mutilation, and one was suicidal prior to the dissolutions.

## CONCLUSIONS

Whether siblings were placed together or apart in adoption was not associated with any specific outcome in this sample. Unlike Barth and Berry (1988a), who found no cases of disrupted adoptions in sibling placements in homes with no other children, in this study, 50 percent of the disrupted and 54 percent of the dissolved placements had no other children in the home at the time of the sibling placement. The majority of children in intact placements had at least one sibling placed with them. Issues emerged in these placements regardless of the ethnicity of the children or families. However, the age of children at removal and placement appeared to influence adoption outcome. The intact sample was characterized by children removed and placed at much younger ages than the children in the disrupted and dissolved sample. These younger children had also experienced less abuse in their prior placements than the older children whose adoptions disrupted or dissolved. The majority of the children in intact placements had not reached the very difficult adolescent years.

Eighty-five percent of the target children in dissolved adoptions were over seven at the time of placement, and seven of these were in pre-adolescence or adolescence at the time of dissolution. Cases in which siblings disrupted and the target did not typically involved older siblings, primarily boys. However, it is important to note that even in cases of intact adoptions, a number of problems were identified that may impact later adjustment and eventual outcome of some of these placements.

The review of case narratives on each of these families and children revealed agency/worker issues that may have also influenced the placement outcomes.

- Although sometimes noted in the records, very little elaboration was provided in the case narrative regarding the sibling's place or role in the birthfamily (i.e., parentified child, protector, etc.) or how the child felt about the role or the expectation to change the role in a new home.

- Learned patterns of relating or getting attention (i.e., sexual acting-out, parentified child) in birthfamilies or dysfunctional sibling relationships were often repeated in adoptive families. It was unclear whether parents were prepared for this possibility and how it might impact their family.

- Many of the target children and siblings had not received therapy for issues of abuse, loss of birthfamily members, or preparation for adoption.

- In most of these cases, the target children and siblings were extremely emotionally needy and were dealing with the trauma of abusive backgrounds. They were typically placed in families that rather quickly became overwhelmed by the responsibility. In some instances, when the families were urged to get counseling, they refused.

- The impact of placing sexually abused and sexually acting-out girls in homes with adolescent boys did not appear to be dealt with adequately in many cases. It was unclear from the records how much and what types of preparation the prospective adoptive families had for the placement of sexually acting-out siblings.

- The decision to place sibling groups in many of these families seemed to exacerbate an already troubled marital situation or family financial strain.

- Frequent worker contact and good preparation of the children and families was characteristic of some of the intact placements and of none of the disrupted and dissolved placements.

- The records did not convey much about the children's feelings of loss and grief associated with removal from their birthfamilies, foster families, or other siblings not placed together.

The specific reasons for sibling separation or placement together were often not provided in the records. It appeared as if deliberate attempts were made to place children who had been together in foster care in the same adoptive family. However, the significance of the relationship (whether functional or dysfunctional) between the children was rarely discussed in the case narratives. Timberlake and Hamlin (1982) suggest that separations of siblings may lead to feelings of guilt among other siblings. Workers must assess the sibling group to determine the feelings each member has about the others and their feelings about separation, consider previous separations, and develop visitation plans and communication in case siblings are separated. Hegar (1993) suggested that workers should engage in individualized evaluations of attachment, permanence, and kinship in selecting permanent homes for foster children. She recommends determining which home can offer the best balance in terms of each of these factors.

Among the many factors that may affect placement outcomes for sibling groups and which should be incorporated into the family selection process are:

1. Adoptive parent preparation for sibling groups
2. Parental motivation for adoption
3. Quality of marital relationship
4. Parenting experience
5. Experience with and behavioral expectations of sexually and physically abused older children
6. Parenting and discipline skills
7. Parent's history of abuse
8. Reasons for adopting
9. Relationship of parents with own birthchildren
10. Willingness to seek counseling
11. Training in understanding sibling relationships
12. Opportunity for adoptive parents to get to know the children and develop a relationship before placement
13. Number of siblings and type of abuse in background
14. Availability of therapy for children
15. Child's willingness and desire to be adopted
16. Child's relationship with siblings
17. Child's feelings of guilt or responsibility for removal
18. Worker assessment and preparation of child, siblings, and adoptive family
19. Child and siblings' behaviors in foster care
20. Availability of family for follow-up contact
21. Loyalty issues
22. Child's feelings of loss or grief for birthfamilies or previous caretakers.

The following chapter explores another controversial issue in adoption placement decision-making: transracial adoptions.

# CHAPTER 9

# Transracial Adoptions

*with Isaac Gusukuma*

Transracial adoptions refer to children from one racial background who are placed for adoption with families of a different racial background. Typically, transracial adoptions involve the placement of ethnic minority children with White adoptive parents. In an effort to promote the adoption of the many minority children in need of homes, state laws as well as national legislation (the Multiethnic Placement Act) have been passed in recent years to prohibit discrimination on the basis of race in adoption. Currently, state laws in Texas prohibit the state agency from using race as a criterion in placement decision-making. In fact, an independent psychological evaluation of a child must be completed to justify any consideration of race or ethnicity in placement planning (McRoy, Oglesby, & Grape, 1997). These policies represent a national and state response to the concern that race matching policies may serve to delay or deny the placement of a minority child for adoption. Transracial placements remain controversial (McRoy, 1989; Silverman, 1993), as many suggest that if systemic obstacles to adoption by minority families were addressed, transracial placements would not be needed (McRoy, Oglesby, & Grape, 1997). Moreover, Sullivan (1994) has noted that specialized minority adoption programs have proven that in reality African American and Latino families are actually available for infants and preschoolers and that most African American and Latino school-age children can be placed inracially if culturally competent services are provided.

Since White infants are in very limited supply, transracial placements of minority children have been used as a means to provide infants and young children for White families (Sullivan, 1994). Barth and Berry (1988a) suggest that "the majority of transracial placements are with foster parents who have privileged legal status for adopting children in their own home" (p. 10). While some previous outcome studies on African American children adopted by White families suggest that child and adoptive parent satisfaction and adjustment do not significantly differ from inracial adoptions, "transracial adoptions may present an additional strain on family resources and may contribute to disruption in families already under stress" (Barth & Berry, 1988a, p. 73).

Several researchers have examined outcomes of special needs children placed in transracial adoptions. Rosenthal, Groze, Curiel, and Westcott (1991) reported the findings of their mailed survey designed to compare transracial and inracial adoptive families of special needs children. Of the sample of almost 300 families, 63 minority special needs children were placed transracially in White families. The average age at placement of the transracial adoptees was 5 years of age, and at the time of the survey, the children were an average of 10.5 years old. These researchers observed that the parent-child relationship scores in the minority inracial group were significantly higher than in the transracial group. However, they noted that the children in the transracial group were more likely to be disabled, to have been in prior psychiatric placement, and to have experienced sexual abuse prior to the adoption than in the inracial group. In their study of adoption disruptions Barth and Berry (1988a; 1988b) stated that disruptions were no more likely in transracial than in inracial adoptions, and in cases in which the child had already attached to the foster family before the adoption, there were no disruptions.

Camarata (1989) reported that in Texas, a clear majority of Mexican American children who are placed for adoption are placed with non-Mexican American families. In Texas, this result is due primarily to the limited number of Mexican American families certified to adopt. Only 12 percent of the families approved for adoption in 1987 were Mexican American, although at the time, 24 percent of the children in care were Mexican American. Camarata concluded that current state agency recruitment policies fail to attract Mexican American families with an income level less than $34,000, which is more than twice the median income for Mexican Americans in Texas, and thus fail to attract the majority of potential adoptive Mexican American families that could meet the needs of Mexican American children in care. In addition, Mexican Americans who do apply to adopt under current standards appear less open to adopt children with special needs. The policy implications of these findings suggest a need to develop improved culturally sensitive adoption policies and practices, particularly in the areas of recruitment, preparation, and post-adoption support services (Camarata, 1989).

Bausch and Serpe (1997) examined transracial placements in California. They found, in 1993 to 1994, that approximately 50% of Hispanic children and more than 80% of mixed Hispanic children were placed with White families through independent adoptions and through private adoption agencies. Similarly, through public agency placements, about 20% of Hispanic and 47% of mixed Hispanic children were placed with White families (Bausch & Serpe, 1997).

Andujo (1988), in her study of Mexican American children placed in White adoptive families, noted that transethnic adopted adolescents tended to have more problems with ethnic identity than same-ethnic adoptees. She recommended that the adoption home study process should include an investigation of the "total psychological and racial milieu of potential transethnic adoptive applicants" (p. 534). Bausch and Serpe (1997) advocated caseworkers to encourage non-Latino adoptive parents to expose Latino children to their heritage to help them feel positive about their ethnic heritage.

In this study, in order to explore whether the transracial nature of the adoption may have influenced adoption outcomes in the cases, the case records of the transracial cases were content-analyzed. Sixteen (20%) of the 80 cases under study were identified as transracial adoptions. Two (12.5%) of the 16 transracial adoptions had disrupted, 4 (25%) had dissolved, and the majority, 10 (62.5%), were still intact. Twelve (75%) of the 16 transracial placements involved Mexican American or part Mexican American children placed with White families. Only 2 (12.5%) involved African American or part African American children, and both were intact adoptions. One transracial case involved a part Native American child and one a Puerto Rican child.

## INTACT CASES

Of the 10 intact cases in this subsample of 16 transracial adoptions, 4 were Mexican American children adopted by White parents. One African American child was adopted by White parents, and another was adopted by a Mexican American adoptive mother and a White adoptive father. Two ethnically mixed Mexican American children were adopted by White adoptive parents, 1 White/Native American child was adopted by White adoptive parents, and 1 Puerto Rican child was adopted by an African American single adoptive mother. Four of the intact transracial adoptions involved either unplanned foster or fost-adoptions, and 2 were out-of-state placements (New York and Missouri). Five of the intact adoptive homes could be characterized as "large adoptive families," having from 5 to 9 adopted children in the homes. The ages of the adoptive parents ranged from mid-30s to late 40s, with 1 set of adoptive parents in their mid-50s at the time of the adoption placement. Transracially adopted children in intact placements ranged in age from $1^1/_2$ years to 13 years of age at placement. One child was less than 2 years of age, 5 were between 4 and 6 years of age, 2 were between 9 and 10 years of age, and 2 were between 12 and 13 years of age. The average age at placement was 7.52 years.

**DISRUPTED CASES**

Two (12.5%) of the 16 transracial adoptions disrupted. A Mexican American child was placed with White parents, and a White/Japanese child was placed with White adoptive parents. The disruptions were due to physically abusive adoptive parents and a sexually abusive adoptive father. One of the disruptions involved an out-of-state placement. One child was almost 6 at placement, and the other was almost 12 years of age. The average age at placement was 8.92 years.

**DISSOLVED CASES**

Four (25%) of the 16 transracial adoptions had dissolved at the time of the study. The dissolved transracial adoptions were as follows. Two Mexican American children were adopted by White adoptive parents. One Mexican American child was adopted by a single White/Native American adoptive parent, and a Mexican American/White child was adopted by White adoptive parents. One child was almost 5 years of age at placement. Two children were between 5 and 7 years old at placement, and 2 of the children were 10 years old at placement. The average age at placement in dissolved transracial cases was 8.46 years. The dissolutions were due to the following: the adopted child's behavioral problems required long-term residential treatment; a single adoptive father was sexually abusive; adoptive parents could not cope with the severe behaviors of the adopted child; and an adopted child sexually abused the adoptive parents' biological daughter.

While 6 (37.5%) of the 16 transracial adoption placements either disrupted or dissolved, an analysis of the transracial adoptions indicates that there appears to be no difference between those placements that remain intact or disrupted/dissolved by age of the child at placement, sibling placements, or by other demographic characteristics of the child or the adoptive parents. All 6 of the disrupted or dissolved transracial adoptions were identified in subsequent coding as "poor" matches, which included: (1) the placement of a child with a single mother with limited income who expressed that she was ready to retire; (2) placement of a 12-year-old child who was very attached to his birthmother with adoptive parents who had requested a child between the ages of 0-6 years; (3) placement of a child who had been physically and sexually abused with adoptive parents who had requested a non-violent, non-abusive, not aggressive or sexually abused child; (4) placement of 2 children who had expressed that they never wanted to be adopted; (5) placement of an older child with adoptive parents who had requested an infant; and (6) the placement of a sibling group who could speak English but whose primary language was Spanish with non-Spanish speaking adoptive parents who lived in another state.

Five of the six disrupted or dissolved transracial adoptions were also subsequently coded as having "serious risk" for the later adjustment of the adopted child. Issues identified as posing a serious risk for future placements included very aggressive sexually acting-out behavior by adopted children; sexual abuse of the adopted child's siblings or the sexual abuse of the adoptive parent's children by the adopted child; and multiple physical and sexual abuse of the adopted child by birthparents, foster parents, or adoptive parents.

Four of the 10 intact transracial adoptions were coded as "good" matches (see Chapter 10). Good matches included the placement of two children with adoptive families who had previous adoption experience, a foster adoption placement in which the sibling group was in the home for four years before the adoption, and the placement of an infant with a foster adoption family that had previous parenting experience.

It should be noted that the majority of transracial adoption case records do not mention the importance of the difference between the ethnic background and heritage of the child from that of the adoptive parents. The transition and placement plans did not include a discussion with the child or the adoptive parents of the impact that the transracial placements could have on their family, how they were feeling about the placement, or about future plans the adoptive parents may have for the child regarding the child's ethnic heritage.

## CONCLUSIONS

Issues associated with the match between adoptive parents and child, transition planning, behavioral issues of the children, and abusive behavior of these adoptive parents seemed to impact the outcome of these transracial placements. The records were almost totally void of any discussion of cultural issues and the impact of transracial adoptions. Therefore, it was impossible to assess whether or not ethnic/cultural differences between parents and child influenced adoption outcome. It was also impossible to assess whether the families or children were prepared to deal with the transracial nature of the adoption.

In the assessment process for transracial adopters, it is essential for workers to explore the familial and community context in which the child will be socialized. Parents will need an understanding of the physical and social needs (Folaron & Hess, 1993) of minority children in their care, and they will need to be prepared to provide them with positive nurturing cultural experiences that will facilitate the development of a positive racial identity (McRoy, 1990; McRoy, 1994). The adoptive parents will need to be aware that they may be questioned about their adoptions and perhaps receive disapproving gestures and comments from minorities and non-minorities (Bausch & Serpe, 1997). Moreover, their older adopted minority children may also challenge their adoptive parents' ability to raise a minority child. Workers will need to prepare parents for handling these issues should they arise. As with all adoptions, it is vitally important to assess adoptive parents' parenting skills and potential for abuse, and the match between parents and children; and to implement good transition planning and maintain close post-placement supervision to facilitate adjustment. Each of these issues is discussed in subsequent chapters.

# Adoption Service Delivery Issues

# CHAPTER 10

# Matching Families and Children

For years, the term "matching" in adoption referred to the process of selecting a family for a child based partially upon the similarity between physical attributes, especially in the situation of infant placements (McRoy & Zurcher, 1983; Child Welfare League of America, 1968). However, in special needs adoptions, "matching" typically refers to the worker's attempt to find appropriate families for children by matching the child's emotional and other needs to the emotional strengths of a particular family (Veevers, 1991). Workers must initially assess a family through a home study process to evaluate the marital relationship, influence of a new family member on the marriage, parental feelings about children and motivation to adopt, expectations of adoptive parenting, disciplinary plans, and many other aspects of parenting (Barth & Berry, 1988a). Parents are told about the types of children who are typically needing placement: sibling groups; children over the age of 6; ethnic minorities; those who have experienced or are experiencing a physical, mental, or developmental disability, and/or have experienced physical, emotional, and/or sexual abuse in prior placements or in the birthfamily.

Once a family has been approved for adoption, adoption workers review the list of child specifications that a family has identified, such as age, gender, number of siblings, ethnicity, and intellectual ability. Some may specify that they will not accept a child who is the product of incest, a child who has been sexually abused or who sexually acts out, or a child with certain kinds of disabilities. Many families initially select a child by looking at the pictures and brief descriptions of the children listed on state adoption exchanges. The families, as well as agency workers, at times make initial choices based upon relatively limited information on a particular child.

Since there is such a large supply of waiting children, workers may encourage parents to "stretch" their original preferences. For example, Nelson (1985) noted that special needs adoptive parents reported that their preferences for a child were "stretched" in the following ways: "(1) fostering attraction to or concern for the child; (2) nurturing the parent's self-confidence by helping them to feel capable of parenting a particular special needs child; (3) clarifying the family's adoption options by letting the family know what kind of child they might realistically be eligible for or presenting only certain children to a family; and (4) failing to provide adequate information on the child's functioning, or not communicating this information effectively" (p. 30). This "stretching" is sometimes encouraged in order to shorten the wait for a child by making the children that are available more appealing.

Barth and Berry (1988a) examined the outcome of matching and stretching in their study of adoption disruptions. They reported that although matching on demographic factors did not contribute to adoption stability, "identifying compatabilities between parents' strengths and resources and children's vulnerabilities and needs" (p. 168) tended to influence adoption outcomes. Zwimpfer (1983) found that the combination of adoptive applicants who are "different" (unsatisfactory or different in some way from the norm for adoptive parents) matched with a child who also tended to be different from those who were typically adopted or who "was considered a poor risk for adoptive placement" (p. 173) may result in an overload of risk factors. The practice of "matching for marginality" clearly increases the chances of adoption disruption.

Partridge et al. (1986) assessed mismatch in special needs adoptions and identified the following three categories of mismatch: (1) child having specific characteristics that adoptive parents viewed as highly negative; (2) child not having specific characteristics considered important to the adoptive parents; and (3) cases in which parents' and child's personalities clashed. As these discontinuities may affect the development of attachment between parent and child, they may in turn influence adoption outcome.

In this study, 6 (15%) of the intact adoptions, 13 (87%) of the disrupted adoptions, and 19 (76%) of the dissolved adoptions were considered to be poor matches. In the analysis of case records, minimal information was available on specific personality clashes. However, the available data did seem to correspond with Partridge et al.'s first 2 categories. These case vignettes illustrate these 2 categories of mismatch.

## MISMATCH: PRESENCE OF CHILD CHARACTERISTICS PERCEIVED AS NEGATIVE BY ADOPTIVE PARENTS

The following cases reviewed in this study involved adoptive parents who specifically stated the gender, age, and type of problems they could accept, but the children they adopted had characteristics that they construed as negative or antithetical to their values and beliefs, and to what they felt capable of handling. Notes taken from such cases are provided below.

> A group of five siblings (three males and two females ranging in age from five to eleven), removed from their birthparents for neglect and abandonment, were placed in foster care for two and one half years prior to their adoptive placement. The oldest child had been sexually abused in one foster placement and was physically and emotionally abused in a crisis nursery.
>
> A couple in their early forties contacted the agency about adopting when their only birthdaughter was about to leave home for college. The couple decided to adopt due to their inability to have more birthchildren and desire to continue parenting. They requested a child who could live up to his/her full potential, regardless of handicaps or problems. Grades were important, and both parents expected their adopted child to adopt their values. When presented with a sibling group of 5, the adoptive parents indicated that they felt they could handle these children although they were aware of their low to average IQ scores. However, once placed, the family had difficulty adjusting to the children's learning and behavioral problems and was unable to adjust to the oldest child's sexual acting out behavior. They had limited coping resources and refused to attend counseling. The parents were described in the narrative as being "fairly rigid" and had difficulty adjusting to five older, acting-out children. The placement disrupted after the children had been in the home for one month.
>
> J., an eight-year-old girl, was placed with an adoptive family after being in three foster placements. The adoptive parents had not

parented before, but had attended MAPP training and felt prepared for J. At the time of the adoption, the adoptive father was in the process of changing jobs to one that would involve less travel. The couple had been married for seven years and had no birthchildren. They were happy to learn that they had been approved to adopt and were looking forward to parenting their new daughter. J. had been sexually abused in one of her prior foster placements and in her birthfamily's home. After she had been in the adoptive home a few weeks, the adoptive mother expressed concern that J. seemed to be much more attached to the adoptive father than to her. J. became very defiant with her adoptive mother, and her behavior was characterized by the mother as disobedient and manipulative. The adoptive parents seemed to have very high expectations of J. and expressed frustration at J.'s "slowness, whining, and maladjusted behavior." The stress led the adoptive parents to seek marital counseling. J. continued to act out at home and seemed very attached to her paternal biological grandparents. J. found it very difficult to adjust in the new adoptive family. Marital problems escalated and the adoption disrupted.

In this case, the adoptive parents held very unrealistic expectations of a special needs child and the affect that this can have on the family. Although they had been introduced to these issues in MAPP training, they had never parented any children. During their home study, they had convinced the worker that they had the flexibility needed to parent a special needs child, but found that they actually had very low tolerance for acting-out behavior and could not understand J.'s needs. They may have already had marital problems prior to the placement, and felt the need to parent children in the hope of avoiding their own issues.

In other cases in this sample, the following mismatch issues were identified: parents felt betrayed by the agency because they did not want a sexually abused adopted child and received one; parents denied that the child had learning disabilities and therefore had unrealistic expectations of the child; parents requested a child with high IQ and no hyperactivity and their adopted daughter had a low IQ and attention deficit disorder with hyperactivity (ADHD); and adoptive parents wanted a White infant and adopted an Asian six-year-old.

## MISMATCH: ABSENCE OF CHILD CHARACTERISTICS PERCEIVED AS POSITIVE BY ADOPTIVE PARENTS

This type of mismatch can be due to differences in parental expectations of the child, and the ability of the child to meet the parents' expectations and the parents' ability to meet the child's needs. This also occurs in situations in which the adoptive parents "stretch" in their selection of a child either because they minimize or the worker minimizes the kinds of behaviors the child is exhibiting and focuses on behaviors they think they can improve (e.g., school performance). The following case notes provide examples of these kinds of mismatches.

N., a sexually and possibly physically abused seven-year-old boy, had been diagnosed with minimal brain damage due to oxygen deprivation at birth. His behaviors were so bizarre that his birthparents signed papers to voluntarily relinquish him but kept his seven-year-old twin sister. At age three or four, he stabbed his sister with a knife and a schoolmate with a fork. He spent three years in two children's homes, a hospital, and a foster home before being placed at the age of 10 with the L. family for adoption. Prior to the selection of the L. family, two families had been identified as possible families and were told about N. Each family became disinterested after reading the background information.

N. often asserted that he had no parents and wanted a new family. Child-specific recruitment was conducted for N. A family was sought that could handle an older child with behavioral problems. When looking at the photo album of the L.'s, his prospective family, he was very excited and began referring to them as Mom and Dad. N. was placed with the L.'s, a couple in their late forties whose 27-year-old birthson lived out-of-state. The L.'s wanted to adopt because they wanted a child in the home, felt they were financially stable, had a good marriage, and had ample time to raise a child. The adoptive parents acknowledged that they were told about the child's background and had talked directly with N.'s foster mother about her experiences with this child. However, the couple had no experience with a special needs child and were not prepared to parent a child with extreme acting-out behavior. While in their home, the L.'s focused primarily on N.'s school work and attempted to improve his grades. Although N. made outcries about the earlier sexual abuse, he was not believed. The family provided a very structured environment that for a time, seemed to improve N.'s behavior. However, once N. began bringing behavior reports home from school, the adoptive father began to beat the child with a belt.

A seven-year-old girl, M., and her sister were removed from their birth home as a result of physical and sexual abuse and neglect. M.'s birthmother was 15 at her birth and involved in alcohol abuse and prostitution. The children had been sexually abused by male babysitters. Before the adoption, M. lived in four foster homes and returned to the birthmother once. Several families were considered for M., but a decision was made to place with the F. family because, according to the case narrative, "they were seen as serving the best interest of the two children. The F. family resided in an area where the children could utilize the same community resources they were accustomed to while in foster care." The adoptive parents chosen for M. had had no previous parenting experience and were pursuing adoption because they could not have birthchildren. They had requested to adopt a sibling group with at least one boy. The father was self-employed and the mother was a homemaker. The total family income was about $15,000, and they had no insurance. M. and her sister were placed with this family about four years after their removal from the birthfamily. M., the oldest sibling, did not want to be placed with the younger sister because she did not get along with her and was still angry about having had to protect her when they were in the birth home.

Prior to the placement, M. exhibited acting-out behavior, was very controlling, had violent thoughts, and still appeared to be grieving the loss of her birthmother. During the home study, the adoptive mother had admitted having a quick temper, having been abused in her first marriage, and that she had always depended on a male to provide for all of her needs. Once M. was placed, the adoptive mother resisted getting M. any counseling. According to the records, during the placement, the adoptive mother referred to M. as "bitch." M. became the family scapegoat and after several months, the adoptive mother began to physically abuse M. This placement appeared to recreate for M. a situation of a very immature, emotionally distraught mother and an abusive home environment.

A couple requested to adopt S., a five-year-old girl who was related to the adoptive mother. They had been involved with S. since her birth and, except for very short periods of time, had been her primary caretakers. The child related to them as her parents in every sense of the word, and the adoptive parents were very attached to S. However, they agreed to not only adopt S. but her siblings, after being informed of the availability of a subsidy for all four children. This family strongly believed in keeping the children within the extended family if possible. This placement initially appeared to be a good match between S. and the adoptive parents, as they had always loved and cared for her. S. did very well in school and was very attached to the family and they to her. However, the addition of the siblings to a family already raising two biological children and S., became an overload. S.'s siblings had a history of school performance problems and problematic adjustment. The adoptive family was resistant to getting counseling, and the adoption of the three siblings disrupted, but S. remained in the family.

In each of these cases, the adoptive parents were presented with and encouraged to adopt children whose behaviors and characteristics were different from those that they indicated they could accept. In most instances, the children had far more severe emotional or learning problems than the parents could handle. In two instances, the family was encouraged to take on a sibling group, but did not have either the emotional or financial resources to deal with the stress and responsibility. Rationale for placement decision-making in the aforementioned cases tended to be based more on finding a family willing to try the placement than a comprehensive assessment of the fit or match between the specific child and family.

The majority of the mismatches occurred in adoptions that eventually disrupted or dissolved. However, in the intact sample, there were 16 cases in which there was evidence from the case narratives that there was a good match between parent and child. These will be described in the next section.

## GOOD MATCHES

Of the 16 (40%) intact cases that seemed to be good matches between parents and children, 10 were foster adoptions, 9 were sibling placements, 6 were minority adoptions, 6 involved good transition planning, and there was evidence that in 12 cases the children as well as the adoptive families seemed well-adjusted. Eleven (69%) of the children were males, and 5 (31%) were females.

Children in the "good match" sample were removed and placed at much earlier ages than the children in the mismatch sample. Age at removal ranged from birth to almost 6 years of age, and age at placement ranged from 1 to 9 years. However, 7 (44%) had been removed before age 1, 5 (31%) had been removed before age 4, and 4 (25%) had been removed between 5 and 6 years of age. Six (37.5%) had been placed between 1 and 3 years of age, and 8 (50%) had been placed between 4 and 7 years of age. The remaining 2 (12.5%) had been placed at 9 years of age.

Probably due to their earlier age at removal and placement, these children had fewer problems than the children in the "mismatch" group. Reasons for removal primarily included medical neglect, physical neglect, and abandonment. One child in this group had a history of sexual abuse, one had a history of physical abuse, and two had a history of both physical and sexual abuse. All of the children in the "good match" group were placed with families who had previous parenting experience as foster, adoptive, or biological parents. Case records were used to develop the following illustrations of good matches.

J., a Hispanic two-year-old male child, and an infant sister were removed from their birthmother as a result of gross neglect. At the time of removal, the child was diagnosed with spinal meningitis, which resulted in paralysis to the right side of his body, hearing loss, and a seizure disorder. Braces were needed to assist the child in walking and a shunt was needed for treatment of hydrocephalus. Three years later, the children were returned to the birthmother after her release from jail for abuse of other children in the home. She immediately voluntarily relinquished the children as she was not capable of handling them. The children were placed in one foster home for five months, but were removed due to the sudden death of the foster father, although the foster mother had become very attached to the children. In his next foster home, the foster mother became very attached to J. and his sister. J. knew little sign language and was unable to communicate very well. While the children were in foster care, the workers placed ads in local newspapers as well as the National Enquirer, registered the children with the CAP book, Spaulding for Children and the Adoption Resource Exchange. During the adoption readiness staffing, caseworkers identified qualifications important to meet the needs of the target child. The workers sought a family with the following characteristics: two-parent Hispanic family, a non-working spouse, skills with special needs children, and no other children in the home so that the children's needs could be met. There was a Court Appointed Special Advocate (CASA) volunteer who assisted in this case. Prospective adoptive families were screened for these criteria. They had seen the children's picture in the newspaper and decided to inquire about adoption. The picture made them realize they wanted to open their home to more children.

The worker selected an out-of-state Hispanic family for J. and his sister. The mother ran a day care in her home, so would be available at home during the day. They had experience as adoptive parents of abused children. J. immediately responded to the adoptive mother and cried when she left after the first meeting. During the pre-placement visits, the adoptive parents visited with the children and J.'s physician and teacher. During this period, the children spent the night with the adoptive family in their home located out-of-state. After the placement, the out-of-state worker had regular contact with the family until consummation, and there were reports of regular telephone contact between the adoptive family and the Texas caseworker after consummation.

One of the dissolved cases was also considered a good initial match. However, other factors led to the dissolution, as indicated in the case notes below.

P., an African American child, had been removed from his birthfamily around one year of age. He had been severely neglected and had witnessed his two younger siblings die in a fire; however, this issue had never been addressed in therapy. While in foster care for seven and a half years, P. was in six African American foster homes. After hearing P. speak on the radio about needing an adoptive home, a single African American male applied immediately to adopt this specific child. The adoptive father had no previous parenting experience, but was willing to work with a variety of acting-out behaviors. At the time of the adoption, P. was diagnosed as emotionally disturbed. P. was described as very bright and had much potential, and the adoptive father was a very intelligent young man who set reasonable limits and was very supportive of P. He was able to express true, deep, emotional feelings towards the child and used an open, honest communication style. The adoptive father's mother was very supportive of the adoption, and P. developed a close relationship with his adoptive grandmother. The worker noted the adoptive father's commitment to the adoption, and he persevered throughout the child's escalating aggressive behaviors after consummation. However, the child eventually became homicidal and suicidal and the adoption dissolved. Although P. was placed in residential treatment, the adoptive father continued to send P. letters and gifts throughout his stay in residential treatment. The adoptive father's commitment and love seemed unconditional. Once P. turns 18, the adoptive father is hoping that they can maintain a mature adult relationship as he is committed to helping the child, despite the dissolution.

Other than a notation that this adoptive father had requested to adopt P., there was no indication in the case record as to the specific reasons why this adoptive father was selected for P. Although in this case the adoptive parent did not have previous parenting experience, a good match appears to have been made. This child had been in many previous placements and was dealing with unresolved issues of grief and loss. It was probably preferable for him to be placed with a single father in a situation in which he could develop a close relationship and not share the attention or have to relate to others. The adoptive father's commitment seemed to be the major factor that led to the maintenance of the relationship even after the dissolution. This child needed someone to believe in him, and throughout the residential placement, he knew that his adoptive father still cared about him and that this was one attachment figure he would not lose.

## CONCLUSIONS

Matching in special needs adoptions should entail an assessment of the adoptive parents' background, family structure, interpersonal character-istics, parenting skills, and the behavioral expectations of the child they hope to adopt (Valdez & McNamara, 1994). An assessment of the child's developmental history as well as current behavior and situation are needed in order to begin to assess compatibility with a particular family. Although speed is very important in making placements, it is even more important to do a thorough assessment in order to ease tran-sition and decrease the likelihood of disruption. Lack of information about the other party tends to set the adoptive family system up for possible failure. Valdez and McNamara (1994) note that about 70% of the children who need out-of-home placement in foster care or adoption have unique needs as a result of having experienced physical abuse, neglect, or sexual abuse. Instead of matching on demographics, some attempts need to be made to match on difficulty of the child and parent's "interpersonal and parenting skills" (p. 397).

Katz (1986) notes that the most successful adopters have a tolerance for ambivalence, find satisfaction in small positive behavioral changes, feel entitled to be parents, set limits, use humor, take care of themselves, and do not allow themselves to feel rejected by the child. These are considered high-level parenting skills that can lead to more positive adoption outcomes. As noted in the case illustrations, parents in this study who had a high level of commitment to the children and are willing to support them and help them work through their losses, anger, and other emotional responses to their abuse or other circumstances that led them to be in the state's custody, are likely to have more successful adoptions.

These illustrations of matching issues suggest the need to have better worker training in the assessment of adoptive families and preparation of children and families for adoption. Rushed placements, encouraging "stretching" by adoptive parents, allowing adoptive parents to take on much more than they can obviously handle, and minimizing behaviors of a child may serve to facilitate movement of children from foster care to adoption but set the stage for disruption or dissolution of the adoption. Given the new federal incentives for moving children out of foster care (see Chapter 1), it is likely that workers may feel even more pressure to expedite adoptive placement decision-making.

Careful attention must be placed on minimizing placement risks by utilizing the research and clinical literature to aid in the development and utilization of more comprehensive, valid assessment tools for families and children. Partridge et al. (1986) suggest that workers, in their zeal to make adoptive placements, sometimes "cross the boundaries of parental capacity" (p. 21).

In order to improve the chances of finding good matches, workers might consider using structured interviews to evaluate parental expectations. Valdez and McNamara (1994) suggest that as part of the adoption process the child's current caretakers complete a standardized measure such as the Child Behavior Checklist (CBCL) (Achenbach &

Edelbrock, 1983), which can be used for children from age four through adolescence to assess severity of behaviors. They also recommend that the caretakers complete the Dimensions of Temperament Survey-Revised (DOTS-R) (Windle & Lerner, 1989) to assess the child's temperament level, and that after the parents have been approved for adoption, the adoptive parents complete the Adult Dimensions of Temperament Survey-Revised (Adult DOTS-R) and the DOTS-R child form to assess their expectations of child temperament (p. 400). This information from standardized measures can be used to assess the child's risk for disruption better and to help in matching the parents' and child's temperaments and parental expectations of the child's temperament.

Besides using written questionnaires to assess what types of children families can parent, it is important to use observational techniques to give the prospective parents an opportunity to evaluate realistically what they can handle. By having them visit children who are developmentally delayed and talk with adoptive parents who are parenting very aggressive children, they can better assess what kind of child problems they can handle. Parents should be encouraged to communicate with their prospective child's teachers, foster parents, physicians, and others who know the child well to gather additional information about the child they are considering for adoption. It is far better to screen out families for specific children before the placement than to have a child experience another rejection as a result of poor placement planning. Some mismatches are unavoidable, as a child's behavior may escalate as he or she reaches adolescence or as previously unknown experiences such as sexual or physical abuse become apparent. Family therapy is essential in these cases since the family and child must work through these issues as well as handle incongruent behavioral expectations (Partridge et al., 1986). The final chapters of this book provide specific recommendations for training workers, parents, and families to facilitate good matches.

The following chapter provides a discussion about transition planning, another significant adoption practice issue that can impact outcomes.

# CHAPTER 11

# Transition Planning

Children often are removed abruptly from their birthfamilies and placed in foster care under emergency circumstances. Insufficient attention is given, at times, to helping the child understand the reasons for the move and express feelings about the loss of birthparents, extended family, community, and school ties. Children are often placed in foster families where they may develop relationships and trust, but typically must be moved again. Often these moves are made very quickly, when it is considered to be detrimental to the child to leave the child in the placement any longer. However, regardless of the reason for the move, the child experiences a loss, and it is important to consider both the short-term and long-term impact on the child.

In arranging for a new placement, it is possible to have a planned transition that can minimize the trauma of separation and loss and facilitate attachment to the child's new adoptive family. Much has been written in the literature about the best approaches to transfer attachment and issues to be considered given the child's developmental stage (Cipolla, McGown, & Yanulis, 1990; Fahlberg, 1991; Hartman, 1979; Holody & Maher, 1996; McRoy, 1996). However, due either to lack of training or large caseloads, it often appears as if workers may engage in poor transition planning, which may lead in turn to rather difficult early adjustments for children in adoption. In many cases, workers must also help foster parents, who have become very attached to children in their care for a long period of time, to deal with their own feelings of grief and loss when the child is removed.

Workers must examine the issue of termination and loss as it affects the child, themselves, and other adults. Termination and transition should be viewed as processes that require time and attention to the child's needs. A child's denial, anger, and sadness about an adoptive placement can be manifested by a return of symptoms, acting-out, withdrawal, or regression (Elbow, 1987). Ideally, the transition process should take several weeks, so that the child has sufficient time to deal with and express the pain of the loss. Others (Jewett, 1982; Lieberman, 1979) recommend that the children be included in planning the transition to reduce their sense of helplessness. This transition time allows the child and the worker to review the purpose of relationships (caseworker-child, substitute care provider-child, and caseworker-substitute care provider), their meaning to the child and the worker, the child's accomplishments, and the impending loss. This review also helps the child master his or her fears and provides a link to the future, which may be frightening to the child without the worker's continued presence and support (Elbow, 1987).

What happens to the child in transition is unique. Before good-byes, the child's life, actions, and emotional energy are directed toward the past. At the point of disengagement, the child turns from emphasis on his or her past toward emphasis on his or her future. It is not uncommon for the worker to have a good-bye interview to help the child prepare to leave the foster home, one week and the following week hear the child ask, "When are you going to find me an adoptive home?" Good transition planning, appropriate preparation, and adequate time for the transition is giving the child direction for the future (McInturf, 1986).

In this study, prior to the adoption placement, children in intact adoptions had been in an average of 2.4 foster placements (range 1 to 6). Children in disrupted adoptions had been in an average of 3.3 foster homes (the actual number ranged from 1 to 9) and children in dissolved adoptions had been in an average of 2.6 foster placements (range 1 to 10). According to the case records, the reasons for frequent foster moves of children in this study included:

- Child behaviors unacceptable and foster parents request move (sexual acting-out, hyperactive, aggressive, hurting foster or biological children)

- Birthparents moved, so child was moved to facilitate visitation

- Sibling separation or reunification

- Placement of child into residential treatment center

- Abuse in foster care (sexual, physical, emotional by foster parent, foster sibling, friend of family, biological sibling)

- Foster parent life stressors (financial problems, death of spouse, birth of child)

- Emergency placement

- Need to move to therapeutic foster placement

- Birthmother took children from foster home—once returned to the agency, they had to be placed with a new foster family

- Overly attached foster mother and foster child (because child would eventually have to move to another setting)

- Too many children in foster home

- Foster sibling dynamics

- Child returned to birthfamily

- Adoptions dissolved or disrupted and children placed back into substitute care but unable to return to same foster home

- Respite care for foster parents (temporary move)

- Poor match between foster parent and child

Very few entries into the case records were found that pertained to the transition process in foster care moves. Sometimes workers make the assumption that the child is too young to understand reasons for moving, so, other than a brief explanation of the facts, nothing else is said about the emotional implications of the relocation. In this study, the child's worker sometimes explained the reason for the move to the child during the actual move. At that time the child is often too frightened and confused to really comprehend rational explanations. Also, many children do not openly express their feelings until trust has been developed. As time passes, the child may become less trusting after experiencing frequent disappointments and may begin hiding many feelings of confusion and grief. There may not be an opportunity to discuss it again until another transition time, when the child is again very emotional. Revelation and communication about the child's past and reasons for placement are essential to build trust and to help the child understand and talk about how the move makes them feel (McRoy, Grotevant, Ayers-Lopez, & Furuta, 1990).

Once children were re-placed, little information was found in the case records on how the children were handling their most recent separation experience. It did seem evident that Lifebooks, sometimes called life story books (a narrative of the child's life often completed by either the worker, foster parent, and/or child), were sometimes used and often contained pictures of previous foster care providers. These were developed during the period of pre-placement planning for the adoption.

Backhaus (1984) reported that the biggest problem in preparing Lifebooks is the amount of time involved. Caseworkers in the Backhaus study specifically mentioned the great amount of time needed (1) to contact previous foster or adoptive families, birthfamilies, and previous workers to get photographs and information, and (2) to establish a relationship with the child and the current adult caretakers. Most workers recognized the futility of expecting a child to participate in the Lifebook process if trust had not been established. However, most believed that Lifebooks helped prepare children for adoption, because the books helped children and adoptive families to be realistic about the past and prevented them from exaggerating or denying it (Backhaus, 1984).

Holody and Maher (1996) have proposed using "here-and-now" Lifebooks to complement the traditional Lifebook model. Used with latency-age children, this approach begins with the child in the present and engages the child in a joint project with the worker, to help the child identify and communicate current feelings and experiences. The book might include a "wheel of the important people in the child's life," memorabilia, and lists of favorite things to do, or favorite friends (p. 329). Not only does this process build trusting relationships between the worker and child, it also helps the child work through feelings and create his or her own personal story.

According to McInturf (1986), depending on the age and cognitive level of the child, it generally takes between one and a half to two months to prepare a child for adoption. During this time the worker does the following: (1) provides the child with facts about his life; (2) helps the child understand that he or she is not to blame for the placement; (3) helps the child explore his or her emotional responses to various placements; (4) encourages the child to disengage emotionally from the birthfamily and say good-bye; and (5) helps the child make a plan for the future. Once these stages are completed, the worker works with the child to prepare the life story. This story can be shared with the adoptive family during pre-placement visits to help them understand the child's prior experiences and feelings about his or her life.

## INTACT ADOPTIONS: GOOD TRANSITION PLANNING

Nine (11.25%) of the 80 cases in the study were identified as having a good transition from the foster home to the adoptive home. All of the nine cases identified as having a good transition involved intact adoptive families. A good adoption transition plan was defined as having a reasonable amount of time between pre-placement, placement, and consummation, which allowed the child and adoptive parents to begin to cope with the move and relationship changes from foster to adoptive care; the adoptive parents receiving full de-identified information on the child prior to placement; evidence of good-bye visits having taken place; and appropriate caseworker follow-up visits with the child and family occurring between placement and consummation, including carefully monitored, post-placement worker-supportive visits.

The following notes from case record reviews revealed the following indicators of good transition planning:

- Transition planning involved the worker, the adoptive parents, the foster parents, and the child.

- Full disclosure of the child's family background, and medical and educational history were provided to the adoptive parents prior to the placement of the child.

- The child's good-bye visits involved meetings with the foster parents, the birthparents, and siblings (as appropriate), and the opportunity for him or her to participate in the completion of the Lifebook.

- The worker and adoptive parents "adhered to the transition plan," yet were flexible and able to adjust as needed to meet the child's needs.

- The worker took into consideration the child's level of adoption readiness.

- Extensive pre-placement visits were held, which allowed the child and prospective adoptive parents to meet in non-threatening environments.

- Caseworker post-placement supportive visits allowed the adoptive parents to work through many personal and family issues that accompany an adoption, as well as allowed the adoptive parents additional opportunities to further meet, contact, or follow up on specific, observed behaviors with the previous foster parents.

Below are notes from cases that demonstrated good transition planning.

H., a nine-year-old female, had been in six foster placements in a little over four and a half years. Before the adoptive placement, the prospective adoptive mother was allowed to begin tutoring H., providing an opportunity for all parties to get to know each other very well prior to the placement. H. asked if the prospective adoptive mother could adopt her. This gave the child a sense that she had chosen her adoptive parents. Additionally, there were at least three pre-placement visits during the month prior to the adoption placement. Individual conferences and meetings were also conducted between the worker and H. and the worker and adoptive parents prior to the placement.

N., a two-year-old African American male who had been abandoned by his birthmother, had been in one foster placement for over a year, when an African American family was selected as his adoptive family. The caseworker, in conjunction with the adoptive parents, developed an extensive and detailed pre-placement schedule. Four days after the initial meeting between N. and his adoptive parents, the parents requested early placement. The caseworker staffed the request, but it was denied. Pre-placement visits with N. and the adoptive parents continued for a month before the good-bye visit was conducted with the foster parents, the placement papers were signed and N. placed with the adoptive parents.

B., a six-year-old male child had been physically, emotionally, and sexually abused in his birthfamily. He had been in two foster homes for a little over a year prior to the planned adoption. Once a family was selected, there was a one month pre-placement period during which time the adoptive parents received full de-identified information on B. and his siblings. The adoptive parents were able to share their family album with the child, and other visits with the caseworker involved "round table" discussions of the upcoming adoption placement with B. and his siblings, visits to their school, and the planning of good-bye visits.

## INTACT ADOPTIONS: POOR TRANSITION PLANNING

In this study, the examination of worker narratives associated with moving children from foster homes into adoption revealed factors that could be identified as poor transition planning. It is possible that more was done to aid in transition, but was not recorded in the case narrative. However, as mentioned earlier, intact adoptions were significantly more likely to have had good transition planning than disrupted or dissolved adoptions. Four (10%) of the 40 cases of intact adoptions, 8 (53%) of the 15 cases of disrupted adoptions, and 8 (32%) of the 25 cases of dissolved adoptions were categorized as involving poor transition planning. Examples of these issues in intact adoptions are presented below.

L., a six-year-old boy with a history of physical and sexual abuse, was removed from his birthgrandmother. During the next two years and two months, this young child was placed in two foster homes and became very close to both foster families. He had a pattern in all of his placements of bonding easily and having good relationships with the male parents but was defiant to females. L. had very difficult separations in both foster placements. The father in his second foster family wanted to adopt L. but because of his difficulty bonding to the foster mother, the foster mother did not agree. According to the worker, L. refused to talk about these foster parents and appeared to be in denial about their decision not to adopt him. The child had been in therapy and had a Lifebook. However, there is no indication in the record that the child's loss issues recognized by the worker were addressed in therapy. There were no good-bye visits mentioned with the foster parents. After five pre-placement visits with the adoptive family over a 15-day time span, L. was placed.

At placement, the worker told the adoptive family that it was up to them to initiate contact with the worker. From the case notes, it appeared as if the worker monitored the placement but did not specifically help the adoptive parents resolve the issue that once again emerged, of the child not bonding to the adoptive mother. The adoptive parents and the worker allowed the child to terminate his own counseling. At the time of consummation, the family was quite upset about the child's behaviors but agreed to the consummation, feeling it was best for the child.

T., a physically and sexually abused seven-year-old, was removed from his birthfamily and was placed in adoption at the age of nine. The child had been in one foster placement for a year and nine months and had developed a very strong attachment. When T. first saw pictures of the adoptive parents, he appeared excited but very apprehensive. Only one day lapsed from the time the child met the adoptive family to their signing adoption papers and taking him out of state to their home. The worker noted that T. was strongly grieving over the loss of the foster family, and that the adoptive parents were trying to be supportive. T. was very attached to a photo album of the foster parents and throughout the placement would get the album out and reminisce about his memories of Texas and the foster family. There is a report in the record that the adoptive parents put the album away "until the child was ready to accept the fact that he was in a permanent home." In therapy, T. asked how long he had to stay with the adoptive family. He also refused to participate in family life and soiled his pants daily. The mother mentioned that T. refused to give anything back to the family, and two weeks before consummation, she mentioned the possibility of disruption.

Although the aforementioned cases involved adoptions that were still intact at the time of the study, it is evident that there are some unresolved transition issues in these cases that may lead to later problems.

## DISRUPTED AND DISSOLVED ADOPTIONS: POOR TRANSITION PLANNING

The majority of cases that involved poor transition planning were either disrupted or dissolved. Over half of the cases that disrupted and almost one-third of the cases that resulted in child removal after consummation were categorized as having poor transition planning. Notes on one case are provided below.

> A sexually abused girl, M., was removed from her birthparents at the age of six. She lived in four foster homes before being adopted at the age of 10. M. was very attached to her last foster mother and wanted to be adopted by her. A prospective adoptive family was selected, and after one pre-placement visit, the parents declined the adoption. M. was described as being very sad about this decision. About three months later, another family was selected for her, and five pre-placement visits were held over one month. After the family read M's record, they mentioned that they were upset at first and did not know if they could handle a child with such an unfortunate background. The adoptive mother also stated that she felt they were being pressured to take M. and that information was being withheld from them. However, after thinking about it, the family agreed to visits. M. reported to the worker that she had acted badly during the visit. The adoptive mother expressed reservations about the placement but agreed to proceed. There was also a notation in the record that the adoptive mother expressed concern that the child seemed unusually attached to the worker. Once placed, M. began to resent the adoptive parents for taking her away from the foster mother and worker. There are no notations in the record that the child's issues of attachment, grief and loss, rejection and abuse, which were recorded by the worker, were addressed before pre-placement planning for the adoption.

Examples of other issues noted in the case records that would influence transition planning outcomes were identified as follows:

- Child very attached to relatives, wanted to be adopted by them but further contact with them was not continued after placement
- Child in seven previous placements
- Target very attached to foster parents, wanted to call them every day

- No pre-placement visits for child who was in one foster placement for almost two years and then placed immediately with adoptive family

- Child had had three long, very significant placements and appeared to attach too easily to adoptive family

- Foster mother had made an excellent transition and good-bye plans, which worker declined

- Move to adoptive family took place after two visits over two days

- Conflict between adoptive mother and last foster mother

The failure to take into consideration the impact of abuse, numerous moves, and interruptions in parenting on children are the primary issues that emerged from the analysis of poor transition planning. The majority of the children in the sample had been abused, and all had suffered the initial loss of being separated from their biological families. In some instances, the separation was temporary and the children returned periodically to their birthfamilies. After each return and removal, these children were often placed in a different foster home. Reasons for removal from birthfamilies generally stemmed from ongoing abuse and neglect. Child abuse literature suggests that children who have been abused and neglected have had their basic sense of security shaken. Separation from their biological families, as well as having been abused, may cause them to blame themselves, feel guilty, and have a low self-concept (McNamara & McNamara, 1990). Once removed from their birthfamilies, they often did not receive therapy to help resolve their grief and feelings about their birthparents. Having never resolved the initial separation, they can move from one home to the next in the foster care system, and never learn to understand about the continuity of relationships or to develop trust and learn to attach.

Although the principles of termination and loss with children parallel those of adults, particular attention must be given to the meaning of the loss for the child. The loss of a relationship is less symbolic of earlier losses than it is real—yet another loss for the child to face and mourn. In social work practice with children, the worker often becomes a transitional object for the child who may have experienced other separations in his or her life (Elbow, 1987). In this study, children in intact placements had an average of six workers, and those in disrupted or dissolved placements had an average of nine different workers while in care (see Chapter 4). Sometimes they became very attached and had difficulty understanding why these losses continued to occur. Lifebooks can include references to a series of caseworkers but seldom mention why the change in workers occurred. This lack of information contributes to the child's helplessness and feelings of "badness for making people disappear."

Moreover, although foster parents are supposed to help children form attachments and aid in transferring these attachments and healthy relationships to other caregivers, these relationships are often terminated with little consideration of the impact on the child or the foster family. In fact, for years foster parents have been trained to be only temporary caregivers, and they have been discouraged from maintaining contact with children once they leave the home (Fahlberg, 1991). In many of the cases of poor transition planning in this study, children were moved either immediately or after a very short period of time with seemingly little concern about the child's obvious attachment to foster parents. However, children who were very attached to foster parents and were moved very quickly with minimal or no explanation experienced adjustment problems in their adoptive placements.

Since these issues were identified in the case records, it is clear that workers acknowledge that the child may be having problems with loss. However, little, if anything, is mentioned in the record about how these problems are being addressed with the child. It is possible that some of these issues were dealt with, yet not reported in the record, or that workers either lacked the necessary skills and/or time to assist the child.

Some may believe that children should not hang on to the past. For example, one worker stated that it was positive for an adopted child (whose younger siblings had remained in the birth home) to see the foster mother caring for a new foster baby, as the child would know that she had been replaced and could more easily detach from the foster parents and attach to adoptive parents. This again points to the need for worker training on research and clinical findings on helping children deal with losses of significant attachment figures.

In numerous case records reviewed in this study, workers indicated that the child was very happy at the initial visit with the new adoptive parents and immediately began to refer to them as "Mommy and Daddy." Upon leaving the foster family's home, workers often noted that the child was happy about leaving a home (where they might have lived for two to three years) and was anxious to move in with the new family. Some records indicated that children were excited about the adoptive parents' new car, or about the child's new room or toys, and couldn't wait to go live with the family. However, once the excitement wears off, these children often grieve their losses. Workers need to have training on children's levels of cognitive development to improve their understanding of children's comprehension of events at various developmental stages.

Children in this study who openly expressed a desire to have contact with foster families were often discouraged from contact both by workers and by their new adoptive parents. Foster parents can play a very strategic role in preparing children for the move and can be supportive throughout a difficult transition. Through joint efforts of foster parents, adoptive parents, and workers, a child can slowly lessen these attachments and form new ones if allowed some control.

Workers must be trained to assess attachment to various caregivers and to work with previous caregivers, new adoptive parents, and the child to develop a plan that will minimize the trauma of another separation and loss for the child. Fahlberg (1991) suggests that pre-placement visits serve to diminish fears and worries of the unknown.

According to Fahlberg, pre-placement visits can be used to transfer attachments, initiate the grieving process, empower new caregivers, and encourage making commitments for the future (p. 179). If foster and adoptive parents work together, they can empower the adoptive parents to serve in the role of parents and reduce the trauma of another move for the child.

Similarly, Fahlberg (1991) suggests that post-placement contacts with foster parents and birthparents, when appropriate, can be used to prevent denial/avoidance.

According to Fahlberg, post-placement visits:

- Resurface emotions about separation at manageable levels
- Provide opportunities for support of feelings
- Provide opportunities to review reasons for the separation
- Decrease magical thinking
- Decrease loyalty issues
- Continue transference of attachment
- Empower new caregivers
- Enhance identity formation (p. 180)

It is essential for children to be given permission from previous caretakers to love their new family and to know that they have not again been rejected. This process can serve to facilitate successful adoptions as the new parents are empowered to act in their new roles and the children can be given permission to form new relationships while maintaining the old ones. Due to the close attachments of many foster parents to the children for whom they provide care, some may need a little time to allow healing of their own grief and loss. However, if the situation becomes unproductive (i.e., some foster parents may try to undermine placement), then worker intervention may be necessary.

Workers should help adoptive parents to understand the foster parents' feelings, to validate the foster parents' importance in the child's life, and to communicate openly when they think the foster parent has done a good job. Lack of validation may be one reason why foster parents, workers, and adoptive parents may end up in a power struggle over what is in the best interest of the child.

Poor transition planning occurs when the child, adoptive parents, or foster parents have not been adequately prepared for the impact of a child's move to a new situation. If the child has not adequately dealt with past losses, a new environment may trigger unresolved issues of loss. Similarly, foster parents may find it difficult to "let go" of a child to whom they have grown attached but are not able to adopt. Adoptive parents must find ways to adjust to a "difficult-to-parent child" or to a child who may be unable to trust due to previous dissolved relationships. Good pre-placement and post-placement services are essential to moderate the transition issues that are evident in any move. Workers clearly need better training in the preparation of children and families for adoption. Suggestions for worker training are provided in Chapter 15.

# CHAPTER 12

# Assessing Potential for Abuse

Much of the empirical literature on special needs adoptions examines the relationship between characteristics of the children, parents, family interaction, and social supports (i.e., Barth & Berry, 1988a; Groze, 1996; Partridge, Hornby, & McDonald, 1986; Rosenthal & Groze, 1992) to various adoption outcomes. For example, factors such as type of adoption, educational level of adoptive parents, match between parent and child, background information deficits, availability of support, child behaviors, age of child, history of abuse, number of foster workers, length of time in institutions before placement, whether siblings are placed apart, age of adoptive parents, and attachment to birthparents are often identified as related to adoption outcomes. The extent and impact of the adopted child's abuse is generally examined with regard to the birthfamily, foster homes, group homes, or treatment facilities (Rosenthal, Motz, Edmonson, & Groze, 1991) and rarely are discussed in relation to the adoptive family. However, in this study, the careful review of case records revealed evidence of children being abused by their adoptive parents. In most of these cases, the abuse was a major factor associated with disrupted or dissolved adoption outcomes.

A number of risk factors for child maltreatment have been identified in the literature, including parental alcoholism; previous history of child maltreatment; impaired parent-child interactions; child misconduct and developmental delays; parental psychopathology; and family stress, including financial strain (Famularo, Kinscherff, Bunshaft, Spivak, & Fenton, 1989). In many of the adoptive families in this study, a number of these risk factors were present. The combination of childhood and/or spousal abuse; loss of both fertility and fantasized birthchild; poor parenting skills; limited or no support; as well as stress associated with parenting children who often had histories of abuse, neglect, possible developmental delays, difficulties in school, and problems in attachment, placed these families and children at risk for maltreatment.

According to case record analysis of adoptive parents' social history, 14 of the adoptive mothers and 10 adoptive fathers had themselves been victims of child or spousal abuse. In 2 families, both the adoptive mother and adoptive father had been victims of abuse. Types of abuse included the following: sexual abuse (6); physical abuse (10—4 had been physically abused by a prior spouse, 1 by a current spouse, and 5 in their families of origin); emotional abuse (3); and in 5 other cases, there was mention of abuse in the record, but the specific type of abuse was not identified. Of the 24 adoptive parents who had themselves been abused, 9 (37.5%) (4 adoptive fathers and 5 adoptive mothers) subsequently abused either their adopted child or other foster children in their home. Kaufman and Zigler (1987) estimated that approximately 30% of persons who have been victims of child abuse will maltreat their children. This is about 6 times higher than the abuse rate in the general population (5%). In this study, 7 (9.3%) of the 65 families in which there was no reported parental history of abuse subsequently abused their adopted or foster children.

There was no indication in the record that any of the abused adoptive parents had received therapy for their own victimization. Their own abuse history may have placed these families at great risk for mistreating children in their care. Although there were no specific indications in the record of either children or adoptive parents as being victims of psychological maltreatment, there is research evidence that suggests that emotional abuse often co-occurs with physical abuse (Egeland, Sroufe, & Erickson, 1983; Garbarino & Vondra, 1987; Herrenkohl, Herrenkohl, & Egolf, 1983). Thus, it is possible that special needs children, as well as adoptive parents who had experienced abuse, may have been victims of emotional abuse.

Case readings revealed allegations of abuse by adoptive parents in 15 (19%) of the 80 cases. Six female and 9 male children were abused in their adoptive homes. As mentioned earlier, there was an indication in the case records of 8 of these abusive families that 1 or both of the adoptive parents had a history of abuse victimization themselves. Two of the adoptions remained intact, 4 disrupted, and 9 dissolved. The following case notes illustrate intact adoptions in which abuse occurred in the family.

## ABUSE IN INTACT ADOPTIVE FAMILIES

L., a five-year-old boy, and J., his three-year-old sister, were placed in a fost-adopt placement with an infertile couple in their late twenties. Shortly after the placement, three other foster children (all toddlers) were also placed in the foster home for an extended period of time although the parents had only expected a temporary placement of two weeks. The family was overwhelmed with parenting five young children, but did not call the agency for assistance. After the adoptive father spanked one of the foster children so hard that bruises were left on the child's body, the parents contacted the agency worker. The case record indicated that the abuse was attributed to parental stress resulting from too many children in the home. Also, according to the home study narrative, the adoptive father had been physically abused as a child. No services other than removing the foster children were reported as being offered. The fost-adoption of L. and J. remains intact.

T., a six-year-old male child who had been physically and medically neglected in his birth home (possibly a fetal alcohol syndrome child), was placed with a couple in their mid-thirties who had been unable to have birthchildren. A review of the case file revealed that the worker had noted during the home study that the "couple yelled and slammed doors during some arguments." One reference had indicated that the couple used spanking as a form of discipline. T. had mild speech problems, was very attached to his foster family, had sexually acted out in foster care, and had not received any therapy. The adoptive parents had stated that they did not want a child needing special education. During the first few months of placement with the adoptive parents, T. reported to the worker that the adoptive mother had bitten his thumb, making it bleed, and that the adoptive father hit him on his head with his knuckles, and hit him with a shoe on his buttocks. The parents admitted that they had wanted the child to act like other "normal" children and may have been pushing him too hard. Despite abuse allegations, the child was not afraid of the adoptive parents—but wanted them to stop hitting him. The abuse allegations were investigated, and the parents were encouraged to go to parent training classes to learn alternative methods of discipline. The parents were very attached to T. and were open to changing their interactions with the child. After attending parenting classes the adoptive parents were allowed to consummate the adoption.

In each of the above-mentioned adoptions that remained intact, neither of the two adoptive families had parented birthchildren or had any previous experience with special needs children. Both couples had chosen to adopt because of an inability to conceive. In one case, there was an indication in the record that the adoptive parent was a victim of physical abuse. The records suggested that a poor match between parents and children, agency inattention to prior abuse, too many children placed in the home, and lack of worker support and attentiveness to the stress the families were feeling may have also attributed to the abuse.

## ABUSE IN DISRUPTED AND DISSOLVED ADOPTIONS

Out of 15 abusive adoptive parent cases, 4 of the adoptions had disrupted. There were 3 cases of physical abuse (2 adoptive mothers and 1 adoptive father were perpetrators) and 1 case of sexual abuse of a male child by an adoptive father. In 2 of the families, there was an indication that the adoptive parent who was physically abusive (1 adoptive mother and 1 adoptive father) had been childhood victims of physical abuse. The children placed in these homes for adoption ranged in age from 3 to 12 (average age, 6.25). Three of the children were female and one was male.

All four families in which disrupted adoptions occurred chose to adopt because they wanted to parent more children. Three adoptive couples were raising birthchildren but were unable to have more, and one couple was infertile, but had adopted other children before the target child was placed. Types of abuse included throwing the child against a wall, spanking, slapping, dragging the child down the street, and force-feeding. Three of the couples also had marital problems, and only one couple had had prior experience with special needs children. Case notes on a disrupted adoption that involved parental abuse are provided below.

> An adoptive couple in their early thirties adopted a three-year-old boy after just consummating the adoption of a sibling group of three

sexually abused children. The case study record included a notation about the adoptive mother's physical abuse as a child and her belief in severe physical discipline as a way to raise children. All four children were removed after investigation of the adoptive mother's reportedly "whipping the sibling group with extension cords and belts and leaving one child unattended in the garage."

There were 9 reports of abusive adoptive parents found in the review of the 25 cases of dissolved adoptions. Children who were placed in these families ranged in age from 2 to 14. The average age was 6.8. Seven boys and 2 girls were involved in these abusive situations. According to case narratives, 2 of the families believed in and used severe physical discipline. Other family characteristics were: 4 had marital problems, 5 of the adoptive parents adopted because they wanted a child and could not conceive, and 2 of the families adopted while in the "empty nest" stage. Of the 3 adoptive parents (2 adoptive fathers and 1 adoptive mother) who became sexually abusive toward the children, 2 had been sexually abused themselves, 1 was suspected to have been physically abused as a child, and 1 adoptive mother had been emotionally abused as a child. In 2 cases, both the adoptive mother and father were involved in the physical abuse of a child in care. In other cases, 3 adoptive mothers and 1 adoptive father physically abused children in their care. Five families were noted in the records as not wanting help with their problems. In one case, the adoptive mother asked for help to address problems in the home, but there was no indication in the records that help was provided.

The following brief case notes illustrate some of the family dynamics in the dissolved adoptions in which abuse had occurred.

An adoptive couple had been married for almost 15 years at the time of their adoption. The adoptive mother had raised a biological daughter from a previous marriage (who was no longer living in the home) when the couple considered adopting. Both parents had graduate degrees and were very committed to opening their home to a sibling group. During the study they indicated that they were willing to accept a child who had experienced all types of abuse. After completion of the home study and parent training, the N.'s were matched with a sibling group of three teenagers (2 males and 1 female). The youngest was a 14-year-old male child who had been sexually abused and who acted out sexually in the foster home and in the adoptive home. This child had received therapy before placement, but it was unclear, according to the case narrative, if the therapy was ongoing after the placement. When the sexual acting-out began, the adoptive mother, who had been sexually abused as a child, initiated sexually abusive behavior with each of the children. For example, at times, as a form of discipline, she would have R., the 16-year-old female, do housework and eat dinner while naked, with the family. Several months later, the adoptive mother began to exhibit symptoms of alcoholism and the adoptive father became homicidal and depressed. The adoptive father was aware of the sexual abuse going on in the family but did not report it. The adoptive mother was close to an emotional breakdown at the time of the adoption dissolution, approximately two years after consummation.

After being abandoned by his birthfamily, ten-year-old B. was first placed in an emergency foster home. However, he remained in the same home for four years until parental rights were terminated. At that time the foster family requested to adopt B. At the time of B.'s adoption, the couple had been married for eight years and were raising two biological children. Within a year after the adoption, the adoptive mother gave birth to twins. Over the years, the couple had been foster parents to 11 children, and had received much training in caring for special needs children. Several of these placements ended early, but according to the foster care records, the reasons for these early removals resulted from child behavior problems. The adoptive parents were active members of a parent support groups and remained very busy in the community and church. B. appeared to adjust well in this family. They were constantly involved in many family activities together including camp outs, picnics and church activities. Prior to finalization, the major behavioral problems B. exhibited stemmed from his anger towards his birthfamily for his abandonment. The adoptive family indicated that they were too busy to seek therapy for B. Despite this, the adoption was finalized 5 years after the initial emergency foster placement. About a year later, B. ran away from home and reported that the adoptive father had sexually abused him. Upon investigation, the adoptive father admitted the abuse and said that he, too, had been abused as an adolescent. Although the adoptive parents were aware of the adoptive father's childhood abuse, they had not reported it during their home study. According to B., he first notified his adoptive mother of the abuse and expected her to protect him. However, it recurred, and this prompted him to run away and never want to return to a family that he could not trust.

These cases also exemplified situations in which poor matches were made in placement decision-making: in three cases, the level of expectations of adoptive parents was too high for the child to meet; 6 of the children were placed with adoptive parents with emotional problems of their own, 3 of which involved issues of past abuse; there were 3 cases where the adoptive parents were reluctant to finalize the adoption but were encouraged to proceed; and 5 cases where the adoptive parents did not want the type of child they received. Five of the target children ended up being placed in residential treatment for a period of time. With appropriate interventions, 2 to 3 of these dissolutions might have been avoided.

Out of 15 cases of alleged adoptive parent abuse, 11 of the children were physically abused and 4 were sexually abused. In 5 cases, the adoptive parents appeared very rigid or had expectations exceeding the abilities of the child (in 3 of these cases, the adoptive father was in the military). For instance, according to notes taken from one case record, "the adoptive parents expected a three-year-old to do the laundry and make his bed so tight that a quarter could bounce off of it."

Three of the families believed severe physical discipline was necessary for children, while four families resorted to severe physical discipline as a reaction to stressors. Stressors that caused problems tended to be a large number of children in the home, adoptive parents' loss of employment, and an inability to cope with a child's severe behavior problems.

There were five cases in which the adoptive parents did not want the type of child they received. In one case, the adoptive mother desired to adopt a male infant with no siblings, yet she consented to adopt a sibling group of two female toddlers. In three cases, adoptive parents wanted children with average or above average intelligence, but the children placed with them included a possible Fetal Alcohol Syndrome (FAS) child, a child with a learning disability, and a child with Noonan's Syndrome (a condition that affects one's mental capabilities).

Out of the 15 families in this subgroup, 12 had had prior parenting experience. However, only 1 family had had prior experience with special needs children. Seven of the 15 families were having marital problems (3 of the disrupted and 4 of the dissolved cases). Seven out of the 15 cases involved an emotionally troubled adoptive parent. In one of these cases, both adoptive parents were unstable. Six of these 7 cases were in the dissolved sample and 1 was in the disrupted.

In the dissolved sample, three of the families had wanted to delay consummation, but seemed to have been strongly dissuaded by the worker, as the problems did not seem intolerable for the family. In other cases, the adoptions were consummated because the parents either minimized the problems or may not have been fully aware of them.

Three of the adoptive parents who engaged in physical abuse had been physically abused themselves as children. Two of the adoptive parents who sexually abused their children had been sexually abused themselves as children. One adoptive mother who was physically abusive had been sexually abused in the past. In one case, both the adoptive mother and father had experienced physical and emotional abuse as children, and they were involved in physical abuse of their adopted children.

Twelve of the couples adopting did so out of a desire to have children and an inability to conceive birthchildren. In five of these cases, the adoptive mother had never had a biological child. Notations in only one out of the 12 case records suggested that problems in the placement may have been associated with the inability of the parents to resolve the fact that they were unable to have birthchildren. All but two of the families dealing with issues of infertility had adoptions that either disrupted or dissolved. Although it is impossible to associate causality with the parent's infertility, a disproportionately high number of infertile couples became abusive to their adopted children.

Neither ethnicity nor age of the adoptive parents seemed to play a significant role in these cases of adoptive parent abuse. The average age of adopted children who were in abusive adoptive families was 6 and a half years of age. The oldest child was 14. Of the children placed in these homes, 4 exhibited moderate to severe behavior problems, 2 mild to moderate, and 12 none to mild while in placement.

There were many worker/agency issues in these cases. Lack of attentiveness to problematic family backgrounds and marital dynamics led to some of these problems. In several cases, mismatches between adoptive parents and children occurred. Support services were desperately needed in many of these placements, yet the records did not reveal that they were provided. Moreover, many of the families were unwilling to participate in therapeutic services. Of these cases, only one adoptive couple asked for intervention, yet did not receive adequate help.

## CONCLUSIONS

Overall, based on case narrative documentations, this group of abusive adoptive families was not well-investigated prior to placement. Seven parents in this sample of 15 cases had some sort of emotional problem. Other issues that were not identified in the screening process were marital problems, expectations of adoptive parents, feelings regarding discipline and special needs, questionable motives for adopting, and the lack of motivation to make a long-term commitment. It is likely that high worker caseloads, the need to place children as expeditiously as possible, the limited number of families seeking to adopt special needs children, and limited training opportunities may have lead to inappropriate placements. Although there is no positive evidence of intergenerational transmission of abuse, if adoptive parents have a history of being abused, this potential risk factor should be considered during the home study process (Kaufman & Zigler, 1987).

In this study, the majority (54%) of the parents who had been victims of abuse themselves did not victimize their adopted children. However, it is critical to consider this issue in adoption decision-making. Some may have resolved the emotional pain associated with the abuse, but others may not. For others, having contact with a child who has been physically or sexually abused may serve as a trigger for unresolved childhood abuse (Johnson, 1990). It is important to use measures such as the Minnesota Multiphasic Personality Inventory (MMPI) or other mental health assessment tools to give an idea of problems the parents may be experiencing. Once information that suggests a possible issue in the parents' background surfaces, it is important to investigate further. In many of these cases, red flags were apparent in either the home study or in reference letters. Any red flag, although not necessarily a definite indicator of a problem, warrants further investigation. In these cases, the following such issues were either not addressed at all or were inadequately addressed: adoptive parent histories of past abuse; comments in letters of reference such as "do not give this family any child that is not very bright"; stated beliefs in the excessive use of corporal punishment; home study assessment of parent as depressed, experiencing unresolved grief; isolated from family, having no close friends; histories of alcoholism or drug dependence; histories of marital violence or past violence involving foster children; and indicators of "bad temper" or the inability to resolve marital conflicts in a rational manner.

Training for prospective parents should include a focus on appropriate disciplinary strategies. Additional training might be needed to address red flag indicators. Parents need to be aware that children who have been abused may have more difficulty attaching, and are likely to test the commitment of the adoptive parents. Some traumatized children have so much anxiety about the possibility of another rejection and loss, that they may provoke the adoptive parents (Sack & Dale, 1982) in such a way that those parents who have experienced physical abuse may be at greater risk to perpetrate physical abuse. Also, parents who have had no prior parenting experience with special needs children need to be prepared for the types of behaviors they may exhibit during the placement.

Post-placement supervision visits should include: (1) visual observation of the child—for example, in one case the adoptive mother had taken the child to a neighbor's house before the worker arrived, so the worker would not see the signs of physical abuse; (2) interviewing family members, especially the target child, separately; (3) pre-consummation physicals for target children; and (4) swift reaction to any call from adoptive parents that sound suspicious—for example, in one case the adoptive mother called the worker the day after the worker had visited with the child and said, "you've got to come see him." The worker was confused by the request and told the adoptive mother it wasn't necessary, as the child had been seen yesterday. The adoptive mother in this case may have been asking for help with her abusive tendencies, but she never asked again. In this same case, a protective services worker had conducted an abuse investigation involving the child during the adoptive placement phase, but the protective services worker did not know the child was in an adoptive placement, and the adoption worker was never alerted that an abuse allegation had been filed.

The above recommendations are costly and time-consuming. However, the risk to the children being placed in what may be the second abusive home must be minimized. Additionally, some of the children who were abused by this group of adoptive parents had never been abused before. If proper screening had occurred, the abuse, loss of family and security, expensive therapy, and residential treatment might have been avoided. Close screening is needed to minimize the risk of physical or sexual maltreatment of children, and mental health evaluations and counseling should be available to all children in care, not just to those who have a reported history of abuse or adjustment problems (Benedict, Zuravin, Somerfield, & Brandt, 1996).

# CHAPTER 13

# Adoption Outcomes: Perspectives of Adoption Supervisors

The research presented in this book has been based upon an analysis of state agency case records on adoptive families and children needing placement. In order to provide further validation of the findings from the case reviews, additional data were sought from others intimately involved in state agency adoptions. Interviews were conducted with 22 state agency adoption supervisors located in each region of the state. These supervisors were asked a series of 25 questions that addressed issues such as their role in the agency, experiences with disruptions/dissolutions, reasons for disruptions/dissolutions, training provided to adoptive parents, adoption preparation process, worker training, and factors contributing to disruption/dissolution or stability. All interviews were tape-recorded and transcribed verbatim. Respondents were assured that neither their names nor specific regions would be identified in presenting the findings of the study.

Due to the differences in the size of the population in various regions and the potential for rural/urban differences, initial analyses were conducted to compare responses from supervisors in large versus small regions. Research team members reviewed and qualitatively analyzed common themes, trends, and patterns of responses. When qualitative differences were found between responses from supervisors located in the two types of regions, they were noted.

This chapter presents a summary of the responses from supervisors. De-identified quotes are used to illustrate their perspectives on factors associated with varying adoption outcomes.

## ROLE OF ADOPTION SUPERVISORS

State agency adoption supervisors in this study were responsible for overseeing adoption and foster care workers, approving home studies and placements, and training staff. For example, supervisors in large regions stated:

> *The primary function is to train staff, because they come to the unit not knowing how to do adoption work. I supervise eight placement workers who handle adoption and foster home cases. I read and approve home studies, attend PPT staffings where adoptions are planned for the child, read for licensing standards, do training for the unit, and serve on several committees.*

In smaller regions, supervisors mentioned assuming additional roles such as recruiting families, reviewing court reports, identifying children who are available for adoption, dealing with adoptive family preservation, conducting MAPP training, supervising recruitment, and supervising placements. In sparsely populated regions, one adoption unit might cover many counties. Therefore, supervisory roles may vary depending on the number of workers and number of counties in the region.

## EXPERIENCES WITH DISRUPTIONS

Most supervisors had personally experienced at least one disruption. Some supervisors indicated a lack of clarity about how to count the disruptions. For example, if a sibling group of seven disrupts, is that seven disruptions, or one? As a whole, the supervisors reported having experienced a range of 0 to 10 disruptions.

Some supervisors described their experiences with disruptions as follows:

> *I am aware of one that was a mismatch between the family and child—they had real inappropriate expectations . . . inappropriate expectations is a big one—the adoptive parents had been told of the limitation of the child but did not "hear" this.*

> *We didn't know the children well enough before the placement. The family's expectations were extremely high for the children, themselves, and the agency, and I went against a gut instinct. When I*

*read the study I knew that. I got the study back three times, and a therapist visited with the family, and I still knew in my heart. I blame myself a lot for that one. It didn't surprise me. . . . I didn't trust my own instincts. . . .*

*We find out information about the children that we didn't know when the children were placed in the home. The adoptive family may not have been prepared to parent children with those types of problems, or they were not accepting of those kinds of kids in their home, i.e., fetal alcohol syndrome or sexual acting-out due to abuse shows up after they were placed. The children that we have are getting more difficult because of their histories, and parenting these kids is real hard.*

*In the past, families were not prepared; caseworkers and psychologists did not know the implications of the children's behaviors, and they didn't know the need for ongoing support, or how adoptive families differed from other families. Now they disrupt because the child has very serious problems that endanger families physically and emotionally. They disrupt after lots of help, counseling, etc. They recognize, after getting an understanding from professionals, the need for residential treatment.*

*The idea of permanency never really sinks in with the adoptive family when it gets real rough. . . . Workers have not been successful at making a connection of "this is forever, this is your child" with the adoptive family. Some adoptive families seem to view these adoptions as similar to that of buying a car—keep as along as it works, return it when it doesn't.*

## REASONS FOR DISRUPTIONS/DISSOLUTIONS

Reasons given for disruptions/dissolutions can be categorized in three groups:

*Adoptive Family–Related Factors*

- Resistance to services
- Abusive adoptive parents
- Lack of preparation to handle child's problems
- Family stress

- Marital problems
- Birthsiblings' interference
- Parental jealousy
- Inability to control child
- Fertility issues
- Divorce
- Adoptive parents burn out
- Unresolved family of origin issues
- Birthchildren in home
- Unrealistic expectations
- Abuse
- High cost of treatment
- Parents had inadequate information on adopted child
- Expectations of adoptive parents
- Adoptive parents' failure to be honest with worker about problems
- Isolation
- Lack of commitment
- Lack of resources
- Not prepared for the long haul—think love is enough

### Child-Related Factors

- Child cannot attach
- Behaviors progressively worsen
- Aggressive behavior
- Behavior endangers adoptive family
- Kids run away
- Sexual acting-out
- Identity issues
- Teen placements difficult
- Adaptability of adopted child

### Agency-Related Factors

- Poor match between child and adoptive parents
- Inadequate assessment of adoptive parents and child
- Unknown information surfacing
- Lack of services

*Below are examples of specific supervisor comments that further elucidate some of the factors contributing to disruptions and dissolutions.*

*Children who are perpetrators . . . parental expectations (a big one) . . . abuse by the adoptive parents. Some children simply can't tolerate the intimacy of family relationships.*

*Kids in the system too long . . . multiple placements, multiple caseworkers where the plan changes. Multiple foster parents. Just a chaotic foster parent experience . . . the level of damage that's been done to a child by the time we get the child can cause the placement to be real difficult.*

*We have to decide how far will, can we, "stretch" this family.*

Supervisors described some of the disruption issues in the following manner:

*One family suspected that the child had multiple personalities. Another child was exhibiting some bizarre behavior and talking of killing the adoptive mother; he was only six.*

*Primarily what I've seen is very physically aggressive, assaultive, unattached teenagers. They are so assaultive that they are a danger to the family.*

*Reason for disruption is primarily unresolved family of origin issues on the part of the adoptive family . . . when you bring in a child of a similar background or scenario, then it just becomes just too much stress.*

*I'd say not a good match and also not a good assessment of the families. And, the families having higher expectations of the child. . . .*

## BEHAVIORS THAT ARE VERY PROBLEMATIC FOR FAMILIES TO HANDLE

Although three supervisors said that no problem was too severe if the adoptive parents were committed to the adopted child, the majority suggested that the following behaviors are problematic for families.

- Sexual acting-out/sexual perpetration
- Physical aggression (toward self, others, or pets) by the adopted child
- Severe property damage (e.g., fire-setting)
- Severe mental disorders
- Substance abuse
- Adopted child's inability to bond with family
- Running away

Supervisors stated:

*Anytime an adopted child hurts a biological child, there will be a breakdown . . . any kind of sexual acting-out . . . is always seen as the adopted child's fault.*

*Extreme sexual acting-out; physically destructive behavior; maybe substance abuse—similar things that cause other children to go into residential treatment—usually occurring at onset of adolescence. Whenever the child becomes a perpetrator.*

*Children who have difficulty in forming attachments; sexual acting-out issues. Parents not understanding that simple limit setting will not work.*

*Long time extensive sexual abuse; if a child has been exposed prenatally to drugs and alcohol and on top of that if you have a lot of neglect and you have sexual abuse going on at a very, very young age, and multiple perpetrators—that is going to be a child that is going to be extremely difficult to deal with along with attachment disorders.*

Clearly, according to adoption supervisors, the most difficult issues for families appear to be sexual acting-out, sexual abuse, and attachment issues.

## PROCESS OF DISRUPTION/DISSOLUTION

Supervisors described the disruption/dissolution process as follows:

*Disruption begins before the placement, with worker not looking for what the child really needs.*

*In the beginning of the placement, there is a honeymoon phase. It seems that most families are trying to make the placement work and don't reach out for help until they are at "the end of their rope." Then interventions occur, and these may reduce stress for some period of time, but not permanently. Eventually, the child may be returned. If the child is returned, they go through pre-placement visits with a foster family, and good-byes. Sometimes adoptive parents are charged with abandonment. Adoptive parents just give up.*

*Once the child is placed, the honeymoon is over, and the family realizes, "oops, this is not really my fantasy child" . . . Then there's denial and trying to work through that . . . typically it gets to a point when the stresses are so high that the family will probably call you at the very end with the child in tow.*

*When families have problems, they isolate themselves and they don't seek out proper resources. . . . If they're being supervised, they won't let the supervising worker know because they are afraid that they won't get to keep the child or that the agency will view them negatively . . . by the time that we find out about it, the family is at the end of their rope and really isn't open to trying to work on the problem.*

*Sometimes the child goes to residential treatment, and the child later returns to the adoptive home . . . problems persist, perhaps are worse . . . placement obviously not working . . . adoption dissolves.*

*Sometimes the match is not there. The worker and/or supervisor may make a poor match, and the adoption dissolves.*

*Many of them start out with problems of behavior that once we try to work with them, sometimes they are not willing to try to do what we are suggesting. They become irritated with the child and are less and less tolerant of their behaviors. The more the child does, the less they want the child in their home.*

*Step one is when the family admits that they're having very serious problems and are thinking about disruption. When they bring it into the public arena, to a friend, caseworker, family, whatever, it's out in the open. That's step one. Step two is talking about it, realizing it is an option, making a decision to disrupt the adoption, and saying to the caseworker, "We're going to do this in the best interest of the child, and we're going to give you plenty of time, and we want this to not hurt the child. So find the best placement for the child." That's step two. Step three is a week later, "Get the kid out of here." Best interest no longer applies. And step four is to move them. Families just cannot tolerate it after they have come out in the open, made the decision. They try very hard to do what's best for the child, but they're done. Usually by that time they just don't have anything left to give, and they will very quickly say, "Move no matter what." So any family that says, "We'll give you a month to move him," you've just got a week if you're lucky.*

*A six-year-old was placed in a home. Shortly after consummation, a 'perfect' toddler was placed also. The family decided to give up the six-year-old and adopt the younger child.*

*There are various patterns. There's not one little road map. Unfortunately, the ones that stand out in my mind are the ones where you do visits, everything's fine, things are going well, we're a happy family. A few little things, but no big deal, and all of a sudden there's a call. Things have gotten out of hand. It's so bad, and it's on and on and on. And I guess I want to go back to the non-disclosure of families not telling us what's going on . . . they were trying for whatever their reasons. I know that some families feel like, "I can handle it." It got to the point where for them it was such a big issue.*

## PREPARATION AND SELECTION OF PARENTS FOR ADOPTION

All supervisors indicated that prospective adoptive parents receive MAPP training. Additionally, in some regions, there are support groups meeting twice a month that prospective adoptive parents are asked to attend. There is some variability in perceptions of supervisors about who makes the final selection of the adoptive home. The majority of supervisors said that the direct services worker and the supervisor make a joint decision. One stated that although the policy calls for a team decision, the children's worker—substitute caretakers—make the decision. Other combinations include: Protective Services worker/worker/direct service worker and supervisor; or family worker, child worker, and one or both supervisors.

## PREPARATION OF CHILD FOR ADOPTION

Again, there was much variation in perceptions of who prepares the child for adoption. Nine (41%) of the supervisors indicated that the adoption worker prepared the child. Five (23%) said the child's worker prepares the child, 2 (4%) indicated the adoption worker and child's worker together via support groups, and 2 (4%) mentioned just the child's worker and adoption worker. Individual supervisors also mentioned foster parents, other counselors, and conservatorship workers as being involved in the preparation of the child for adoption. According to several supervisors:

> *The sub-care worker . . . is the one who prepares the child, but that person is not an adoption worker and is not familiar with adoption policy or casework practice. Nobody in the adoption unit works with the child toward the placement.*

> *The caseworker for the child will begin talking with the foster parents or the adoptive parents . . . and the counselor to coordinate the early preparation for the child. A lot of that's done through the counseling setting, too. And then, the adoption workers will do a formal adoption preparation class with kids to talk specifically about adoption issues in a group setting.*

Supervisors listed specific strategies for preparing the child, such as good-bye visits with siblings, medical assessments, meeting the adoptive parents, playing games, reading books on adoption, registering the child on adoption exchanges, talks with the child, counseling, and Lifebooks. However, supervisors differed in their assessment of the child's adoption preparation process. Most supervisors thought there was inadequate/mediocre/minimal preparation of children and families for adoption. Only 4 (18%) supervisors thought that they did a good to adequate job of preparation, and only 1 (4.5%) felt that adopted children receive a great deal of preparation. Some of the attitudes are expressed in the following quotes:

> *The child is not adequately prepared.... Most kids do not have Lifebooks. They are photo albums rather than Lifebooks, the therapeutic kind that goes into why your mommy couldn't raise you, etc.*

> *Not adequate in most cases—work is done by highly inexperienced caseworkers who aren't investing the time necessary to adequately prepare a child.*

> *From the point a child comes into care, a Lifebook is started ... the idea is that the child is supposed to be prepared all along as things are coming up. This is generally done with early conversations between the child's worker and the foster parent helping prepare the child in conjunction with the child's individual therapist. And then we try to work real closely with the foster parents and the adoptive parents during a transition—kind of a team transition into the adoptive placement. And again, a lot of that has gotten easier since we do more dual licensed placements—that we don't have this big moment in the child's life when he moves from a foster home to an adoptive home ... I really support this concept.*

> *Preparation is not adequate when the workers see the kids just once a month instead of once a week.*

> *I think we are doing a good job on our understanding of how we are supposed to prepare kids. ... I think that the failing, if there is one, would come in the quality of individual casework based on that caseworker or that group of caseworkers, working as a team—their own skill level, the quality of their work.*

*In the past, I don't think enough work has been done around preparing kids for adoption. . . . You're going to have to go over those past issues with the child about why they were removed, again. And so I say you can't do enough.*

*Preparation is an ongoing process, and it really should begin when the child enters the system.*

*Kids who need the most often seem to get the least.*

*Not enough preparation is done with the younger kid.*

## MOST DIFFICULT ISSUES IN NEW PLACEMENTS

The following issues were identified as being most difficult for the child in a new placement.

- Attachment
- Loss of biological or foster family, and everything else in the child's life/change of environment
- Coping with sibling loss if placed apart from other birthsiblings
- Dealing with anger/rage
- Adjusting to the adoptive parents
- Developing/maintaining trust
- Identity, new role in the adoptive family
- Learning new rules
- Dealing with fears
- Sibling group living apart and now coming together for adoption
- Problem behaviors of adopted child

The issues of loss and attachment were seen as the most difficult in most placements. Two workers stated:

*Issues that are related to attachment and bonding are most difficult . . . they are going through a grieving process for having left an environment . . . They [the children] are not real sure they are going to stay there, and after the first few weeks, . . . they really start testing these parents to see if they're going to be moved again.*

*The child loses everything: the foster parents, the home that they've
gotten accustomed to, the school, their friends, the pets, everything.
There are major losses for the child. They have to start all over
again.*

## SUCCESSFUL COPING STRATEGIES

Supervisors listed the following specific strategies for adoptive families
and children as well as agencies to facilitate coping with special needs
adoptions:

*Adoptive Families*

- Patience
- Flexibility
- Use Lifebooks
- Have empathy
- Be consistent
- Get early and appropriate therapy
- Identify resources
- Identify problems early
- Have support systems
- Perseverance, forgiveness, openness, acceptance
- Let child develop at his/her own level
- Pre-placement services and mandatory training
- Allow for contact with siblings not placed in home
- Foster adoptions

*Adopted Children*

- Continuing contact with foster families and siblings
- Preparation for adoption

*Agency/Worker*

- Encourage foster parent adoptions
- Minimize moves
- Help family find ways to express love
- Skilled, professional foster parents
- Treatment plan with treatment team
- Family therapy

- Placement rules (e.g., don't place a child older than or same age as children in home, match intellectual ability, etc.)
- Help family bond
- Use rage therapy
- Keep in close contact with the adoptive parents and child
- Identify problems early
- All parties need time
- Provide children with adequate preparation and follow-up

Additional comments from supervisors on ways to prepare children for adoption included:

*The support systems of the adoptive family have been real helpful. This includes other children that have been adopted who can help the children. The parents are helpful to other new adoptive parents. The buddy system and going to support groups. Getting the family into therapy as soon as you can after a problem has been identified and not wait until everything explodes. Stay in real close touch with the family . . . The families have access to that worker at any time that they are having a problem. Just knowing that they aren't stranded helps.*

*I think continuing to talk with the child, and having the adoptive parent talk with the child about the reason that he couldn't go home and what has happened helps him understand. He should understand, "You've been in foster homes. They've given you some things you are bringing with you, and we are going to combine them." And the parents should not be trying to make these children forget their past. They should be using Lifebooks to help them understand how they got where they are and to sit down and let the child talk about it . . .*

*I think in today's society and with today's problems, what you need in a foster parent is a professional, therapeutically trained and skilled parent who has a realistic expectation of what these kids are like, what they are going to do, and has real tangible skills in addressing them . . . . I think they should have a real clear-cut plan.*

*[The adoptive parents] going though the Lifebook with the adopted child seems to be the most ideal strategy to use because they can add to the end of the book family pictures right away, showing the child*

*moving along in addition to the history . . . The family has to have the patience of Job and the flexibility of Mr. Stretch. Those families are getting harder and harder to find.*

## UNSUCCESSFUL COPING STRATEGIES

A number of factors may lead to problems in special needs adoptive families. Supervisors identified unsuccessful adjustment strategies for adoptive families, adopted children, and agencies. Examples of each are given below.

### Adoptive Family Strategies

- Seeking some type of fulfillment from the child
- No strategy or plan
- Expectations (too high, unrealistic); failing to discuss expectations
- Adoptive parents not accepting desire for contact with biological and foster families
- Too much control
- Not taking responsibility/blaming child
- Punishing vs. logical consequences
- Inadequate preparation
- Being rigid
- Denial of problems
- Failing to keep child informed of his/her status
- Putting Lifebooks away and not taking time to review with child

### Adopted Children

- Child behaviors—acting-out, being violent
- Inadequate preparation
- Inability to let go of biological family
- Non-attaching behaviors
- Not integrating/accepting family values
- Lack of trust, due to prior history of disappointments and broken promises

### Agency/Worker

- Poor matching (using physical appearance, etc., as the criteria)
- Inadequate preparation of adoptive parent or adopted child

Examples of unsuccessful coping strategies are given below.

*Trying to make the child meet needs of the family; expecting the child to give something back.*

*High expectations, too much control . . . blaming the child for situations. There have been some families that say things like, "this child can't do anything right."*

*They're going to try and manipulate one parent against the other. They're going to pick on younger children. They're going to have school problems. They're going to be horrible. They are not going to obey, and they're going to be tearing up their room and screaming and hollering. And a lot of this is their anxiety about whether anyone wants them, and the low self-esteem that all our kids have. A lot is testing. "Are they really going to take me when I'm bad? If I can just be horrible and they're still going to keep me, I guess maybe I can begin to trust."*

*I think one of the things, which is kind of hard for us to identify sometimes, is when the child is not accepting of the family. When they start acting-out, we can identify it. . . . But the subtle ones are much more difficult—when the child withdraws and almost refuses to be a part of the family. And the reason I say it's hard for us to identify or understand sometimes is because as we go in there, the families may say something to the effect like, "Things aren't going well." And we'll say, "Well, what's going on?" They can't pinpoint it . . .*

## FACTORS THAT CONTRIBUTE TO ADOPTION STABILITY AND ADOPTION DISRUPTIONS

Supervisors identified adoptive family factors, child factors, and agency factors that contributed to adoption stability or instability. They are as follows:

*Adoptive Family Factors Contributing to Stability*

- Ability to learn from mistakes
- Acceptance of adopted child
- Commitment to a lifelong process
- Accept supervision
- Flexibility

- Good family communication
- Good, stable marriage
- Help the adopted child cope with loss
- More adoptive parents know about the child the better
- Ongoing support
- Preparation
- Realistic expectations
- Stable adoptive parents

*Adopted Child Factors Contributing to Stability*

- Adequate preparation and readiness
- Fewer number of placements for child
- Minimal or no abuse and neglect history

*Agency Factors Contributing to Stability*

- Fewer moves for the adopted child
- Help the adopted child cope with loss
- Skilled, experienced workers
- Well-managed cases
- Available funds for post-adoption services
- Assessment should be thorough and lead to a good match
- Adequate preparation of families

The most common factors that impact dissolution were the child acting-out, not being what the adoptive parents expected, or reaching adolescence (at which time they begin acting-out, etc.); these factors sometimes combined with a difficult time in the family's life cycle and the situation just becomes too disruptive to the family. As one supervisor stated:

> Pre-adolescents and early adolescents seem to be the ones facing dissolution. . . . Then they hit the most difficult developmental stage. This seems to be the point at which the family and the child can no longer tolerate each other—that is where the acting-out comes into play.

## RECOMMENDATIONS FOR ADOPTIVE FAMILIES

Supervisors provided very specific recommendations for families who adopt special needs children. Their advice included the following:

- Accept the biological family
- Be willing to take the risk
- Be flexible
- Examine motivation for adopting
- Do not expect to "get" something from the child
- Seek formalized respite care
- Have a good therapist
- Recognize the long term commitment

Other supervisors stated:

> *I think that their reason has to be much beyond that they love children. They have to really be prepared for what they're stepping into, realistic, that there's joys, but it is very, very challenging . . . they have to be the type of people that are open to having a lot of people involved in their lives . . . they carefully assess their family and make sure that it is a commitment that everybody in that family is wanting to make, and is capable of making.*

> *Have a good therapist . . . Have mental health checkups . . . attend support groups . . . be around other people who share the same experiences, who have been through it, because nobody else knows . . . be open to therapy . . . Keep educating yourself about adoption, that it's a lifelong experience.*

> *Get into counseling day one . . .*

> *It's going to take a lot of time and energy, and really the rest of your life, but it's very worth it.*

## RECOMMENDATIONS FOR AGENCY AND WORKERS

Worker training and experience was the most frequently stated recommendation by supervisors. Supervisors' comments included the following:

- Training, training, training
- Do better family assessments
- Know the adopted child a lot better
- Know the adoptive parents better

- Know placement issues and adoption theory
- Look to the "fit" in the future, not just "fit" for now
- May need to wait before placing the adopted child to get the best fit
- Need for more family assessment tools
- Use the foster parent profile to identify possible issues
- Remove worker bias from placement decisions
- MAPP training
- Placement rules (don't place a child who will be older than biological children or same age as biological children; match intellectual abilities; etc.)

The following quotes from supervisors are also illustrative of agency/worker issues.

*I think there should be a longer engagement before the wedding.*

*I see a real problem develop when the placement worker sees him/herself as an advocate for the family and goes after what the family wants versus what is the best placement for the child.*

*I think that the agency has to be prepared to stand behind these kiddos and the families . . . forever . . . for counseling and post-adoption services for the issues that will always be there.*

*Siblings are an important part of identity and attachment issues.*

*I think that there is a group of children that falls between the cracks. . . . There needs to be an in-between kind of placement for those children, kind of like long-term respite . . . where we won't have to remove those children from that family. Where the family can stay involved and still have custody of the children, but as an agency we could provide the financial support or whatever they need for that placement.*

*I think there are certain kinds of problems that require you to have a different family concept or a different family approach. For example . . . children with attachment problems . . . I think you just then look to a family that has different expectations or different approaches to a child . . . maybe you find a more distant family. Or maybe your family becomes more of a sponsor family as opposed to an everyday family.*

*And again, a lot of that has gotten easier since we do more dual licensed placements—that we don't have this big moment in the child's life when he moves from a foster home to an adoptive home.*

## CONCLUSIONS

Adoption unit supervisors provided very candid responses to questions on their experiences with adoption disruptions and dissolutions. They identified numerous, very critical issues associated with agency practices, adoptive parents, and adopted children that should be addressed.

Since supervisors tended to have limited knowledge of dissolutions as they occurred after finalization, many of their comments and illustrations were based upon their experiences with disruption. They noted that they have very little information on outcomes of placements after they have been consummated. Therefore, they are unaware of many children whose adoptions dissolved and who returned to the state's custody.

In identifying factors that have led to disruption or stability, regional supervisors noted a number of adoptive family characteristics, including commitment; adequate preparation; utilizing resources; need for flexibility; strong stable marriages; open, honest communication; realistic expectations; mental stability; willingness to allow child to discuss previous history and families; and ability to attach. These were all factors that we also noted in the review of case records as influencing adoption outcomes.

Supervisors emphasized that more extensive training is needed for workers to make better matches between children and parents. Specifically, workers need training in assessment of the child, the family, the marriage, abuse, loss, identity issues, self-esteem, matching children and families, and other possible issues developing in a family system. Some supervisors suggested the need for a longer pre-placement period to facilitate the adjustment.

Other supervisors noted that the types of children the state is placing today are very different from those placed a few years ago. These children have often come into the system after having been severely abused and neglected, and are also experiencing the affects of parental substance abuse. Attachment is a major issue for many of these children. In many cases, they need long-term therapy to work through their issues of loss, anger, feelings of low self-esteem and distrust, and need much better preparation for adoptive placement. Workers need to share realistically with families the impact of loss, abuse, and neglect on the child. Workers must receive training in assessment so that they can be better able to identify potential children's problems and to scrutinize families more carefully in order to make better matches.

Just as the state is mandated to provide all factual information about the child's background, parents must be helped to trust and feel secure in their adoptions so that they will also reveal trouble spots in the adopted child's and family's adjustment. Only if these problems can be identified early in the placement can counseling be sought before the family has given up on the child.

As one worker suggested, there may be a need to reassess the types of children coming into care and better define the types of familial situations they may need. Considering subsidizing foster families to help with children while allowing the children to maintain contact with their families of origin may serve to reduce some of the trauma children experience over the loss of their birthfamilies. This may also help to alleviate the financial stress many families experience while seeking medical or psychological treatment for their children. Also, there may be some children for whom permanent foster care and ongoing contact with their birthfamilies is the ideal. Since one of the most difficult issues adopted children must deal with is their grief over the loss of their birthfamilies, much more attention should be given to issues of open adoptions for older children.

The following chapter examines these issues from the perspective of post-adoption service providers.

# CHAPTER 14

# Adoption Outcomes: Perspectives of Post-Adoption Service Providers

To gain additional knowledge about issues associated with state agency adoption outcomes, telephone interviews were conducted with 12 post-adoption service providers located within 12 regions in the state. As these therapists provide services to children after the placement, they know first-hand about the problems experienced by children and families. These providers generally contract with the state to provide post-adoption services.

The interview protocol consisted of 18 open-ended questions that were designed to elicit information about post-adoption workers' experiences with special needs adoptive families. All of the interviews were tape-recorded and transcribed verbatim in order to have an accurate record of the participants' comments. Providers were assured that their specific responses would not be identifiable in any reports published from the data.

Due to the differences in population size and resources available in small, rural regions and large, urban regions, initial analyses were conducted to compare responses from providers in both types of regions. Content analysis of the interview responses yielded a variety of patterns and themes, which will be presented below. However, as noted below, only a few regional differences emerged in the responses of post-adoption service providers.

## ADOPTED CHILDREN

### Characteristics of Children and Families

Post-adoption service providers viewed special needs adopted children as unique because of their history of physical and/or sexual abuse, neglect, and behavioral and neurological problems. Others noted specific psychological issues, such as identity problems, unresolved grief, loss, separation, lack of permanence, and attachment problems, as characteristic of the children for whom they have provided treatment. For example, one provider discussed what she was seeing:

> *Lots of these children. . . . have been abused in foster homes—by older foster children and some by foster parents. This continuation of abuse happens very frequently, and children have a difficult time developing trust.*

Providers reported several differences in relationships in adoptive families and in birthfamilies. Primary differences pertain to commitment, attachment, family history, and problem ownership. Adoptive families may know that there was a previous family, but little may be known about the past. Attachment issues remain a problem and concern in adoptive families. Three post-adoption providers stated the following:

> *I don't think that the biological children that we work with are generally as disturbed as these particular post-adoptive children.*

> *Basically, biological families have created their own systems from day one. And so, the dysfunctional or acting-out behavior in the biological family at least is expected. . . . When an adoptive family comes together, it's like two foreign family systems coming together, and it immediately throws them into crisis.*

> *Well, primarily, it is the history of the children. They come from a bad situation. A lot of them are suffering from the past that they have not dealt with . . . the primary issue is that a lot of these children have not dealt with their issues, and it just goes on and on until it blows up.*

## Contributors to Successful Adjustment of Adopted Children

The majority of post-adoption service staff believed that the successful adjustment of the adopted child is related to the adoptive parents. Families must be open, honest, devoted, and nurturing. They must set clear rules and boundaries, provide competent parenting, and have strong marriages. Families who are in tune with the child's needs, have realistic expectations, have had adequate adoptive parent training, seek out help early, and are willing to help the child are the most successful. Service providers in rural areas also mentioned factors such as time, prayer, and information as being important in the successful adjustment of adopted children. Those in larger regions also emphasized the importance of love, consistency, and children's ability to bond and express affection. Service providers stated:

*It is those children that are able to express a bond and affection to the adoptive family, those who can "give back" to the adoptive families in some small way—it may be a hug or some joy. . . .*

*When parents are very open and honest about birthparents, non-judgmental, and empathetic. Mother is usually very devoted to children . . . would rather fight than switch.*

*I think when it's a family that has a good marriage, it's clear about what their rules are in the family, what the boundaries are . . . these adoptions seem to work.*

## Difficult Issues for Adopted Children

Post-adoption service providers indicated that adopted children often deal with issues associated with their relationship to the former family and/or their new adoptive family. Those issues related to the former family included loss, separation, attachment, bonding, and loyalty. Issues pertaining to the new adoptive family included not knowing the rules, not liking the biological children in the home, living in a home with inexperienced parents, not being what the adoptive family expected, having adoptive families that lacked knowledge of available resources, accepting the new adoptive family, believing the new family would be a permanent placement, and developing trust in the new family. Providers stated:

*I guess the most difficult issue related to the adoption that we have seen has been the child having issues of separation from wherever he was before.*

*The family often has an unrealistic picture of what this child is like. Helping them to come to grips with, "this child is not the child I dreamed about."*

*Attachment issues are paramount. I think it's just that when they first go to the family, they don't know what the rules are.*

## Problem Behaviors: Impact of Child's Age and Developmental Stage

Almost all providers agreed that age at placement has an effect on the problems experienced by the adopted child. Older children may have more memories of abuse, yet young children who were abused as infants may act out pre-verbal abuse. One worker suggested that the most difficult age is 4, others suggested age 7, while others suggested the teen years. Recognizing that different issues arise at different developmental stages, some explained their impressions of the impact of age as follows:

*Some of my most disturbed children are my younger children right now that were severely abused and have no memory of that. They're acting-out and they don't know why they are; they're just reacting.*

*We did a survey from March 1990-December 1992 and found that kids start having signs of problems at 7 years. They begin aggressive behavior, stealing, lying, and acting-out.*

*Most of the children coming in for services are in pre-adolescence or in adolescence . . . a child that may have been sexually abused and is now in adolescence is bigger, stronger and may begin to act out.*

Other workers noted that although age at placement is a factor, other important factors, such as the severity of the abuse or family dysfunction, also greatly contributed to the severity of the child's behavior.

### Reasons for Children's Inappropriate Behavior

The majority of all post-adoption service providers identified loss, sadness, and anger as the reasons for the acting-out behaviors. This anger is often projected onto the adoptive parents. More specifically, service providers stated:

> *They have anger and rage ... but because the adoptive family is available, that is transferred to them.*

> *Every child has grief issues, anger, sadness. ... Workers have not done as well helping kids understand removal. Every kid that's abused deals with anger.*

> *Many deny that the birthparents abused them and project the anger they feel towards the birthparents—especially the birthmother—onto the adoptive mother.*

> *It's rare for adopted kids to involve the bios in sex ... because the bios tell the parents. With adopted kids they protect each other [and] don't tell the parents. ... These kids generally don't try to hurt the parents because they don't have enough self-esteem to think they can hurt the parent.*

> *They have tremendous rage. They're angry, angry, angry. I don't think any of us have any sense of how angry these children are ... Sometimes when they tell me their story, I can hardly hear it ... It's just too awful, too horribly awful.*

### Children's Acting-Out Behaviors

The majority of post-adoption providers indicated that children may act-out with inappropriate behaviors as a means of coping with the new placement. Specific counterproductive behaviors include the following:

- Recreating the abusive relationships
- Joining gangs
- Running away
- Stealing
- Lying
- Bed-wetting

- Aggression
- Sexual acting-out
- Antisocial behavior
- Trying to wedge adoptive parents apart
- Not learning or ignoring rules
- Sabotaging relationships with other family members
- Hanging on to birthparents
- Testing
- Not attaching due to fear or distrust

Providers gave the following illustrations of the above-mentioned behaviors:

> *They manipulate the families. They get between the couple. They cause serious trauma to the parents.*

> *Deliberately sabotaging relationships, abuse to other siblings in the home, pushing forbidden buttons of the parents . . . acting-out is especially present around the end of the six-month trial period before adoption finalization—kid wants to make sure the parents will accept him/her.*

> *When they start getting into substance abuse, when they start getting into gangs, when they start not being able to deal with the issues of bonding and attachment—that they're so distrustful they'll push people away. . . . They'll try to escape in one way or another. . . .*

## Therapeutic Interventions to Address Loss

All providers had worked with some children who openly expressed a desire to have contact with their birthfamilies. Providers suggested that most children desire this contact even though they may not state it openly. The following statements from providers illustrate the range of responses pertaining to contact with birthfamilies.

> *I'd say they probably do want contact. For a lot of them, that's not an OK thing to even talk about in their family. They know that to make a statement such as that would cause serious problems.*

*Most do wonder where their birthparents are and wish for contact. However, only a fraction have contact with birthparents and another fraction with some member of [the] extended birthfamily.*

*About half have contact—some visits do take place, but some kids just want to know what's happening with their birthfamilies and for them to know what's happening with them (birthfamilies) rather than having direct contact.*

Most providers believed therapy can help children resolve some other issues of loss of contact with birthfamilies and previous caregivers. However, two providers stated that they were not sure that the children could ever completely work through this. Another felt that the issues should be dealt with prior to an adoptive placement. Four therapists suggested the need for the adopted child to be able in some way to reconnect with the past via case records, tapes, or visits to former homes. Therapeutic interventions included:

- Showing the child the case record
- Saying good-bye to the past through letter-writing, visiting former homes, and phone calls
- Adoptive parents' giving the child permission for the adopted child to contact the birthparents
- Bringing the birthfamily into therapy
- Participating in ropes therapy (trust building)
- Participating in rage therapy, art therapy, music therapy, holding therapy, family therapy, role-playing, play therapy, and group work

*We teach the families how to hold the child, how to talk with them, how to get that eye contact, how to begin to do that attachment work with that child . . . to get through that rage.*

*I've had a couple where we brought back the birthfamily to work through it . . . but I think that most of them that I have now are still having an element of anger that they've not been able to resolve because the birthfamily has not been part of the puzzle.*

*We've been real impressed with the adoptive families' [not all adoptive parents] ability to learn the meaning of some of these*

*behaviors. They've developed a real understanding of the depth of the*
*grieving and loss and lack of roots that a child may be growing up*
*with.*

## ADOPTIVE PARENTS

### Revelation of Background Information to Adoptive Parents

Detailed background information on special needs adopted children
was either not shared at all, or not completely shared, with adoptive
parents until the Texas disclosure law was passed in 1989. There are
many adoptions that occurred before this date that involved parents
who were not completely informed about the child's background.
However, several providers reported that the families neither heard nor
completely understood all that they were told. Others stated that
background information "just isn't always available." Only one
provider from a large, urban area indicated that she had never
experienced cases in which the family had not been told about the
child's past. Five providers in small regions indicated that they had
encountered cases in which the family did not receive full disclosure of
information about a particular child. Two stated that almost everyone is
not told something, and two others stated that the adoptive parents did
not remember being told or did not hear everything they were told
because they were anxious to adopt.

Providers have learned that agencies have withheld from adoptive
parents the following types of information: extent of drug abuse history
by the birthparents, extent of sexual abuse, and the number of previous
placements of the child. In some instances, a child may have
experienced abuse, but if the adopted child never disclosed it, the
agency or the adoptive parents would have no knowledge of it. One
post-adoption service provider commented:

> *We've had cases where families have told us they've been told [that]*
> *Medicaid will pay for everything, which is absolutely not true ...*
> *families were told that schizophrenia is not inherited. ... Generally,*
> *families don't process everything they read when they go in and read*
> *the charts ... sometimes you have to read between the lines, and*
> *sometimes there's a lot of jargon that families don't understand.*

## Most Difficult Issues for Adoptive Parents

Providers in large urban areas reported that the most difficult issue for adoptive parents was the contrast between what the parents expected and the reality of what they encountered in parenting their child. The majority of the providers in small, rural areas identified specific behaviors such as sexual acting-out and aggression. These behaviors probably contributed to adoptive parents viewing the child as not fitting into their fantasy of what parenting would be like. The following quotes from providers illustrate these perceptions.

*It's a big adjustment that most people are not really geared for. . . . It is hard enough to adopt, but when you adopt special needs children you need to go an extra mile.*

*It's difficult for parents to really understand the dynamics of attachment, especially if the child has been in multiple placements. Coming to grips with different value systems—the fact that the children do have different value systems, and may not ever completely embrace their [adoptive family's] value system.*

*I think the immediate most difficult issue is the child not behaving the way they expected him to, the child not blending into their system and meeting their expectations as quickly or as well as they would want to. On top of that, many parents are shocked that they are not in love with this child for a long, long time.*

*Sexual abuse is the most frightening for adoptive parents.*

*Just the sheer work of parenting these children . . . these kids have to be supervised all the time.*

## Adjustment of Adoptive Parents

Post-adoption providers indicated that a number of factors can impact the adjustment of adoptive parents, including:

- Personality characteristics (being open, honest, empathetic, flexible, having a sense of humor)
- Availability of support from within the family or from other adoptive families or respite care

- Seeking therapy before the problem becomes too severe
- Letting go of expectations
- Religious beliefs
- Giving the child time to adjust
- Parenting ability/skills
- Having knowledge about the effects of sexual abuse.

Others suggested:

> *Give the child space without crowding the child—give the child time to adjust. People must be aware of what they are getting into. They need to have commitment.*

> *I think parents must be able to delay their gratification—and to maybe redefine what parenting is going to be for these children.*

> *Parents must let go of expectations of selves as parents or the relationship between parent and child. Be laid back.*

### Counterproductive Behaviors of Adoptive Parents

Providers described a variety of counterproductive adjustment activities that some adoptive parents engage in, as follows:

- Becoming abusive to the child
- Trying to make the child like the parents' fantasy child
- Blaming the child
- Maintaining unrealistic expectations
- Shaming the child
- Using traditional parenting techniques for non-traditional children
- Bringing up own sexual abuse issues from the past
- Not recognizing the child's behavior as dysfunctional

More specifically, providers commented:

> *They hide things for a long period of time until it is intolerable . . . they're just going with it and hoping it will all work out . . . But yet, they could have gotten help way back before it got this bad. They'll wait until the child needs residential placement or something because*

*he's so disturbed, and sometimes they, themselves, have made it worse.*

*They are more rigid than they were before sometimes. They blame the kid. Sometimes they see the child as the embodiment of evil.*

## SIBLING ADJUSTMENT ISSUES

Adopting a special needs child impacts the entire family system—including the siblings already in the home. Three providers indicated that the new child's behavior is one of the most difficult issues for the siblings. For example, the new child may steal or destroy their belongings. Some are angry about having to help with the new child. Some feel the loss of the parents and the parents' attention due to the new child, while others may fear that removal could happen to them. Sibling rivalry and jealousy can lead to further problems. Also, some adoptive parents have noted that the children already in the home may pick up negative behaviors of the new adoptive children to get parental attention. Other comments included:

*I think the basic thing is lack of preparation for these children who are already in the home . . . they become very territorial, especially if it is biological children.*

*They're giving up the family as they've known it. That's an issue of real big loss for the siblings. . . . Most of the time, we have found that the adoption is not something they want.*

*I have had kids tell me, "I'm so tired of Mom being angry all the time." Just the neediness that these kids have, the family will never be the same.*

### Counterproductive Sibling Adjustment

As mentioned earlier, siblings often have a very difficult time adjusting to the new child especially when they have not been prepared. Among the counterproductive behaviors are the following:

- Acting-out
- Running away
- Abusing or scapegoating the adopted child

- Undermining the adopted child's placement
- Setting up or being unkind to the adopted child
- Withdrawing
- Becoming sad
- Telling the adopted child's story at school

Post-adoption service providers gave the following examples of counterproductive sibling adjustment:

> *Sometimes siblings become very sad . . . they try to pull the attention back to themselves . . . sometimes they are very unkind to the new child.*

> *Some handle it by withdrawing from family or by doing some super-duper acting-out to get their own attention needs met.*

### Strategies for Facilitating Sibling Adjustment

Service providers tend to agree that it is important for the siblings to be part of the adjustment process, somehow connected to the new child—as mentors and/or as part of the problem-solving process. However, as one worker noted, "it is important for siblings to have their own interests with which they can continue. When siblings are adequately prepared, they do a better job of adjusting to the new placements." Other providers advised parents to make space for their biological children or other children already in the home. Specific worker comments are as follows:

> *I think the times when this [adoption] works is when everybody has their input into what it means and how they're going to have to change.*

> *Coming to an understanding of accepting people for who they are and having patience.*

### EXPERIENCES WITH DISSOLUTIONS

Service providers in large areas had seen 2 to 12 cases of dissolved adoptions, and workers in small rural areas had worked with anywhere from 1 to 6 dissolutions in the last few years. Behaviors of the adopted child are the primary reason given for adoption dissolutions by these post-adoption service providers. These behaviors included smearing feces on the wall, self-abuse, violence, running away, chronic stealing, and life-threatening acting-out. Other adoptions dissolved because of adoptive family issues or specific circumstances, such as the child was incarcerated, the adoptive parents were getting a divorce, the adopted child was in treatment and did not want to go home, the adoptive parent was abusive, the adoptive mother died, problems occurred regarding the family of origin, marital problems occurred, the family could not afford continued residential treatment, the family disengaged from the child, the adoptive parents were rigid and conservatively religious, the family blamed the child and was not involved in therapy, there was no bonding with the adoptive parents, and jealousy/sibling rivalry occurred. Specific provider comments included:

> *A lot of times it is a situation where the adoptive parents can no longer deal with the child's behaviors as he or she become an adolescent . . . the child is perhaps in residential care or psychiatric care . . . and families were no longer able to cope financially or emotionally.*

> *The family was always saying how everything was the child's fault. And they had done all they could, but yet these were the families that really weren't wanting to be involved in the therapeutic process. They just wanted somebody to fix their kid . . . They never really bonded with the child, the child never bonded with them, and it was always the child's problem.*

## Problems with Which Families Can't Cope

Although two providers indicated that different families can handle different behaviors and some families can handle almost anything, the majority of providers indicated that there are adopted child behaviors that may create problems that are likely to be beyond the coping ability of most parents. These include:

- Sexual acting-out between siblings
- Sexual acting-out in general
- Substance abuse
- Chronic runaways
- Biological and/or younger children threatened or in danger

- Lack of funds for residential treatment center
- Chronic mental illness
- Aggression (including rape) or signs of aggression (hoarding knives, etc.)
- Defiance at home and school
- Severe depression, psychoses
- Severe medical problems
- Becoming a danger to self and others

Providers in large urban areas identified severe aggression as the most difficult issue for adoptive families, while workers in rural areas identified inability of adoptive parent or adopted child to attach as the most difficult issue. Two providers stated:

> *You know the parents get pretty heartbroken. They say . . . "this child never attached to me." Like if there was some attachment maybe they could extend themselves further.*

> *The fact that this child may never bond or attach to them [is the most difficult issue]. And then they learn, particularly due to some type of impairment, that they might not have been fully aware of, that this child may never be independent.*

## Factors That Lead to Residential Treatment

The most common factor that leads to residential treatment is children being a danger to themselves or to others. Others mentioned adopted children being in trouble with the law, sexually acting-out, not taking medications, having no emotions, having attachment difficulties, not trusting, and being the victims of sexual abuse. Several post-adoption service providers commented as follows:

> *I think where the family feels at any minute they're going to do something to them or something to their sibling.*

> *Aggression is first. Sexual abuse would be next. Usually when the child becomes aggressive with his parents or others in the home.*

> *The raping of a little sister, or threatening to; things involving knives—every one of the dissolutions I worked with involved knives.*

## The Process of Dissolution

Although one provider stated that there is no typical process of dissolution, the majority of respondents suggested similar dissolution scenarios, such as:

> *The adoptive parents are at the end of their rope, worn out and tired . . . the parents are angry . . . the adoptive parents feel helpless and hopeless . . . they have tried therapy or residential treatment . . . the family needs a respite. They may try residential treatment again as a last hope. Once in treatment, 66% of the adopted children do not return home or the adoptive parents don't want them to return. While the child is in treatment, the wound in the family heals, and there is no place in the family for the adopted child to return . . . or the family wants to help the child, but can't afford continued residential treatment. The case may go to the agency [and] the adoptive parents may experience a sense of failure or relief, and the adopted child may also feel relieved.*

Another provider phrased it in this way:

> *The family has parented the child for 7 to 9 years or so, and when they heard about post-adoption services, they're in pretty much a state of need . . . we've put the child in and out of treatment, outpatient or inpatient. They're exhausted, and once I get the child into a placement, this family is kind of relieved, and so they back off a little bit. We try to keep them connected. . . . When it gets close to the time for the child to be discharged then they panic. . . . They're desperate, and they may try to get CPS to take back this child because they don't feel like this child can come back into their home and everybody can be safe. And maybe they're so exhausted financially, they don't feel like they can continue to provide for this child, or maybe, even at this point, they don't want this child back. . . .*

## FACTORS THAT CONTRIBUTE TO ADOPTION STABILITY

Post-adoption providers viewed strong marriages, good support systems, commitment of the adoptive parents, ability to deal with issues and behaviors, strong families, realistic self-perceptions, and healthy adoptive parents as important factors contributing to adoption stability.

Other factors mentioned by individual providers were the following: religious connection, financial resources, practicing and teaching values to kids, consistency, family commitment to the adoption, functioning level of the child, early intervention, united front of families, strong faith, ability to keep going when frustrated, having full information on child, tolerance of bizarre behavior, parental history of having survived a trauma, flexible families, getting family therapy, and willingness to seek help.

It is interesting to note that the providers, like the supervisors, primarily mentioned adoptive family factors rather than child factors as contributors to adoption stability. The following three quotes are particularly illustrative of this belief:

> *I think the primary thing is the healthy functioning of the adults. That's the primary thing. Secondarily is the level of functioning of the child.*

> *Stability—a good strong support system . . . ability to be frustrated and keep on trying.*

> *A serious commitment on the part of the mother; it helps if the father is as committed.*

## FACTORS THAT CONTRIBUTE TO ADOPTION DISSOLUTION

Similarly, when identifying factors contributing to adoption dissolution, post-adoption providers also primarily listed factors associated with the family. These included:

- Adoptive parents that can't separate child's behavior from themselves as parents
- Pre-conceived fantasy child and subsequent disillusionment
- Isolated families
- Inflexible, rigid adoptive parents
- Lack of support
- Adoptive parents who want a child versus wanting to parent
- Adoptive parents who don't listen to reality in training because they want a child so much
- Adoptive parent history of being victims of abuse or neglect

- Unrealistic expectations
- Unhealthy adoptive parents
- Lack of resources
- Lack of information

Although the majority of comments focused on familial factors, child and agency factors were also mentioned as contributors. Child factors were identified as follows:

- Adopted child's unresolved issues
- Extreme behaviors
- Kids who don't want to be adopted
- Violence by adopted child
- Inability to bond
- Functioning of adopted child
- Temperament

"Worker," or agency, factors contributing to dissolutions are identified below:

- Required MAPP training doesn't meet the adoptive parents' needs
- Hurried placements
- Social workers not knowing the adoptive parents
- Poor follow-up
- Adoptive mother made to feel that she is the problem
- Lack of outside intervention

Post-adoption service providers clearly expressed concerns about adoption dissolutions and stressed that adoptive parents must receive full information, workers must make good matches based on a thorough assessment of the adoptive parents and the child, and families must be given ongoing support, therapy, and respite care. They advocated for services to be provided early to prevent dissolution. A sampling of the comments from service providers on dissolution issues is illustrated below.

*The state does not have a good mechanism to handle these situations.*
*There are families that have extended every resource that they have,*
*including financial resources, and they're almost to the point where*

*they need to be hospitalized themselves. Then the state says to them, "we're going to charge you with abandonment and take you to court if you try to give the child to protective services to relinquish."*

*It really depends on how in-depth you get with these people that are wanting to adopt special needs children . . . just glancing at my caseload, I'd say one-third of them should not have been placed. And I keep thinking, "who did these placements?"*

*Too many sloppy placements because of the rush to get the kid out of foster care by or before six months.*

*Problems occur with the ones who wanted only one or two children and got talked into taking more.*

*We need to have a lot more contact with the workers. I don't think that most of the workers know all that the family goes through once the adoption is finalized.*

*A lot of these children that are coming into the system are more and more damaged. I mean it is not getting any easier. That's why post-adoption services are growing and growing.*

*Parents don't always "hear" the behavior problems when they are shared with the parents . . . parents believe, "oh, it won't happen to me."*

*I think that when they get into adolescence, that's when they begin to have severe problems. So this family may keep this child for 5, 6, 7 years before they get to a point where they're screaming for help.*

*I give subcontractors a handout that talks about all the issues of post-adoption services and what that entails and what that means. And it's kind of like news to them that they're supposed to be dealing with this.*

*Always ask the fundamental question: Are the parents involved in this adoption because they want to have a child . . . or want to parent?*

*Dissolutions do not simply fix the problem. There is tremendous grief and guilt over dissolutions by both parents and children—residential treatment doesn't make this go away.*

*Some of the most recent theories on adoption are maybe that adoption shouldn't even happen. Adoption totally changes a child's life.*

## COUNSELING METHODS

Although individual therapy is the most commonly followed by residential treatment, other types of therapy and assistance offered by workers were the following: family treatment, respite care, couples therapy, group treatment, art therapy, play therapy, and parenting training. Rural programs were more likely to contract out services or provide referrals rather than provide therapy themselves. Providers commented:

*As far as family therapy, we're most often working on how to cope, behavioral problems, attachment issues. I think that attachment and coping skills are probably the most important issues.*

*I don't see a lot of therapy that is effective. I believe it is important that all receive family therapy.*

*The problem is that funds are real limited . . . top priority for services are the individual child and the parents and then the siblings.*

The majority of rural and urban service providers indicated a preference for family therapy. However, some noted that the selection of therapy depends upon the family's needs. Two other providers stated:

*I prefer family therapy, if the family is ready.*

*I know of one therapist that is doing better with the families—the therapist does "holding type" of therapy and works with the parents. Other therapists draw in the parents when the therapy is almost over as part of closure.*

## FINANCING THERAPY

Most post-adoption providers suggested that adoptive parents don't pay for treatment out of their own funds—most have insurance, subsidy, or Medicaid; or the state agency pays. Providers commented:

> *This past year, we have had four families out of 23 that paid with insurance. The families have not paid out-of-pocket fees, but we did have some who arranged third party payment out of their own insurance.*

> *Very few of our families pay out of pocket. All of our families are on some sort of subsidy.*

## KNOWLEDGE NEEDS: POST-ADOPTION PROVIDERS

Post-adoption providers generally mentioned several categories of knowledge needed to provide post-adoption services:

- Knowledge of child issues (attachment, identity issues, normal child behavior and development, grief, and loss)
- General issues (adoption, resources, post-adoption services, neurological problems, physical diseases)
- Knowledge of families (family dynamics, creating an adoptive family)
- Therapeutic knowledge (family therapy, assessment, working with families of special needs children, dynamics and effects of abuse, childhood depression, ADD, supporting adoptive parents)

Additional comments by providers included:

> *I think they have to have a real understanding of the issues that a child who is going through separation stuff or has experienced traumatic separation in their lives will be dealing with and what the implications are later on.*

> *Good solid knowledge of family dynamics, developmental levels of children, effect of types of abuse in families, physical diseases . . . knowledge of grief, anger, pain—be able to differentiate each situation from the other . . . be shockproof.*

*Understand that parents are doing the best that they can do.*

## KNOWLEDGE NEEDS: ADOPTION WORKERS

Post-adoption providers were very specific in identifying the types of knowledge that adoption workers need. They emphasized that workers need to understand abuse and its effects, specific types of abuse, and the dynamics of abuse. Two post-adoption providers suggested that adoption workers need to know the same things as post-adoption workers, and three mentioned the need for an understanding of attachment issues. Others gave specific suggestions to adoption workers, which included:

*Love is not enough.*

*Be honest with parents.*

*Be realistic about the kids.*

Providers also identified specific types of knowledge that adoption workers should have, such as:

- Matching kids and families
- Creating an adoptive home
- Communication between workers
- Fighting bureaucracy
- Dealing with the child's problems
- Needs of the child
- Assessment
- Insurance coverage
- Effects of separating siblings and reuniting them
- Child development
- Trust issues
- Legal system
- Family code
- Family dynamics

Other suggestions for adoption workers included:

*They need to have contact with post-adoption workers to understand what happens five years later after consummation.*

*They should have at least 10 years of experience in family dynamics to understand the effects of abuse on kids before doing adoption work.*

*They need to be able to assess a family's ability to really cope with severe differences in their children. They must be able to modify expectations of children.*

*I think that they need to have a sensitivity that sometimes they have to fight the bureaucratic system that they work in. . . .*

*Workers need to have knowledge of the dynamics of an abused/neglected child in the family system and the effects of abuse and neglect on that child. . . . They need to understand the needs of the child, especially the abused child.*

## SUGGESTIONS FOR ADOPTIVE FAMILIES

Service providers gave a variety of advice to adoptive families, which primarily emphasized the need to be realistic about what adoption of special needs children will be like. Several workers suggested intensive parent education or experience and looking at oneself, one's family, and one's marriage to see if one can really do this. They also recommended having a strong support system and adequate training regarding special needs adoption. Specific suggestions are given below.

*My first recommendation is that they better learn all that they can . . . they definitely need to be hooked up with a support group. They've got to have some other families that they can talk to.*

*They need to be mentally and physically healthy themselves and have successfully dealt with issues themselves, have a strong marriage, and a strong support base.*

*Adoption will tear the family apart if there are other problems.*

*Be willing to deal with almost anything. Do this at a time in your life when you feel like you have energy to focus 85% of your attention to this issue.*

*Parent education is a must. Often the parents may be told something, but they don't really hear or understand it.*

Other suggestions included:

- Have one parent at home, not working, for a while
- Learn how to deal with sexual issues
- Spend time in a family with a special needs child
- Expect changes in your family—from all members
- Get MAPP or other training; learn all you can
- Understand effects of abuse
- Understand attachment issues
- Examine motivation, commitment
- Learn how to access special education
- Don't express anger toward or disapproval of birthparents
- Be strong advocates with the school system
- Expect that therapy may be needed off and on for life
- Take care of yourself
- Understand level of supervision these children will need
- Be supportive to the child and to each other
- Don't expect love in return
- Don't try to fit the child into your definition of what the child should be
- Find out about the child in school
- Don't believe that with prayer alone they can make it

## CRITERIA FOR THE SELECTION OF ADOPTION STAFF

Based upon their experiences in working with adoptive families, post-adoption providers identified specific criteria staff should meet if they are responsible for matching children and families, which is as follows:

- Maturity
- Previous exposure to adoption
- Master's degree
- Willingness to listen to adoptive parents' expectations

- Good social workers
- Good diagnosticians; being able to identify unresolved issues in adoptive parents

## CRITERIA FOR THE SELECTION OF ADOPTIVE FAMILIES

Based upon their clinical work with adoptive families, providers were able to delineate specific attributes that are needed by special needs adoptive families. The following factors should be considered in the selection process:

- Flexible parenting style—avoid families with rigid expectations
- Support systems available—linkages with other families
- Avoid families that have high expectations
- Assess mental health of adoptive mother
- Advocacy skills
- Willingness to use resources
- Church involvement
- Choose adoptive parents that have a realistic understanding of their weaknesses and strengths
- Select experienced families that have previously weathered traumatic situations
- Select families open to therapy
- Use caution with sibling placements
- Give preference to families with children
- Choose families with strong marriages

Specific provider comments:

*Workers have the attitude, "We are beggars so we can't be choosy"—but they must be very selective in who is raising these children. They need to select out those who want a child and keep those who want to parent.*

*Weed out people who themselves had been abused or neglected and had not truly resolved these issues. Weed out those who are rigid, have too high of expectations.*

*It's hard if you've been the worker for the child to be objective about the child. The worker's viewpoint is unrealistic. Their contacts are very different than living with the child.*

## MATCHING CHILDREN AND PARENTS

Providers suggested better matching of children and parents in terms of temperaments, personalities, expectations, amount of energy needed to parent a particular child, ability of adopted child to attach, and the adoptive parents' need for attachment.

In the case of adolescents, one provider emphasized the need to let them have input in the selection of adoptive parents. Another suggested using research findings in selecting parents for special needs children. Several providers emphasized the need to be open about the children's limitations with prospective adoptive parents, and to have longer pre-placement visits to assess the match between the adoptive parents and the child. Other specific comments included:

*They could make better placements by doing personality testing and matching better the personalities of the families and the child. If you have a child that is not going to excel in sports, you don't want to put that child with a family that thinks sports is all there is.*

*Really pay attention to where these people are coming from . . . it is a field you can't short-cut . . . it is a lifetime commitment. And people really have to realize it is a lifetime commitment regardless of what happens.*

*Agencies need to take a closer look at sibling placements. If they are going to adopt out a sibling group, then don't have separate foster placements for the sibs.*

## CONCLUSIONS

Post-placement providers' comments seemed to validate the findings of the case reviews of stable and disrupted or dissolved adoptions. Many of the adoptive family, child, and agency factors that were identified through the case record analysis as relating to adoption outcomes were also mentioned by professionals who work directly with special needs adoption families and children. The providers offered extremely useful, detailed feedback on adoption dissolutions, which can be used in training post-placement providers and adoption workers, as well as adoptive parents. The following points have been emphasized throughout this chapter:

- Families must receive full disclosure of information on the children they are interested in adopting. To withhold any information is a disservice to the child and to the family.

- Adoption is a lifelong experience, and contact with the family must not cease once the adoption is finalized. Many children and families may need ongoing treatment, and families should be encouraged to seek help as needed before significant problems arise.

- A family's adoption of an infant or a very young child does not mean that there will not be problems or that criteria for their selection or training can be any less stringent than that for older children. Pre-verbal children who have suffered abuse, neglect, fetal alcohol syndrome, problems resulting from lack of pre-natal care, or other problems, may begin to show the effects of abuse at later ages.

Post-placement providers identified a number of positive adoptive parent attributes, including flexibility, commitment, availability of support network, willingness to seek help, strong marriage, mental and physical health, and preferably coming from non-abusive backgrounds. According to these service providers, families should exhibit a willingness to acknowledge their children's interest in birthparents, accept bizarre behaviors, and deal with very angry, unattached children. Moreover, families of special needs children must be able to abandon their image of a fantasy child and accept the reality of the child they adopted, have a sense of humor, and have good parenting ability, especially with aggressive kids. Those families will be most successful if they understand the effects of abuse, have previous parenting experience and experience with difficult situations, and understand that the adoption will affect all family members. Parents should have a willingness to learn all they can about the child, understand normal and abnormal behavior, have a willingness to become a child advocate at school, and desire to parent rather than just have a child.

In order to select such adoptive parents, post-adoption providers suggested the need to have well-trained social workers who are able to utilize assessment tools to assess the fit, or compatibility, between the adoptive parents and child. Issues such as temperament, personality, interests, ability to attach, other siblings in the home, strengths and weaknesses of adopted child and parents, energy level of parents, and amount of energy needed for the child should all be considered. Adoption workers must also realize that they may not be totally objective about a child on their caseload, as their contact with the child is very limited. They may be more likely to minimize the child's problems and influence the adoptive parents' expectations about the child's behavior. Lengthier pre-placement visitation periods may be needed to give the family and child an opportunity truly to learn about one another. In addition, both the adoption worker and the prospective adoptive parents should have contact with both the foster family with whom the child has spent much time and the foster parent's caseworker, as a part of the preparation of a family for a particular child.

Some post-placement workers suggested that although the MAPP training may be better than previous methods of family preparation, it still may not adequately prepare a family for the realities of special needs children. Also, during the training process, the family has not yet received a special needs child, and therefore has no "context" in which to fit the new knowledge gained in the training. As a result, they may be less likely to "hear" the realities of life with a special needs adopted child. They must have ongoing support and training once the child has been placed in the home.

Repeatedly, post-placement workers emphasized the absolute need of support for adoptive families. Families need to become involved with support groups or other adoptive families before adopting so that they can become more aware of the realities of adoption. This involvement should continue once the child is placed and even long after finalization, so that they will not feel isolated when dealing with the inevitable problems these children will have.

Special needs adopted children have experienced significant losses. They are often grieving for their birthfamilies and foster families, and this grief may be expressed through anger. Many have lived in so many places that they can no longer trust or attach. They may be expressing the anger, abuse, or lack of attachment and trust that they have experienced by rejecting the adoptive parents. The adoptive mother is often especially vulnerable, as many of these children may displace anger toward their own birthmothers to the closest female in their presence, their adoptive mother.

Adoptive parents who lack an awareness of the problems these children have experienced, or who have sought adoption as a means of getting a child rather than as a result of their commitment to parenting a special needs child, will have difficulties which could lead to dissolution. Post-placement providers recommended that attention be called to the myriad of adoptive family problems contributing to dissolution and problems associated with the child, as well as to worker error.

Once these families come for treatment, post-placement providers tend to prefer family treatment. However, due to costs, this is sometimes not possible, and only the child and the adoptive parents are involved. In some rural areas, family therapy is not as readily available, and individual therapy is the only option. Most post-adoption workers suggested their interest in providing ongoing group therapy for both parents and children, as the other members serve as a support and provide affirmation that they are not in these difficult family situations alone.

Providers noted that often when services are contracted, many subcontractors may not fully understand the unique dynamics associated with adopted children and their families. They must be familiar with issues associated with attachment, abuse, neglect, multiple placements, and adoptive family dynamics. Workers providing such services should be certified as post-adoption specialists, and should be required to receive ongoing training in these areas.

Opportunities should be made available for post-adoption providers, supervisors, and adoption workers to interact routinely and provide feedback about adoptive placements. These kinds of interactions can serve to improve the process of screening adoptive families and provide ongoing services to children and families.

# Implications for Training and Practice

# CHAPTER 15

# Implications for Training: Families and Workers

*(with Steven Onken)*

In the field of child welfare, protective service workers, foster care workers, and adoption workers make daily decisions that have serious and far-reaching consequences for children and families. The termination of parental rights is one of the most radical intrusions the state can make into parental and family rights. Yet there is no more fundamental responsibility of the state than to provide protection for children at risk of maltreatment (Hughes & Rycus, 1989). Workers and their supervisors must balance the conflicting elements of the protective needs of children with the inherent rights and capacities of birthfamilies. Impacting this picture further is family preservation, whether it is within the birthfamily, foster family, or adoptive family.

An agency's ability to meet its goals and objectives is increasingly dependent upon developing the competencies of its staff, as well as those of foster and adoptive families. A common observation made by workers, supervisors, foster parents, and adoptive parents is that the child who comes into protective services today is a more "damaged" child. Schmidt, Rosenthal, and Bombeck (1988) found that "Despite the information given the [adoptive] families verbally or in writing, in meetings with the foster families or residential staff, or through video tapes and observation, they expected a less difficult child" (p. 125). To the extent that basic training opportunities met the needs of foster and adoptive families in the past, they often fall short of the far more complex and specialized competencies that are required today.

To discharge these complex and difficult responsibilities, all parties (workers and families) must have considerable value-based competencies and corresponding specialized knowledge and skills. Opportunities for workers and families to acquire these values, knowledge, and skills are often limited. Often, formalized opportunities to gain such competencies consist of orientation, basic job skills training, and occasional in-service for workers; training components in plans of service for biological families; and pre-placement training and some in-service training for foster and adoptive families. Though a starting point, such training opportunities alone may fall short of the needs of today's children, families, and workers.

This chapter discusses the training needs that have been identified from the findings of this research study. It begins with foster and adoptive family needs, and then discusses worker and supervisor training needs. Although this research was based upon one large state agency, it is likely that many of the practice issues and training competencies are applicable to most agencies placing special needs children in adoption. The chapter is designed to offer specific training competencies that will improve the provision of quality, progressive training, and development for staff, foster families, and adoptive families. According to Schmidt et al. (1988), agencies have an "enormous challenge to make the [foster and] adoptive experience more real, to cut through the idealism of parents and workers, and find ways to help families expect and live with reality" (p. 126).

## FOSTER AND ADOPTIVE FAMILY TRAINING NEEDS

The literature available on parent training for adopting special needs children tends to call for a person-centered, worker empowerment, and/or family empowerment approach (Denning & Verschelden, 1993; Hegar & Hunzeker, 1988; Tremitiere, 1979). Hasenfeld (1987) defines empowerment as the process through which individuals obtain resources—personal, organizational, and community—that enable them to gain greater control over their environment and attain their aspirations. The person-centered approach "puts the focus where the agency believes it should be, on client self-determination, building on already existing parental skills, self-assessment of strengths and weaknesses, and the ability of the applicants to be the primary active decision-makers in the building of their families through adoption" (Tremitiere, 1979, p. 685).

The worker is responsible for:

- Educating the applicants about what to expect and what skills can be used to meet the needs of the children
- Increasing the applicants' knowledge and expertise in handling their own and their children's needs (develop coping skills, enhancing self-concept)
- Enhancing the personal skills of the applicants to manipulate their environments effectively to obtain needed resources and achieve desired outcomes

It is clear that effective parenting of special needs children is not just the result of more knowledge or more information. It also requires specific skills and attitudes that are used every day with children. In the case studies provided for this research on special needs adoption outcomes several adoptive family training needs were identified in the course of data analysis. These will be identified in terms of pre-placement competencies, placement and post-placement competencies. Many of these competencies are appropriate for foster as well as adoptive families.

## PRE-PLACEMENT TRAINING COMPETENCIES

In many of the case narratives reviewed in this study, researchers picked up "red flags" in the home study and screening process that raised serious questions regarding the family's ability to parent a child with special needs. As noted in other sections of this book, these red flags—past abuse, harsh discipline, and so forth—occurred more frequently with parents whose child's adoption later disrupted or dissolved. The following pre-placement training competencies should be incorporated into training goals for foster and adoptive parents. Each competency can be assessed using the following scale: below expectations, meets expectations, and exceeds expectations.

- The adoptive parent is able to articulate in depth her or his reasons for wanting to adopt a special needs child.
- All members of the adoptive family are willing to and engage in the home study and initial screening process.
- The adoptive parent is aware of her or his idealism, including the expectation for a less difficult child, regardless of the amount of information provided on the child. The adoptive parent is aware

of her or his limitations in parenting a special needs child without special training, support, and assistance, and can identify ways to lower expectations and gain a more realistic picture of what the future will be like.

- The adoptive parent understands the impact of any abuse or neglect that she or he has experienced on her or his ability to parent the child effectively.

- The adoptive parent is aware of her or his own strength and limitations in parenting, and her or his emotional responses to difficult issues such as sexual abuse and the potential for these responses to interfere with effective parenting.

- The adoptive parent develops a thorough understanding of family boundaries and roles and how to adapt and maintain these once the adopted child is in the new home.

- The adoptive parent understands the impact of siblings placed together and can identify actions to take to address resulting issues, such as preparing for the consequences of multiple placements for the siblings or differences of family environment in the foster families prior to the adoptive placement.

- The adoptive parent understands the lifelong process of adoption and the uniqueness of adoptive families, including the continual discussion of the adoption as children develop, discussion of the adopted child's interaction and relationship with siblings, what to do when the child wants to know more about the biological parents, the importance of letting the child grieve, and opportunities to participate in mutual aid groups and to educate other adoptive families.

- The adoptive parent can identify when to use a Lifebook with the child and demonstrate how to use it.

- The adoptive parent understands the potentially traumatic outcomes of the separation and placement experience and the impact on the adopted child's contact, interaction, and relationship with biological and/or foster parents and siblings.

- The adoptive parent understands principles of learning theory and behavior modification, including positive reinforcement, differential reinforcement, extinction, time out, shaping of behavior, and modeling strategies.

- The adoptive parent grasps family systems theory and its application in understanding interactions and relationships of family members, family roles, power, communication patterns, dysfunctional behaviors, and other family processes.

- The adoptive parent can identify the benefits of family-based interventions and reasons families may be resistant to participating in them.

- The adoptive parent is aware of her or his own cultural background, including values, beliefs, and traditions, and understands how these can interfere with one's ability to parent an adopted child.

- The adoptive parent understands transracial adoption issues, including developmental issues, racial awareness, and the formation of racial/ethnic identity; understands how her or his own cultural background may be different from those of the adopted child and the child's birthfamily; and recognizes ways in which an ethnocentric perspective can interfere with one's ability to parent a child from a different cultural group.

- The adoptive parent is aware of the impact of transitions between biological, foster, and adoptive homes on the child's feelings about removals and placements, and how the permanency of this latter move uniquely impacts these issues.

- The adoptive parent can identify stages of the individual life cycle and possible subsequent changes in an adopted child's behavior as he or she matures in the adoptive home (e.g., sexual abuse issues may not surface in any significant way until the child reaches adolescence), as well as stages of the family life cycle and how adoption adds a new dimension to these traditional stages.

- The children of adoptive parents can identify, within an age-appropriate context, factors that contribute to an adopted child's possible adjustment problems within the adoptive family, and can participate, within an age-appropriate context, in management methods to handle such problems.

- The children of adoptive parents can identify and discuss, within an age-appropriate context, the issues involved in their own adjustment to the adopted child.

- The adoptive parent can list the various causes for disruption and dissolution and the ways that such causes can be identified and addressed early in the adoption process.

- The adoptive parent is aware of the legal ramifications of terminating an adoption and is able to make an informed choice before adopting a special needs child.

- The adoptive parent knows how to observe children's physical, cognitive, social, and emotional development, and can recognize when development is delayed or follows abnormal patterns.

- The adoptive parent knows the importance of early identification of developmental disabilities and delays, of referring children for comprehensive assessment, and of seeking the proper developmental, educational, social, and recreational services for the child.

- The adoptive parent displays mastery of specialized training in the use of community resources, such as working with school systems to advocate for the child's education needs, dealing with health care providers, and so forth.

- The adoptive parent is fully aware of the adoption agency, its resources, and her or his entitlements and rights.

## ADOPTIVE FAMILY POST-PLACEMENT TRAINING COMPETENCIES

Once the child is placed, there are additional training competencies to facilitate the development of a good relationship in the newly formed family. According to Ward (1979), adoptive families must develop a sense of entitlement and develop appropriate warm and reciprocal family relationships. Serious stresses for the relationship can result if this sense of entitlement does not occur (p. 100). The following list of training competencies should also be evaluated using the following scale: below expectations, meets expectations, and exceeds expectations.

- The adoptive parent can implement problem-solving strategies, can apply these strategies to the adopted child's problems and needs, and can teach other family members to use problem-solving methods to resolve family problems.

- The adoptive parent can identify the severity of some of the adopted child's behaviors within their own specific family context and demonstrate child management methods to handle such problems.

- The adoptive parent demonstrates consideration and use of family-based interventions as needed.

- The adoptive parent can identify strategies to address issues resulting from the role that the child occupied in the birth and/or foster family (e.g., a parentified child will be more challenging to parent and may have a difficult time allowing adoptive parents to parent any younger siblings placed together).

- Within an age-appropriate context, the adoptive parent's biological children residing in the home can identify factors that contribute to an adopted child's possible adjustment problems within the adoptive family, and can participate in management methods to handle such problems.

- The adoptive parent can recognize age-appropriate sexual knowledge and awareness in children and can identify abnormal and/or precocious sexual knowledge or preoccupation.

- The adoptive parent is aware of the problems resulting from and consequences of sexual abuse on the adopted child and on the adoptive family, and can seek appropriate assessment and supportive and/or therapeutic services.

- The adoptive parent has a thorough knowledge of the physical, cognitive, social, and emotional development of adopted adolescents and knows how developmental variables affect the adolescent's behavior.

- The adoptive parent can identify strategies that address the emotional, social, and environmental factors contributing to the adopted adolescent's behavior.

- The adoptive parent knows the behavioral indicators and dynamics of adolescent depression, suicide, and other emotional disturbances, and can seek appropriate assessment and supportive and/or therapeutic services.

* The adoptive parent is able to discuss the adoption with the adopted child as he or she develops and the adoption with all siblings at different stages, including providing an understanding of the grief and loss process.

* The adoptive parent is able to implement strategies to lessen the traumatic outcomes of the separation and placement experience, addressing such issues as the adopted child's continued contact, interaction, and relationship with biological and/or foster parents and siblings.

* The adoptive parent is able to take actions to address problems arising from siblings being placed together.

* The adoptive parent takes advantage of opportunities to participate in mutual aid groups and to educate other adoptive families.

* The adoptive parent is able to assert and claim her or his legitimate rights and resources from the agency.

## WORKER TRAINING NEEDS

The majority of public agency workers in this nation do not have social work or related degrees. Those with relevant degrees may not have had academic courses specific to agency functions such as out-of-home care and child protective service investigations. "This lack of formal social work education, along with other factors, such as the steady increase in multiproblem clients, contributes to the training challenges in public agencies" (Denning & Verschelden, 1993, p. 570).

## WORKER MATCHING AND TRANSITION TRAINING COMPETENCIES

Matching and transition planning were critical issues in many of the cases in the study. The following training competencies are based on the analysis of these issues and can be assessed using the following scale: below expectations, meets expectations, and exceeds expectations.

- The worker can conduct a thorough assessment and screening of the needs of the child requiring adoptive placement, including engaging the child in the matching process, gathering pertinent data, and documenting this information.

- The worker knows age-appropriate communication strategies and techniques to communicate with and involve the target child in the matching/transition stages, including age-appropriate participation in all phases of the matching, selection, transition planning, and implementation.

- The worker is able to select the most appropriate, least restrictive, most home-like placement setting to meet the child's developmental and treatment needs, including consideration of long-term foster care, therapeutic placement, or adoptive placement.

- The worker can conduct a thorough assessment and screening of the limitations of the adoptive family being considered in a specific adoption match, including engaging the adoptive family, gathering pertinent data, and documenting this information.

- The worker knows strategies to empower adoptive parents in the matching process, including involvement of them in all phases of the matching, selection, and transition planning and implementation.

- The worker is able to use the comprehensive assessments of the child and adoptive family to draw accurate conclusions as to the strengths and limitations of a particular match, educate members of the selection team, and facilitate a match selection that most closely meets the child's developmental, cultural, and treatment needs and the adoptive family's capabilities and expectations.

- The worker is able to provide accurate and comprehensive documentation on the case and notes specific factors and reasons that were considered in the selection of an adoptive family. In one case in the study, the location of the adoptive home was the only selection criteria identified in the record. In another case, there was no documentation that any outreach was done to find the best home for a child.

- The worker is able to educate the potential adoptive family thoroughly about the limitations and concerns that this adoptive family and this adopted child present for this specific match, elicit from them an understanding of the accommodations that will need to be planned and implemented to address these limitations, and document this information. As mentioned in Chapter 10, very little attention was given in the case records to matching children and families. In some cases, the workers' case narratives minimized the problems in all areas: severity of neglect by birthparents; ability or inability of birthparents to care for children; trauma suffered by children; effects of loss, separation, and abuse of children; and the target child's behavior.

- The worker can conduct a thorough professional assessment of adoptive parents' reactions during the selection and transition phase in order to complete early identification of possible adoptive parent factors that may impede successful placement, including: (1) past exposure to abuse; (2) abuse and neglect tendencies (severe discipline practices, firm belief in "spare the rod, spoil the child," etc.); (3) sexual issues (unable or unwilling to participate in discussions about sex, sex education, sexual abuse, etc.); (4) inflexibility; (5) marital difficulties; (6) developmental and life cycle issues (empty nest syndrome, needing a child to feel complete, etc.); and (7) unrealistic expectations.

- The worker is able to recognize biological and/or foster relationship continuation needs, educate adoptive parents to these needs and involve them in the development of appropriate contact objectives during the transition phase, and formulate and implement meaningful, achievable contact and visitation plans.

- The worker is able to recognize children with very strong attachment(s) to biological and/or foster family members and is able to identify and screen out adoptive families that have an issue with such attachment. Should the adoptive family change their minds about this attachment issue during the course of the home study or adoption training, the issue needs to be explored in much more depth during the matching process to ensure that the adoptive family is not responding in the "socially appropriate way," and rather have actually had a true change in beliefs.

- The worker can develop and implement individualized transition plans that take into account the adoptive parents' and adopted child's strengths and limitations, and builds on strengths to reduce transition-induced stress and to maintain identity and continuity of the adopted child.

- The worker recognizes and understands attachment and bonding issues and dynamics and can develop transition plans incorporating strategies to address these needs.

- The worker understands separation, loss, and transition dynamics and can establish realistic time frames that work to minimize the amount of stress induced by these forces in the adopted child during the transition phase.

- The worker can identify the unique transition planning needs of sibling placements, and can develop an individualized transition plan that addresses these needs, including intensive preparation work with the adoptive family.

- The worker can identify the unique transition planning needs of a child that may be moving from a more restrictive treatment setting into a less restrictive adoptive setting, and can develop a long-range transition plan that addresses these needs, such as readjustment into a family setting with the accompanying set of responsibilities and intimacy dynamics.

- The worker understands parentified child dynamics and can develop individualized transition plans, including intensive preparation work with the adoptive family that helps the child make the transition into a non-parentified role and that minimizes the amount of stress induced by these dynamics.

- The worker can develop and implement individualized good-bye visits that occur within realistic time frames, taking into account the biological and/or foster parent and adopted child's attachments to each other, allowing and encouraging expression of emotions felt at the time, and taking the time to process these emotions to the extent possible in order to acknowledge and validate transition-induced stress.

- The worker understands the importance of establishing and maintaining cooperative and professional relationships within the organization, with provider organizations, and with foster and adoptive families and is able to work collaboratively with these parties.

• The worker knows the necessity of regular, frequent visits and processing time with each party to encourage the adoptive parents' and adopted child's relationship with each other during the transition stage, and can identify those placement situations that will require more intensive monitoring (such as the placement of a child who sexually acts out, an older child, a parentified child, a sibling placement, etc.).

## POST-PLACEMENT WORKER COMPETENCIES

According to Ward (1979), "Once a child has been placed, the caseworkers must focus on the family-in-crisis as client. The welfare of the child demands the switch from the child orientation appropriate for pre-placement to a family orientation" (p. 102). Adoption workers must use this family orientation, and monitor the placed child and other members of the family closely and accurately. Specific training competencies necessary to accomplish this responsibility are listed below.

• The worker can accurately identify and assess physical, emotional, and behavioral indicators of sexual abuse in children and in families and can assess individual, family, and environmental contributors to sexual abuse.

• The worker is able to write concise, summarized, meaningful documentation, including assessments, case plans, and other supporting documentation into the case record in a timely manner.

• The worker is able to prioritize case needs, develop appropriate, time-limited case goals and objectives, formulate observable, behavioral measures of these goals and objectives, and develop meaningful action and service plans for these goals and objectives.

• The worker is able to recognize biological and/or foster relationship continuation needs, develop appropriate contact objectives, and formulate and implement meaningful, achievable contact and visitation plans.

- The worker can communicate with, interview, and interact with children using a variety of age-appropriate methods and strategies to elicit and transmit information and understanding.

- The worker understands the importance of establishing and maintaining cooperative and professional relationships within the organization, with provider organizations, and with foster and adoptive families, and is able to work collaboratively with these parties.

- The worker understands separation, loss, and transition dynamics, and can develop partnerships with adoptive families in identifying and using strategies to address these needs.

- The worker recognizes and understands attachment and bonding issues and dynamics and can develop partnerships with adoptive families in identifying and using strategies to address these needs.

- The worker is aware of and can use alternative approaches and support strategies in handling the conflicting worker roles inherent in special needs adoptions, for example monitoring/enforcement versus support/counseling.

- The worker understands the value of ongoing in-service training for refining and developing observation and assessment skills and case planning and action planning techniques, and participates in such ongoing in-service training.

- The worker is able to demonstrate to adoptive parents mastery of periodic and ongoing specialized training in the use of community resources by teaching and role-modeling such skills as working with school systems to secure services to meet the child's education needs; and working with health care providers to secure preventive, routine, and acute health care, and so forth.

- The worker is able to demonstrate advocacy skills and strategies in locating, securing, and providing services that help adoptive parents meet case goals and objectives, including teaching and role-modeling self-advocacy skills to adoptive parents and their children that advance these goals and objectives.

- The worker understands the importance of ongoing in-service training for refining and developing in-depth empathic skills and techniques, including the use of developmental and theoretical frameworks and processes in understanding a person's response to a given situation, and participates in such ongoing in-service training.

- The worker knows the necessity of regular, frequent visits and processing time with each party to encourage the adoptive parents' and adopted child's relationship with each other, and can use strategies that enable all parties to participate in and attend to such visits and activities.

- The worker can identify indicators of high-risk placements (those placement situations that will require more intensive monitoring and services such as the placement of a child who sexually acts out, an older child, a parentified child, or a sibling placement, etc.) and can mutually develop intervention strategies with the adoptive family to address such risks.

- The worker is aware of the personal psychological stresses associated with special needs adoptions that adoptive parents and family members experience and is able to involve such family members in identifying and implementing strategies to prevent emotional distress and burnout.

- The worker knows the importance of continuing supportive and treatment services after the consummation and knows strategies to assure that these services are provided to the child and the adoptive family.

- The worker understands post-adoption services and can engage the adoptive family in understanding, seeking out, and securing such services as needed.

- The worker can identify indicators of high-risk placements that merit post-adoption services and can use strategies to engage the family in securing such services.

- The worker understands family preservation services and can access and use such services to prevent the placement of an adopted child out of his/her adoptive family.

- The worker has a thorough knowledge of the physical, cognitive, social, and emotional development of adopted adolescents and knows how developmental variables affect the adolescent's behavior.

- The worker is aware of the adoptive family's need for support, reassurance, and/or possible assistance when their adopted child reaches adolescence and can mutually develop a strategy with the adoptive family that reconnects the family with an adoption worker's expertise at that point in time. The worker can identify strategies that address the emotional, social, and environmental factors contributing to the adopted adolescent's behavior.

- The worker knows the behavioral indicators and dynamics of adolescent depression, suicide, and other emotional disturbances, and can seek appropriate assessment and supportive and/or therapeutic services.

- The worker can assess an adolescent's need for specialized residential placement, treatment, or other special services, and knows how to locate and refer adolescents to these resources.

## WORKER DISRUPTION AND DISSOLUTION COMPETENCIES

As some adoptions may disrupt or dissolve, it is essential that workers have specific competencies to be able to effectively handle these situations. Among these competencies are the following:

- The worker is able to conduct a comprehensive assessment of the factors leading to the adoption disruption or dissolution, including engaging all parties in the assessment process, gathering pertinent data, and documenting this information.

- The worker is able to use the comprehensive assessment to draw accurate conclusions as to the limitations and problems contributing to the adoption disruption or dissolution, identify strategies that will work to address these factors in the future, and educate all parties regarding these factors and strategies.

- The worker is able to use the comprehensive assessment to facilitate a new placement option or match selection that most closely meets the child's developmental, cultural, and treatment needs, including the elimination of factors that contributed to the past adoption disruption or dissolution.

## SUPERVISOR TRAINING COMPETENCIES

In addition to the competencies needed by workers, the following additional supervisor competencies are needed:

- The supervisor understands the value of ongoing in-service training for workers and can assess needs and plan and implement training workshops and activities to meet such needs.

- The supervisor recognizes and understands attachment and bonding issues and separation, loss, and transition dynamics between worker and child and can assist the worker in minimizing the amount of stress experienced by the child during the transition phase from one worker to the next.

- The supervisor understands the importance of the case-planning process and is able to develop worker skills in prioritizing case needs; developing appropriate, time-limited case goals and objectives; formulating observable, behavioral measures of these goals and objectives; and developing meaningful action and service plans for these goals and objectives.

- The supervisor understands the importance of establishing and maintaining cooperative and professional relationships within the organization and with provider organizations, and is able to develop collaborative worker relationships with these parties.

## CONCLUSIONS

The person-centered family empowerment approach and strengths-building model that this chapter has outlined for family and worker training is also applicable as a framework from which to provide worker supervision. Such supervision would also reinforce and model worker empowerment and lessen burnout.

The list of specific worker competencies may seem overwhelming, but are necessary for quality practice. As Denning and Verschelden (1993) note, "every effort should be made to overcome the powerlessness felt by child welfare workers by providing opportunities for their increased participation in, and ownership of the process" (p. 578). Similarly, the competencies for adoptive families are designed to improve family relationships and increase the likelihood of healthy family functioning and stable placements. The following chapter presents practice recommendations.

# CHAPTER 16

# The Challenges of Special Needs Adoptions: Practice Recommendations

This research was designed to enhance child welfare practice knowledge about factors that may lead to intact placements, adoption disruptions, and dissolutions. Data gathering strategies included: (1) approximately 2,800 hours of intensive reviews of state agency case records from 40 intact, 15 disrupted, and 25 dissolved adoptions; and (2) telephone interviews with 22 adoption supervisors and 12 adoption service providers from all 12 service regions in the state of Texas. It is admirable that a state agency would be so committed to improving practice in special needs adoptions that the agency allowed outside reviews of their closed case records and encouraged all interviewees to share their experiences openly with the research staff. Upon completion of the study, the agency shared copies of the final report (McRoy, 1994) with staff throughout the state and requested that the author give presentations of the findings to agency personnel and post-adoption service providers. Because of the very close scrutiny each case was given, individual case feedback and recommendations were given to the state agency to disseminate to supervisors in each region. This chapter presents a synopsis of the findings of the study and provides very specific recommendations for practice.

## LIMITATIONS OF THE STUDY

The primary limitation of the study was the use of case narrative records that were prepared by protective services or adoption caseworkers assigned to the child's case. The content of narratives and the amount of related information at times varied from region to region and from worker to worker. However, this process made it possible to follow the child's journey systematically through the state agency system from the point of initial investigation through the close of the case at consummation or to the end of the recorded narrative in open cases. The second limitation of the study was that the sample was not entirely random (see Chapter 2), as the difficulty in obtaining cases listed on the closed subsidy list made it necessary to obtain additional cases from regional supervisors. A variety of efforts, detailed in Chapter 3, were utilized to minimize selection bias. Although the findings may be limited in generalizability, they are consistent with those of other researchers in special needs adoptions and lend themselves to many specific child welfare practice considerations in special needs adoptions.

## KEY FINDINGS AND RECOMMENDATIONS

### Characteristics of the Sample

The cases selected in the intact and in the disrupted/dissolved sample were very similar in their distribution across regions of the state, number of in-state and out-of-state placements, reason for adopting, and characteristics of birthparents. Children in disrupted/dissolved adoptions were older at time of removal from their birthfamilies and were more likely to be exhibiting aggressive, acting-out behaviors prior to removal than children in intact adoptions. Children in intact and disrupted/dissolved placements were similar with regard to the following characteristics: number of foster placements, number of siblings, number of siblings placed with the target child, racial background of children and parents, and number of out-of-state placements. Adoptive parents of children in these groups were similar with regard to income, education, and occupation. However, parents in disrupted/dissolved placements were more likely to have abuse in their backgrounds, to have less experience with special needs children, and less experience with parenting in general than parents in intact placements.

## Indicators of Disruptions, Dissolutions, and Intact Adoptions

The children in intact placements, on average, had been less traumatized, were younger, and had fewer externalized behaviors than the children in disrupted/dissolved placements. Adoptive parents in the intact group had more stable marriages, greater flexibility, more realistic expectations, more experience in parenting special-needs children through foster care or adoption, a greater commitment to the adoption, and willingness to seek needed help than parents in the disrupted/dissolved group. Children in disrupted/dissolved adoptions had been removed and placed at older ages, had been more severely traumatized, were exhibiting more aggressive and sexual acting-out behaviors, had experienced numerous moves, and were at greater risk at the time of the adoptive placements.

### Foster Parent Adoptions

Both legal risk adoptions and unplanned foster adoptions allow the child and family to develop a relationship before the adoption. Twenty-two (27.5%) of the cases in the study were foster parent adoptions. These were much more likely to be intact than non-foster parent adoptions. Most of the 16 intact foster parent placements were considered well-functioning, primarily because these families had adopted very young children with relatively few behavioral problems.

The study findings suggest that the least disruptive placements occurred with parents who had experience parenting special needs children before, and with those who had had previous experience as foster parents with the child or children they planned to adopt. Since preference is often given to foster parent adoptions, it is critical that these initial placements represent good matches and chances for permanence between children and families.

### Single-Parent Adoptions

Nine (11%) of the cases reviewed in the study were single-parent adoptions, and six had disrupted or dissolved at the time of the study. As in previous studies, the majority of the single-parent adopters were people of color, as were the majority of the children adopted by single parents. The unsuccessful adoption outcomes were less related to the type of adoption than to the fact that the children placed were dealing with significant issues of loss and abuse, and parents chose to adopt children with characteristics that they had stated that they could not handle, but accepted them for placement anyway.

Single parents should preferably have strong family and/or social networks to provide support in these adoptions. Single parents can be good resources for special needs children, but it is important to recognize that financial resources may be limited and that placing several special needs children with single parents will significantly increase the risk of disruption.

## Sibling Placements

Fifty-seven percent of the cases reviewed involved sibling placements. Of this group, more than half were intact placements. The number of siblings placed with the target child ranged from 1 to 6. Although sometimes noted in the records, very little elaboration was provided in the case narrative of the sibling's place or role in the birthfamily (i.e., parentified child, sexual acting-out, protector, etc.) or how the child felt about the role or the expectation to change the role in a new home. The records did not convey much about children's feelings of loss and grief associated with removal from their birthfamilies or foster families or other siblings not placed together. Many of the target children and siblings had not received therapy for issues such as abuse and loss of birthfamily members, and had not been adequately prepared for adoption. The choice of either placing siblings together or splitting sibling groups did not seem to be the most significant factor leading either to intact or disrupted/dissolved adoptions. Among the factors that seemed to have an impact on outcome were adoptive parent preparation for sibling groups, parental motivation for adoption, quality of marital relationship, parenting experience, behavioral expectations, sibling interaction patterns, relationship with own birthchildren, and willingness to seek counseling.

Sibling placements should be considered on a case-by-case basis. It is critical to assess attachment, behavioral problems, previous interactions when placed together, and current interactional patterns before making the decision to place siblings in the same adoptive family. In cases in which sibling placements are not possible or preferred due to the dysfunctional interactional patterns between them, some means of contact should be arranged so that they can maintain a sense of continuity.

**Transracial Adoptions**

Sixteen of the cases involved transracial adoptions. The majority of these adoptions involved Hispanic children placed with White families. Six of the transracial adoptions had disrupted or dissolved. However, since the case records were almost totally void of any discussion of cultural issues and the impact of transracial adoptions, it was impossible to assess whether or not ethnic and cultural factors were even acknowledged in placement decision-making.

Although it was possible for workers to consider these factors at the time the cases in this study were active, in 1995 the Texas Family Code was amended to stipulate that any employee who denies or delays a placement in order to seek a same-race family is subject to immediate dismissal (Texas Family Code, 1995). In fact, in Texas an independent psychological evaluation of the child must be now be completed to justify any consideration of race or ethnicity (McRoy, Oglesby, & Grape, 1997). In addition, the Multiethnic Placement Act of 1995 prohibits any foster care or adoption agency that receives federal financial assistance from denying a placement solely on the basis of race; but it allows for consideration of the cultural, ethnic, or racial background of the child and the capacity of the foster parents to meet the needs of a child of this background. The act also requires that agencies engage in diligent recruitment efforts for foster and adoptive parents that reflect the diversity of children needing placement. These various state and federal laws were enacted in hopes that minority children could move quickly from out-of home care into adoption with available White families, as many believe that locating minority families necessitates delays in the placement process (McRoy, Oglesby, & Grape, 1997). However, such transracial placements introduce another set of issues for the children and families involved.

As stated early, any older child placement presents a number of adjustments for children and families. In the case of transracially placed children, preparation in cultural sensitivity and differences and ways to enhance the child's positive self-image must be provided. Folaron and Hess (1993) recommend that agencies seek culturally competent social workers who are prepared to: (1) assess risk factors in the adoptive family environment, including lack of support for children and families due to racism; and (2) assist and educate parents, caregivers, and school personnel about the challenges minority children face in society and about the social and cultural needs of minority children. Case records should contain evidence that an assessment was made of the social-cultural milieu in which the child would be raised. Ongoing post-placement supervision and services should include discussions of ethnic differences and how to facilitate the adjustment of the child and family. Moreover, efforts should be made to eliminate barriers to same-race placements (Gilles & Kroll, 1991) and increase the number of minority families interested in adopting.

**Transition Planning**

Over half of the disrupted cases, 32% of the dissolved cases, and 10% of the intact cases were characterized by poor transition planning. The failure to take into consideration the impact of abuse and numerous moves and interruptions in parenting on the children is the primary issue that emerged from the analysis of transition planning. Although the records contained information that suggested that workers acknowledged that the child may be having problems dealing with the loss of previous caretakers, little, if anything, was mentioned about how these problems were being addressed with the child.

Lifebooks and placement genograms (Groze & Rosenthal, 1993; McMillen & Groze, 1994) can be useful tools for visually tracing the child's history and helping the child explore feelings toward former caregivers and the meanings of past relationships. Using a cognitive restructuring process, children may be able to link their past with their present, which may facilitate attachment in the future.

**Matching Children and Families**

Fifteen percent of the intact adoptions, 87% of the disrupted adoptions, and 76% of the dissolved adoptions were considered to be poor matches between parent and child. Forty percent of the intact adoptions were identified as good matches, and 10 of these were foster adoptions. Rushed placements, encouraging "stretching" by adoptive parents, allowing adoptive parents to take on much more than they could obviously handle, and minimizing behaviors of a child may serve to facilitate movement of children from foster care to adoption, but set the stage for disruption or dissolution of the adoption.

## Supervisors' Concerns

Adoption supervisors interviewed in this study commented that workers often don't know children well enough before the placement, and family expectations are too high for the children. In some cases, workers learned about important background information about the children after they have been placed in the adoptive home. Similar to the findings in the case analyses, the supervisors noted that poor matches, inadequate assessments of the adoptive parents, and unknown background information surfacing after placement are among the agency factors leading to disruptions and dissolutions. Supervisors observed that disruptions are often associated with the following child behaviors: sexual acting-out, physical aggression toward the adoptive family's biological children, and difficulties in attaching. They expressed concern that adoptive families often fail to disclose difficulties the family is experiencing until it is too late. Workers need additional training in how to assess family problems and in developing trusting relationships with adoptive families so that they will reveal problems before it is too late.

Supervisors also noted that many of the caseworkers are highly inexperienced and weren't investing the time necessary to prepare the child adequately for adoption. As one supervisor noted, "Workers tend to see the children once a month instead of once a week. This is insufficient, as preparation is an ongoing process which begins when the child enters the system."

Supervisors stated that adoption workers must realize that they may not be totally objective about a child on their caseload, and that their contact with the child is often very limited. They may be more likely to minimize the child's problems and influence the adoptive parents' expectations about the child's behavior. Lengthier pre-placement visitation periods may be needed to give the family and child an opportunity truly to learn about one another. In addition, the adoption worker should have contact with the foster family with whom the child has spent much time. The prospective adoptive parents should be in contact with the foster parents and foster parents' caseworker as part of the preparation of the family for a particular child.

Adoption supervisors and workers need feedback about dissolutions. They often receive little information on outcomes after consummation, yet this information could improve practice.

**Post-adoption Providers' Concerns**

Post-adoption providers have a great deal of insight into the problem of adoption disruptions and dissolutions and should be utilized to provide ongoing de-identified feedback, as well as regular training for adoption workers and supervisors. These kinds of interactions can serve to improve the process of screening adoptive families and providing ongoing services to children and families. These providers emphasized the need for providing families with ongoing support, therapy, and respite care.

**Training Recommendations**

The findings of this study lend credence to the comments made by several adoption supervisors who were interviewed:

> *Training, training, and training is needed to make better matches between parents and children.*

> *Post-adoption workers should be involved in providing training for workers involved with foster parents and adoptive parents and children.*

> *Training for staff should be broken out by program area and specialized training is needed for all staff handling adoption and foster care caseloads.*

Worker and supervisor training needs include the following: assessing adoption readiness; assessing children, families, marriages, abuse, loss, and identity; matching; transition planning; recognizing potential problems; understanding the child's desire for contact with birthfamily or previous caretakers; and knowing the impact of the new child on the entire family system.

The specific training competencies identified in this book resulted from close scrutiny of case records to assess problems or potential problems in such areas as assessment, securing supportive or therapeutic services, and development of service plans. In this study, the factors that influenced outcomes included the match between the adoptive parent and child, transition planning, specific behaviors of the child, parental expectations, marital issues, parenting style, commitment to the adoption, the child's previous history of abuse, frequent foster moves, foster parent adoption, and availability and utilization of therapy. Similarly, Festinger (1986) reported the following reasons for disruption in her study of 78 disruptions and 105 intact adoptions: family expectations and coping problems, family motivation for adoption, children's expectations, mismatch between the parent and the needs of the child, marital conflict, environmental influences on the children, environmental stressors on the family, motivation of the child, alleged parental misconduct, and physical illness of the adoptive parent. She suggested that agency issues such as staff discontinuity and inadequate training and preparation for adoption workers significantly impact the quality of service. Moreover, workers need to assess their powers of self-persuasion, as they may be likely to convince themselves that a placement is appropriate (Festinger, 1990). They need training in assessing a family system and anticipating areas of risk and vulnerability to facilitate early intervention. The findings of this study support the need for worker training in recruitment, assessment, tracking, and provision of pre- and post-placement services for families and children. A foster care and adoption worker certification program that is competency-based and culturally contextualized would be ideal.

## PRACTICE RECOMMENDATIONS

### Family Preservation

According to a recent United States Department of Health and Human Services study, the incidence of child maltreatment was seven times greater for families earning less than $15,000 a year than it was for families earning a greater income (Zigler & Stevenson, 1993). Health problems, spousal violence, early childbearing, drug and alcohol abuse, communication and relationship skill deficits, poor child management skills, and single parenthood are also factors that have been identified with abusive parents (Videka-Sherman, 1991; Garbarino, 1992; Zigler & Stevenson, 1993). Similarly, in this study, birthparents typically came from low-income families in which a previous history of abuse, as well as substance abuse, was common. The study findings suggested that children who were removed from these families as a result of abuse or neglect were generally placed in unrelated out-of-home placements. It is important to assess whether sufficient attention has been given to family reunification. According to Pinderhughes (1995), assessments should be made of the competence of the caregiver, an exploration of services that can empower the parents, the linking of the parents to informal and formal support services, and the reviewing of the extended family supports and resources before making the out-of-home placement. In many cases in this study, the records did not provide evidence that sufficient efforts were made to empower the family or extended family to assume responsibility for the child or children.

## Size of Caseloads/Controlled Caseloads

In some cases, workers seemed unable, due to time constraints, to conduct a thorough preparation of the child for adoptive placement and in-depth post-placement supervision. Although it is clear from the findings in this study that worker error accounted for many of the problematic outcomes, it is important to note that these errors occurred in relatively few cases, as most special needs adoptions remained intact.

In cases in which placements dissolved, workers did not set out to make poor matches or to overlook risk factors in case assessments. It is possible that many lacked the advanced training and sufficient experience necessary to handle the volume of cases to which they were assigned, were responding to pressure to place quickly, and/or felt that they made the best or only choice possible given limited family resources. High staff turnover was also a factor associated with large caseloads. Worker caseloads must be reduced in order to serve children and families better.

## Documentation in Case Records

Workers must be trained in the necessity of accurate and complete documentation of all case activities. In many cases, assessment data and service plans were incomplete. Workers need extensive training on (1) strategies for obtaining background information from multiple sources (previous caretakers, school, therapists, etc.) in order to assess a child's case, and (2) recording behavioral observations and interpretations of a child's behaviors and attitudes. Workers must give much more attention to the assessment of the child's grief and loss issues.

Each case record should include evidence of planning the placement and post-placement services, which takes into consideration unique characteristics of the child and family. These records should include comprehensive documentation and narrative accounts of the worker's interactions with the family and child. This will lead to better practice if there is an ongoing record of indicators of the child's adjustment and will provide much-needed information in preparing prospective adoptive families for the types of behaviors they can expect.

## Use of CASA Volunteers

Court Appointed Special Advocates (CASAs) or other child advocacy organizations can provide assistance to the worker throughout the pre- and post-placement process. Spending time with the child provides a rich source of information, but time constraints sometimes make this a formidable task for the caseworker. Adoption supervisors commented that knowing the child better would have helped in decision-making. Most of the time, the need for in-depth knowledge of the child was vital for appropriate placement. A CASA assigned to a case can be a valuable source of information for the caseworker.

## Recruitment/Selection/Training of Families

Increased recruitment of prospective adoptive families will increase choice in the selection of families. Ongoing recruitment would avoid "stretching" families beyond the type of child they are initially willing to consider or accept for adoptive placement. In foster care placements as well, matching is important. For example, a very disturbed, acting-out child should not be placed with a couple who has never parented.

During the adoptive parent group preparation training, close relationships are often formed between families. Ongoing relationships can be fostered by providing name and address lists of participants and having reunions or picnics for cohorts. Establishing a "buddy system" between adoptive families is also useful, so that they will have another family to share the joys as well as difficulties of parenting. These buddies could emerge during the MAPP group training process.

MAPP-trained prospective adoptive families might be considered as respite care providers to give them an opportunity to gain experience in parenting special needs children prior to their adoption. This is essential, as adoptive families in the intact sample were much more likely than families in the disrupted/dissolved group to have had previous experience with special needs children.

**Improved Family Assessments**

Improved means of assessing marital relationships, levels of commitment, emotional stability, and reasons for adopting are needed for foster and adoptive families. In this study, troubled marital relationships, emotional problems of one partner, or differing levels of commitment to the adoption aggravated an already tenuous adoptive family system.

If adoptive parents choose to adopt a special needs child solely to fulfill a specific need that they have, this should probably be considered a "red flag." Parenting non-special needs children for one's own need fulfillment is risky in general, but with traumatized children, the risks are even greater. Parental motivation for adoption should be child-centered or altruistic in nature, rather than for personal fulfillment. As one post-adoption provider stated (Chapter 14), "be selective in who is raising these children. . . . Select out those who want a child and keep those who want to parent."

As Kirk (1981) suggested, adoptive parents experience a role handicap. They have not been prepared to function as adoptive parents and must be trained by the agency. They are parenting children who have endured many stresses and may not readily fit into another family or meet the parental expectations and needs of the family. Adoptive parents of special needs children must understand that if they are adopting to meet their own needs, the adoption will not work. They must be prepared for all that is necessary to meet the needs of the child; they will not be "traditional parents" with a traditional parent-child bond. They must be willing to accept that an attachment may never occur with some of these children.

**Detecting Potentially Abusive Families**

Case readings revealed allegations of adoptive parent abuse in 15 of the 80 cases reviewed. Six female and 9 male children were abused by adoptive parents. Thirteen of these cases had either dissolved or disrupted. Moreover, 14 of the adoptive mothers and 10 adoptive fathers in the sample had been victims of child or spousal abuse. Of these, 9 subsequently abused adopted or foster children in their care. There was no indication that any of these abusive families had received therapy for their own victimization. Prior history of abuse had not been sufficiently identified or addressed in the screening process with these adoptive families.

Adoptive parents' and foster parents' history of abuse and potential for abuse of a child are often not detected through the conventional adoptive parent training program and home study reports. In some cases, when evidence of abuse or abusive behavior in the background was noted in the record, there was no indication of how or whether the worker explored these issues with the family. Hampton (1991) has noted that about 30 percent of parents who experience abuse as children will later become abusive themselves. This study has provided detailed information about the instances of adoptive parent abuse, but there were also instances of foster parent abuse that must be noted. Eight children in the study were removed from foster homes because of suspected or actual emotional, physical, or sexual abuse in the home. In the four cases of sexual abuse, older cousins, an older foster brother, the foster father, and an unknown party were the alleged perpetrators. Accusations of physical abuse included the following types of harm: sibling burned with a curling iron, unexplained marks and bruises, and foster parents hitting the child. Other forms of abuse included requiring foster children to bathe in cold water, to sleep in the tub or on the floor, to stand in a corner for hours, verbal abuse, and allowing other children in the home to stab the child with a fork if he put his elbows on the table. It is essential for workers to assess and monitor foster families carefully and to provide them with ongoing parenting skills training.

### Unrealistic Expectations

Some families chose to adopt because their own biological children were grown and no longer living at home (another type of loss). Several of these families had indicated to the worker that they were adopting because they felt their marriage would be stronger if they had children in the home again. These, as well as couples who were infertile, may have had unrealistic expectations that the adopted children would save or strengthen their marriage or be a replacement for birthchildren. These expectations may have set the child up for failure and impacted adoption outcomes.

### Addressing Issues of Loss and Infertility

The literature suggests that therapists and workers must be prepared in special needs adoptions to deal with issues of loss not only with children, but with adoptive parents as well (Berman & Bufferd, 1986). Some parents are dealing with the empty nest syndrome and want to relive their birthparenting experiences through adoption. Single parents may either be single by choice, or may choose to parent after "giving up," for whatever reasons, on a dream to marry and have birthchildren (Keck & Kupecky, 1995). Others may have chosen to adopt because of infertility. Although often addressed in infant placements, infertility is rarely discussed in depth in assessments for older child placements. In this study, 30 out of 80 cases had experienced infertility, which constitutes a significant loss.

In order to be successful in adoption, parents need to acknowledge these losses and deal with their feelings about them. Many adoptive families in the study were dealing with the aforementioned issues which, according to the records, were either not addressed by the worker, or the worker made the incorrect assessment that the family had resolved its loss issues. For example, in one case, the worker noted that the adoptive mother was experiencing profound grief associated with the loss of a child several years earlier, but there was no mention in the record about the worker's perceptions of how this grief might influence the adoptive mother's parenting ability. If these issues are not addressed, families may find themselves very disillusioned with their adoptions and have difficulty adjusting to children who also are suffering from great losses.

**Sharing Background Information**

Although the families in the study, according to most case recordings, had an opportunity to read the entire background history on the child or children they were adopting, there was no indication in the record as to how the family responded to this information. In some cases, the family read the adoption readiness summary rather than the whole de-identified case record. It is possible that adoption workers may have minimized the seriousness of the behavioral problems many of these children were experiencing or may have been unaware of important issues due to lack of documentation or the incomplete record-keeping of previous workers. Perhaps, in an effort to find a family for a particularly hard-to-place child, workers place more emphasis on the positive and do not talk as much about problems. In addition, the parents may have been too unrealistic in their interpretation of the types of problems these children had and the rate that their behavior would stabilize after placement.

Families must receive full disclosure of information about the children they are interested in adopting. To withhold any information is a disservice to the child as well as to the family. Barth and Berry (1988a) reported that the amount and type of preparation provided to adoptive parents is crucial. In their study of California special needs adoptive families, Barth and Berry found that families that had high-risk placements had received overly positive and less realistic information about the children they had adopted. Having accurate information may screen out families that cannot handle specific kinds of behaviors and result in more intact placements with families who are prepared and have realistic expectations of the behavior these children may exhibit.

**Contact with Previous Caregivers**

In order to understand not only what has happened to the child in the past, but to understand better how the child is reacting to past traumas, it may be helpful for families to meet the child's most recent foster parents to gain a better understanding of the child's current behavior. Also, foster parents should be asked about the child's behavior upon being placed in their home, to determine how the child reacted to the transition.

**Team Approach to Facilitate Transition**

As one provider indicated, for every hour a worker spends with a child, one hour should be spent with foster parents—if the worker helps foster parents deal with grief and loss they may feel when an adoptive placement is planned for the child, they are also helping the child. The team approach is ideal—much more input from foster parents is needed regarding the type of family the child needs (strengths, skills, etc.), how to help the child make the transition from the foster family to the adoptive family, and positive behavior management strategies that work with this particular child.

**Willingness to Seek Therapy**

Some of the families in the study were unwilling to seek treatment or to follow clinicians' advice. It is essential to advocate for children and help parents to understand the need for therapy.

**Child-Focused Units**

Adoption units should be focused on meeting the child's needs for an adoptive family. If a child must wait in foster care, then emphasis should be placed on making it a productive time for the child; in other words, a child with a history of abuse or neglect should receive a psychological assessment and developmental screening/assessment to insure an appropriate, timely, and effective plan of service. Consistent or stable subcare can allow the child to grieve the loss of the birthfamily and stabilize behaviors before an adoptive placement is considered. For many children, ongoing contact with their birthfamilies could lessen the grief, loss, and identity crises they may experience. Specialized services or units have been found to increase the success of placing developmentally disabled children (Coyne & Brown, 1986). Similarly, child-focused, specialized services should be designed to prepare families and children for adoption. Specific training and counseling should be provided, given the unique needs of children and families seeking to adopt these children.

**Risk and Strength Assessments**

Children in care may not exhibit overt symptomatology, but yet have suffered abuse. It is important to screen all children in care for possible sexual abuse, as well as depression and anxiety that may result from the abuse.

Risk and strength assessments should be conducted on children and families before placement, including assessment of environmental opportunities and the resources of birthfamilies, foster families, and adoptive families. Intensive adoptive family preservation efforts should be offered for high-risk placements that are allowed to proceed. There may be some placements that are at such high risk that children may need to be in therapy or allowed to stabilize before adoption is considered an option.

**Attachment**

Once children are placed in foster care, they now often spend less continuous time in care than before; they often exit the system, return to their birthfamilies, and later reenter the system. This process may serve to reduce the number of children in care, but it causes more adjustment problems for children. According to Tatara, Shapiro,

Portner, and Gnanasigamony (1988), during the three-year period prior to their study, 26% of the children in care in 23 states had been placed in three or more foster placements. Several studies have reported that the number of moves in care has been associated with the development of emotional disturbance (Eisenberg, 1962; Maas & Engler, 1959; Pelton, 1989). Children in these ambivalent situations often find that they experience divided loyalty between two sets of parents and experience a great deal of uncertainty about the future: loss of friends, family, and familiar environments; confusion; and feelings of rejection, distrust, and grief. Rosenthal (1993), in a study of attachment in special needs adoptions, found that as children move from place to place they must unattach from previous caregivers and attach to new caregivers. This process of reattachment becomes even more difficult in cases in which children have histories of abuse. Although much more research is needed on this topic, it is clear that adoptive parents must be prepared to help mediate the effects of multiple placements by providing consistent, positive caregiving. Often therapeutic interventions are also needed to help the child overcome negative behavior patterns symptomatic of abuse history and multiple caregivers.

**Addressing Feelings of Guilt**

Adopted children may blame themselves for being placed for adoption, especially in cases in which they made the outcry related to the abuse in the birthfamily. They, too, may experience feelings of rejection by birthparents and divided loyalty between birth and adoptive parents (Berman & Bufferd, 1986). In this study, several siblings were feeling guilt about their adoptive placements, and at least two were suicidal. Others found it difficult to relate to adoptive parents, since they felt very emotionally attached to their birthfamilies or foster families. These issues must be addressed in adoption preparation classes and post-adoption services, as well as in therapy with adopted children.

**Contact with Birthfamilies**

Both foster parents and adoptive parents must be helped to understand the importance of the biological parent to the child (Kates, Johnson, Rader, & Strieder, 1991). There may be some cases of severely disturbed adopted children who need to have contact and involvement with their birthparents in the therapeutic process, to help them come to terms with the removal from the birthfamily and to give permission to attach to the adoptive family (Blotcky, Looney, & Grace, 1982).

Sometimes the child needs to hear from birthparents that it wasn't the child's fault. After some time has passed, the birthparents may be able to distance themselves from the problem, admit their failings to the child, and allow the child to express anger toward them. This process could potentially move both child and birthparent toward healing.

**Ongoing Evaluation of Services**

Workers should track children's plans of service to insure that recommended services are provided and goals/objectives for the child are completed in a timely manner. Goals and dates for completion could come up on the computer screen as a reminder anytime the worker opens a case file.

In many instances, longer pre-placement periods will be needed to facilitate child and family adjustment. In addition, the findings of the study suggest the need for longer post-placement periods in order to work with the family and child to stabilize the relationship and family system.

**Post-adoption Services**

Post-adoption services are needed as older adopted children have a significantly higher incidence of behavioral disorders than children who were adopted as infants (Dickson, Heffron, & Parker, 1990; McRoy, Grotevant, & Zurcher, 1988). As reported in other studies, the child behavior that seems to be most associated with adoption disruptions/dissolution is sexual acting-out. Clearly there is a need for ongoing therapy with children who have been or are suspected of having been sexually abused. It also suggests the need for intensive training of prospective adoptive and foster parents to handle this behavior, as well as other aggressive acting-out behaviors. After consummation, families should be encouraged to participate in adoption support groups and to continue counseling as needed. In this study, post-consummation services were typically used for families who had identified themselves as having severe problems. Families should be encouraged to seek help early, and even for problems that are moderate. Services should be established with a preventive, educational approach so that parents would not feel like failures if they use them. Family members should be seen both separately and together, and workers should visit the family often and have at least biweekly phone contact with the families. Subsidies should be available for families to offset costs for counseling and even residential treatment, if needed. The public adoption agency, like most private agencies, must acknowledge that adoption is a lifelong process and be committed to helping families long after the consummation.

## Disruptions and Dissolutions

In most cases, children were removed less than a month or two after the initial discussion of problems with the agency. Similarly, Barth and Berry (1988a) noted that adoptive parents whose adoptions disrupted sought agency help much later than those who were able to give early, clear signals of their distress and work through problems to remain intact. Workers must keep in close contact with families and intervene to provide services before the family has become disengaged from the child and made a determination that the child must be removed.

In this study, case record data suggested that families in dissolved/disrupted adoptions tended not to communicate that problems had developed until they were just about at the point of giving up on the adoption. In some cases the families had hinted or indirectly mentioned problems at an earlier point, but there was no written documentation that the worker addressed the issue. Therefore, the problems may have escalated to the point that the family felt the adoption would not work. In one case, the child was receiving individual therapy for quite a while, but no progress was being made. Either the family did not tell the worker of the situation, or the worker made the assessment that all that could be done was being done. According to the record, no alternate plan was instituted, although progress was not being made and the adoption disrupted a few months later.

## Bringing Closure to Relationships

If an adoption disrupts or dissolves, it is important for the worker to intervene with the child, as well as the family, in order to bring closure to relationships. The worker must address issues such as the family's ambivalence about terminating the placement, and give an objective assessment of the situation rather than projecting blame. The worker must also help the child understand the disruption and not feel solely responsible (Elbow & Knight, 1987). In some instances, it is important for another worker, perhaps a more objective worker, to handle the disruption counseling. This might be accomplished by a post-placement therapist. It is essential that the child have a good-bye visit with the adoptive family, and for the worker to explain the reasons for the disruption and to talk about the gains the child made in the placement. A conference with the family is important in order to tell them about the plan for the child, to discuss whether there will be any ongoing contact with the child, and to discuss the family's assessment of their strengths and weaknesses in parenting the child.

**Assessing Dissolutions**

Placement staff should know about and have input in service plans for the children from disrupted/dissolved adoptions who may be returning to the system. They should be involved in assessing what went wrong and what the consequences for the child and family are. Adoption worker input is also needed to set up the child's care plan to remediate before another placement is attempted.

**CONCLUSIONS**

In 1997, Barth called on agencies "to reexamine every aspect of adoption practice and have the courage to act on that analysis" (p. 305). The state of Texas began this process several years ago when the state agency initiated this study. They should be commended for caring enough about the children in their care to invest in this kind of research, and for having the willingness to share it with other public and private agencies for the benefit of all children and families. Since this study began four years ago, the agency has implemented a computerized data entry and tracking system in order to begin to rectify some of the problems in documentation, tracking, and coordinating service plans for children. The agency has also demonstrated a consistent commitment to advanced, high-quality training for supervisors and workers.

Complex challenges will continue to face adoption professionals in the future as they strive to serve the growing number of children in care, many of whom have been drug-exposed, are HIV positive, or have AIDS, and who have been physically or sexually abused or neglected in their birth homes. Many of these children are older and exhibit aggressive, sexually inappropriate behaviors, and are often unlikely to return to their biological families. Although the number of children and complexities of their backgrounds have increased, there has not been a comparable increase in child welfare staff. As a result, caseloads as well as turnover rates remain high (Hess and Folaron, 1991). These factors can limit the development of close relationships to the children needing placement and limit the time available to screen foster and adoptive families carefully.

Some states are currently contracting with private agencies to handle their special needs adoptions, or are considering doing so (Child Welfare League of America, 1997). However, this practice introduces new issues of how to determine costs of various contracted services, financial incentives for speedy placements, interagency communication and coordination, and territoriality (e.g., public agency staff being comfortable with and trusting the family choices and placement decisions of private agency staff).

Adoptions practice will become even more challenging in the future as new federal laws require that workers concurrently provide reunification and placement services in order to reduce the time that children remain in foster care. These new policies will certainly promote a sense of ambivalence on the part of workers; children; and birth, foster, and adoptive families. Only if funding is provided for more training, recruiting adoptive and foster families, hiring a larger number of child welfare staff, and contracting for more post-adoption services workers in the area of adoptions and foster care service delivery, will we be able to offset the current service delivery problems associated with overworked staff and rushed placements.

Adoption is a lifelong commitment. This is true for parents as well as for the adoption agency. The agency must be willing to be there to provide support for the child and family well after consummation. Problems that stem from the child's early experiences in the birth home or foster home, may not be reflected in the child's behavior for many years after the adoption. Supervisors as well as post-adoption providers in this study echoed the need for training for workers as well as families. Families need training in child development, behavioral management, and the impact of abuse and multiple moves on the child. Ongoing training and support must be available to families in order to help them feel empowered to maintain a sense of unconditional commitment to their placed child (Kates et al., 1991).

The intricacies of special needs adoptions, as outlined in this book, will hopefully serve to encourage public and private adoption agencies to reexamine their practices and case documentation and to provide adoptive parents with new insights on factors that can impact outcomes. Now that the soaring number of children in foster care once again has captured the nation's attention, state and federal policy makers must advocate: (1) to help provide support and reunify children and their birthfamilies when possible; (2) to minimize the risks involved in achieving permanence through adoption for the thousands of children who have experienced trauma in their lives, yet who dare to trust, love, and belong to a family again; and (3) to provide assistance to the thousands of families who are willing to provide a loving home and give the children a chance for a better future.

# References

Achenbach, T., & Edelbrock, C. (1983). *Manual for the Child Behavior Checklist/4-18 and 1991 Profile*. Burlington, VT: University of Vermont, Department of Psychiatry.

Aldridge, M., & Cautley, P. (1976). Placing siblings in the same foster home. *Child Welfare, LV*(2), 85-93.

Andujo, E. (1988). Ethnic identity of transethnically adopted Hispanic adolescents. *Social Work, 33*(6), 531-535

Bachrach, C. A. (1983). Children in families: Characteristics of biological, step-, and adopted children. *Journal of Marriage and the Family, 45*, 171-79.

Backhaus, K. A. (1984). Life books: Tool for working with children in placement. *Social Work, 29*, 551-554.

Barth, R. P. (1988). Disruption in older child adoptions. *Public Welfare, 46*(1), 23-29.

Barth, R. P. (1991a). Adoption of drug-exposed children. *Children & Youth Services Review, 13*, 323-341.

Barth, R. P. (1991b). Research on special needs adoption. *Children and Youth Services Review, 13*, 317-320.

Barth, R. P. (1997). Effects of age and race on the odds of adoption versus remaining in long-term out-of-home care. *Child Welfare, LXXVI*(2), 285-309.

Barth, R. P., & Berry, M. (1988a). *Adoption and disruption: Rates, risks, and responses*. New York: Aldine de Gruyter.

Barth, R. P., & Berry, M. (1988b). Predicting adoption disruption. *Social Work, 33*(3), 227-233.

Barth, R. P., Courtney, M., Berrick, J. D., & Albert, V. (1994) *From child abuse to permanency planning*. New York: Aldine de Gruyter.

Bausch, R. S., & Serpe, R. T. (1997). Negative outcomes of interethnic adoption of Mexican American children. *Social Work, 42*(2), 136-143.

Benedict, M. I., Zuravin, S., Somerfield, M., & Brandt, D. (1996). The reported health and functioning of children maltreated while in family foster care. *Child Abuse and Neglect, 20*(7), 561-571.

Berman, L. C., & Bufferd, R. K. (1986). Family treatment to address loss in adoptive families. *Social Casework, 67,* 3-11.

Berry, M. (1994). Has permanency planning been successful? In E. Gambrill & T. Stein (Eds.), *Controversial issues in child welfare* (pp. 261-266). Boston: Allyn & Bacon.

Berry, M., & Barth, R. (1990). A study of disrupted adopted placements of adolescents. *Child Welfare, LXIX*(3), 209-225.

Blotcky, M. J., Looney, J. G., & Grace, K. D. (1982). Treatment of the adopted adolescent: Involvement of the biological mother. *Journal of American Academy of Child Psychiatry, 21*(3), 281-285.

Boneh, C. (1979). *Disruptions in adoptive placements: A research study.* Unpublished manuscript, Massachusetts Department of Welfare.

Boyne, J., Denby, L., Dettenring, J. R., & Wheeler, W. (1984). *The shadow of success: A statistical analysis of outcomes of adoptions of hard-to-place children.* Westfield, N.J: Spaulding for Children.

Branham, E. (1970). One-parent adoptions. *Children, 17,* 103-107.

Brodzinsky, D. M. (1987). Adjustment to adoption: A psychosocial perspective. *Clinical Psychology Review, 7*(1), 25-47.

Bush, M. (1984). The public and private purposes of case records. *Children and Youth Services Review, 6,* 1-18.

Camarata, C. (1989). *Profile of Hispanic adoptive families in Texas.* Austin, TX: Office of Strategic Management, Research and Development, Texas Department of Human Services.

Child Welfare League of America (1968). *Standards for adoption services.* Washington, DC: The Child Welfare League of America.

Child Welfare League of America (1989). *Standards for services for abused or neglected children and their families.* Washington, DC: The Child Welfare League of America.

Child Welfare League of America (1997). Child welfare privatized: Kansas is the first state to try it. *Children's Voice, 6*(3), 27-29.

Cipolla, J., McGown, D. B., & Yanulis, M. A. (1990). *Using play techniques to assess and prepare older children for adoption.* Chelsea, MI: National Resource Center for Special Needs Adoption.

Coyne, A., & Brown, M. E. (1986). Agency practices in successful adoption of developmentally disabled children. *Child Welfare, LXV*(2), 45-52.

Coyne, A., & Brown, M. E. (1986). Relationship between foster care and adoption units serving developmentally disabled children. *Child Welfare, LXV*, 189-198.

Denning, J. D., & Verschelden, C. (1993). Using the focus group in assessing training needs: Empowering child welfare workers. *Child Welfare League of America, LXXII*(6), 569.

Derdeyn, A. (1990). Foster parent adoption: The legal framework. In D. M. Brodzinsky & M. D. Schechter (Eds.), *The Psychology of adoption* (pp. 332-348). New York: Oxford University Press.

Dickson, L. R., Heffron, W. M., & Parker, C. (1990). Children from disrupted and adoptive homes on an inpatient unit. *American Journal of Orthopsychiatry, 60*(4), 594-602.

DiLeonardi, J. (1993) Families in poverty and chronic neglect of children. *Families in society, 74*(9), 557-562.

Egeland, B., Sroufe, D., & Erickson, M. (1983). The developmental consequence of different patterns of maltreatment. *Child Abuse & Neglect, 7*, 459-469.

Eisenberg, L. (1962). The sins of the fathers: Urban decay and social pathology. *American Journal of Orthopsychiatry, 32*, 5-17.

Elbow, M. (1987). The memory book: Facilitating terminations with children. *Social Casework, 68*, 180183.

Elbow, M., & Knight, M. (1987). Adoption disruption: Losses, transitions, and tasks. *Social Casework, 68*, 546-552.

Fahlberg, V. (1991). *A child's journey through placement.* Indianapolis, IN: Perspectives Press.

Famularo, R., Kinscherff, R., Bunshaft, D., Spivak, G., & Fenton, T. (1989). Parental compliance to court-ordered treatment interventions in cases of child maltreatment. *Child Abuse & Neglect, 13*, 507-514.

Feigelman, W., & Silverman, A. R. (1977). Single-parent adoptions. *Social Casework, 58*, 418-425.

Festinger, T. (1974). Placement agreements with boarding homes: A survey. *Child Welfare, LIII*(10), 643-652.

Festinger, T. (1983). *No one ever asked us . . . A postcript to foster care.* New York: Columbia University Press.

Festinger, T. (1986). *Necessary risk: A study of adoptions and disruptive adoptive placements.* Washington, DC: Child Welfare League of America.

Festinger, T. (1990) Adoption disruption: Rates and correlates. In D. M. Brodzinsky & M. D. Schechter (Eds.), *The psychology of adoption* (pp. 201-239). New York: Oxford University Press.

Folaron, G., & Hess, P. M. (1993). Placement considerations for children of mixed African American and Caucasian parentage. *Child Welfare, LXXII*(2), 113-125.

Garbarino, J. (1992). *Children and families in the social environment.* New York: Aldine de Gruyter.

Garbarino, J., & Vondra, J. (1987). Psychological maltreatment: Issues and perspectives. In M. R. Brassard, R. B. Germain, & S. N. Hart (Eds.), *Psychological maltreatment of children and youth* (pp. 25-44). New York: Pergamon Press.

Gardiner, E. A. (1987). The fost-adopt program: A review of the literature. Washington, DC: Child Welfare League of America.

Gilles, T., & Kroll, J. (1991). *Barriers to same race placement.* St. Paul, MN: North America Council on Adoptable Children.

Glaser, B., & Strauss, A. (1967). *The discovery of grounded theory.* Chicago: Aldine.

Glidden, L. M. (1989). Parents for children, children for parents: The adoption alternative. *Monographs of the American Association on Mental Retardation, 11.*

Glidden, L. M. (1991). Adopted children with developmental disabilities: Post-placement family functioning. *Children and Youth Services Review, 13*(5-6), 363-377.

Glidden, L. M., & Pursley, J. T. (1989). Longitudinal comparisons of families who have adopted children with mental retardation. *American Journal of Mental Retardation, 94*(3), 272-277.

Glidden, L. M., Valliere, V. N., & Herbert, S. L. (1988). Adopted children with mental retardation: Positive family impact. *Mental Retardation, 26*(3), 119-125.

Groze, V. (1986). Special needs adoptions. *Children and Youth Services Review, 8,* 363-373.

Groze, V. (1996). *Successful adoptive families: A longitudinal study of special needs adoption.* Westport, CT: Praeger.

Groze, V., & Rosenthal, J. A. (1991a). Single parents and their adopted children: A psychosocial analysis. *Families in Society, 72,* 67-77.

Groze, V., & Rosenthal, J. A. (1991b). A structural analysis of families adopting special needs children. *Families in Society, 72,* 469-82.

Groze, V., & Rosenthal, J. A. (1993). Attachment theory and the adoption of children with special needs. *Social Work Research & Abstracts, 29*(2), 5-12.

Hampton, R. (1991). Is violence in Black families increasing? A comparison of 1975 and 1985 national survey rates. *Child Welfare, LXIX*(6), 513-23.

Hardy, D. R. (1984). Adoption of children with special needs: A national perspective. *American Psychologist, 39,* 901-904.

Hartman, A. (1979). *Finding families: An ecological approach to family assessment in adoption.* Beverly Hills, CA: Sage Publications.

Hasenfeld, Y. (1987). Power in social work practice. *Social Service Review, 61,* 469-483.

Hegar, R. L. (1986). *Siblings in foster care: A descriptive and attitudinal study.* Unpublished doctoral dissertation, Tulane University.

Hegar, R. L. (1988). Sibling relationships and separations: Implications for child placement. *Social Service Review, 62*(8), 446-467.

Hegar, R. L. (1993). Assessing attachment, permanence, and kinship in choosing permanent homes. *Child Welfare, LXXII*(4), 367-378.

Hegar, R. L., & Hunzeker, J. M. (1988). Moving toward empowerment-based practice in public child welfare. *Social Work, 33*(6), 499-502.

Herrenkohl, R. C., Herrenkohl, E. C., & Egolf, B. P. (1983). Circumstances surrounding the occurrence of child maltreatment. *Journal of Consulting and Clinical Psychology, 51,* 424-432.

Hess, P. M., & Folaron, G. (1991). Ambivalences: A challenge to permanency for children. *Child Welfare, LXX*(4), 403-423.

Holody, R., & Maher, S. (1996). Using lifebooks with children in family foster care: A here-and-now process model. *Child Welfare, LXXV* (4), 321-335.

Hornby, H.C. (1986). Why adoptions disrupt . . . and what agencies can do to prevent it. *Children Today,15,* 711.

Hughes, R. C., & Rycus, J. S. (1989). *Target: Competent staff: Competency based in-service training for child welfare.* Washington, DC: Child Welfare League of America.

Ingrassia, M., & McCormick, J. (1994, April 25). Why leave children with bad parents? *Newsweek,* 51-56, 58.

Jewett, C. (1982). *Helping children cope with separation and loss.* Harvard, MA: Harvard Common Press.

Johnson, T. C. (1990). Important tools for adoptive parents of children with touching problems. In J. McNamara & R. McNamara (Eds.), *Adoption and the sexually abused child* (pp. 63-75). Portland, ME: Human Services Development Institute, University of Southern Maine.

Kadushin, A. (1970). *Adopting older children.* New York: Columbia University Press.

Kadushin, A., & Seidl, F. (1971). Adoption failure: A social work post mortem. *Social Work, 16,* 32-38.

Kagan, R., & Reid, W. J. (1986). Critical factors in the adoption of emotionally disturbed youths. *Child Welfare, LXV*(1), 63-73.

Kates, W., Johnson, R. L., Rader, M.W., & Strieder, F. (1991). Whose child is this? Assessment and treatment of children in foster care. *American Journal of Orthopsychiatry, 61*(4), 584-591.

Katz, L. (1986). Parental stress and factors for success in olderchild adoption. *Child Welfare, LXV*(6), 569578.

Kaufman, J., & Zigler, E. (1987). Do abused children become abusive parents? *American Journal of Orthopsychiatry, 57*(2), 186-192.

Keck, G., & Kupecky, R. (1995). *Adopting the hurt child.* Colorado Springs, CO: Pinon Press.

Kirk, D. (1981). *Adoptive kinship.* Toronto: Butterworths.

Lahti, J. (1982). A follow-up study of foster children in permanent placements. *Social Service Review, 56,* 556-571.

Lawder, E. A., Poulin, J. E., & Andrews, R. G. (1986). A study of 185 foster children 5 years after placement. *Child Welfare, LXV*(3), 241-251.

Lieberman, F. (1979). *Social work with children.* New York: Human Sciences Press.

Maas, H. S., & Engler, R. E., Jr. (1959). *Children in need of parents.* New York: Columbia University Press.

Marx, J. (1990). Better me than somebody else: Families reflect on their adoption of children with developmental disabilities. *Journal of Children in Contemporary Society, 21*(3-4), 141-174.

McInturf, J. W. (1986). Preparing special needs children for adoption through use of a life book. *Child Welfare, LXV*(4), 373-386.

McKelvey, C., & Stevens, J. (1994). *Adoption crisis.* Golden, CO: Fulcrum Publishing.

McKenzie, J. K. (1993). Adoption of children with special needs. In R. E. Behrman (Ed.), *The Future of Children, 3*(1),(pp. 62-76). Los Altos, CA: Center for the Future of Children, The David and Lucile Packard Foundation.

McMillen, J., & Groze, V. (1994). Using placement genograms in child welfare practices. *Child Welfare, LXXIII*(4), 307-317.

McNamara, J., & McNamara, B. (1990). *Adoption and the sexually abused child.* Portland, ME: Human Services Development Institute, University of Southern Maine.

McRoy, R. G. (1989). An organizational dilemma: The case of transracial adoptions. *Journal of Applied Behavioral Science, 25*(2), 145-160.

McRoy, R. G. (1990). Assessing cultural and racial identity. In S. Logan, E. Freeman, & R. G. McRoy (Eds.), *Social work practice with Black families.* White Plains, NY: Longman, Inc.

McRoy, R. G. (1994). *A study of adoption dissolutions in Texas*. Report submitted to the Texas Department of Protective and Regulatory Services.

McRoy, R. G. (1994). *Study of adoption dissolutions in Texas: Final report*. Unpublished manuscript.

McRoy, R. (1996). Racial identity issues for black children in foster care. In S. Logan (Ed.), *Black family strengths, self help, and positive change*. Boulder, CO: Westview Press.

McRoy, R. G., Grotevant, H. D., Ayers-Lopez, S. A., & Furuta, A. (1990). Adoption revelation and communication issues: Implications for practice with adoptive families. *Families in Society, 71*(9), 550-558.

McRoy, R. G., Grotevant, H. D., & Zurcher, L. A. (1988). *Emotional disturbance in adopted adolescents: Origins and development*. New York: Praeger.

McRoy, R. G., Oglesby, Z., & Grape, H. (1997). Achieving same-race adoptive placements for African American children: Culturally sensitive practice approaches. *Child Welfare, LXXVI*(1), 85-104.

McRoy, R. G., & Zurcher, L. A. (1983, 1986). *Transracial and inracial adoptees: The adolescent years*. Springfield, IL: Charles C. Thomas.

Meezan, W., & Shireman, J. F. (1982). Foster parent adoption: A literature review. *Child Welfare, LXI*(8), 525-535.

Meezan, W., & Shireman, J. F. (1985a). Antecedents to foster parent adoption decisions. *Children and Youth Services Review, 2/3*, 207-224.

Meezan, W., & Shireman, J. F. (1985b). *Care and commitment: Foster parent adoption decisions*. New York: State University of New York Press.

Mica, M. D., & Vosler, N. R. (1990). Foster-adoptive programs in public social service agencies: Toward flexible family resources. *Child Welfare, LXIX*(5), 433-446.

National Conference of Commissioners on Uniform State Laws (1994). *Uniform Adoption Act*.

National Commission on Foster Care (1991). A blueprint for fostering infants, children & youth in the 1990s. Washington, DC: Child Welfare League of America.

Nelson, K. A. (1985). *On adoption's frontier: A study of special needs adoptive families*. New York: Child Welfare League of America.

Newlin, P. B. (1997). Family preservation: Where have we been? How can we as social workers continue to collaborate? *Proceedings of the BiRegional Conference for Public Health Social Workers* (pp. 60-78). National Maternal and Child Health Clearinghouse.

Partridge, S., Hornby, H., & McDonald, T. (1986). *Legacies of loss—visions of gain: An inside look at adoption disruption.* Portland, ME: University of Maine Center for Research and Advanced Study.

Pelton, L. H. (1989). *For reasons of poverty: A critical analysis of the Public Child Welfare System in the United States.* New York: Praeger.

Pinderhughes, E. E. (1995). Toward understanding family readjustment following older child adoptions: The interplay between theory generation and empirical research. *Children and Youth Services Review, 18,* 115-138.

Proch, K. (1981). Foster parents as preferred adoptive parents: Practice implications. *Child Welfare, LX,* 617-625.

Risley-Curtiss, C. (1996, February). Foster children at risk for sexually transmitted diseases. *Family in Society, 77,* 67-80.

Rosenthal, J. A. (1986). *Final report on factors associated with Oklahoma special needs adoptive disruptions.* Unpublished manuscript.

Rosenthal, J. A. (1993). Outcomes of adoption of children with special needs. In R. E. Behrman (Ed.), *The Future of Children, 3*(1), (pp. 77-88). Los Altos, CA: Center for the Future of Children, The David and Lucile Packard Foundation.

Rosenthal, J. A., & Groze, V. (1992). *Special-needs adoption: A study of intact families.* New York: Praeger.

Rosenthal, J. A., Groze, V., & Aguilar, G. D. (1991). Adoption outcomes for children with handicaps. *Child Welfare, LXX*(6), 623-636.

Rosenthal, J. A., Groze, V., Curiel, H., & Westcott, P. A. (1991). Transracial and inracial adoption of special needs children. *Journal of Multicultural Social Work, 3*(1), 13-32.

Rosenthal, J. A., Motz, J. K., Edmondson, D. A., & Groze, V. (1991). A descriptive study of abuse and neglect in out-of-home-placement. *Child Abuse & Neglect, 15,* 249-260.

Rosenthal, J. A., Schmidt, D., & Conner, J. (1988). Predictors of special needs adoption disruption: An explanatory study and literature review. *Children & Youth Services Review, 10,*101-117.

Sack, W. H., & Dale, D. D. (1982). Abuse and deprivation in failing adoptions. *Child Abuse and Neglect, 6,* 443-451.

Sandmaier, M., & Family Service of Burlington County (1987). *When love is not enough.* Washington, DC: Child Welfare League of America.

Schmidt, D. M., Rosenthal, J. A., & Bombeck, B. (1988). Parents' views of adoption disruption. *Children and Youth Services Review, 10*(2), 119130.

Seelye, K. G. (1997, November 17). President is set to approve sweeping shift in adoption. *The New York Times,* p. 3.

Shireman, J., & Johnson, P. (1976). Single persons as adoptive parents. *Social Service Review, 50*, 103-116.

Shireman, J., & Johnson, P. (1986). A longitudinal study of Black adoptions: Single parent, transracial, and traditional. *Social Work, 31*(3), 172-176.

Silverman, A. R. (1993). Outcomes of transracial adoption. *Future of Children, 3*(1), 104-118.

Smith, S. L., & Howard, J. A. (1991). A comparative study of successful and disrupted adoptions. *Social Service Review, 65*(2), 248-261.

Staff, I., & Fein, E. (1992). Together or separate: A study of siblings in foster care. *Child Welfare, LXXI*(3), 257-270.

Sullivan, A. (1994, Spring). On transracial adoption. *Children's Voice, 3*(3), 4-6.

Tatara, T., Shapiro, P., Portner, H., & Gnanasigamony, S. (1988, July). *Characteristics of children in substitute and adoptive care: A statistical summary of the VCIS National Child Welfare Data Base, based on FY 85 data.* Washington, DC: American Public Welfare Association, Voluntary Cooperative Information System (VCIS).

Texas Family Code. (1995). *Race or ethnicity.* Sect. 162.308.

Timberlake, E., & Hamlin, E. R. (1982). The sibling group: A neglected dimension of placement. *Child Welfare, LXI*(8), 545-552.

Tremitiere, B. T. (1979). Adoption of children with special needs: The client-centered approach. *Child Welfare, LVIII*, 681-685.

Urban Systems Research and Engineering (1985). *Evaluation of state activities with regard to adoption disruption.* Washington, DC: Urban Systems Research and Engineering.

U.S. Department of Health and Human Services. (1988). *Study of national incidence and prevalence of child abuse and neglect.* Washington, DC: U.S. Department of Health and Human Services.

Valdez, G. M., & McNamara, J. R. (1994). Matching to prevent adoption disruption. *Child and Adolescent Social Work Journal, 11*, 391-403.

Veevers, H. M. (1991). Which child—Which family? *Transactional Analysis Journal, 21*(4), 207-211.

Videka-Sherman, L. (1991). Child abuse and neglect. In A. Gitterman (Ed.), *Handbook of social work practice with vulnerable populations* (pp. 345-379). New York: Columbia University Press.

Ward, M. (1979). The relationship between parents and caseworker in adoption. *Social Casework, 60*, 96103.

Ward, M. (1984). Sibling ties in foster care and adoption planning. *Child Welfare, LXIII*(4), 321-332.

Ward, M., & Lewko, J. H. (1987a). Adolescents in families adopting older children: Implications for service. *Child Welfare, LXVI*(6), 539-547.

Ward, M., & Lewko, J. H. (1987b). Support sources of adolescents in families adopting older children. *American Journal of Orthopsychiatry, 57*(4), 610-612.

Ward, M., & Lewko, J. H. (1988). Problems experienced by adolescents already in families that adopt older children. *Adolescence, 23*, 221-228.

Washington, V. (1994). *Families for kids of color: A special report on challenges and opportunities*. Battle Creek, MI: W. K. Kellogg Foundation.

Westhues, A., & Cohen, J. S. (1990). Preventing disruption of special-needs adoptions. *Child Welfare, LXIX*(2), 141-155.

Wimmer, J. S., & Richardson, S. (1990). Adoption of children with developmental disabilities. *Child Welfare, LXIX*(6), 563-569.

Windle, M., & Lerner, R. M. (1989). Reassessing the dimensions of temperamental individuality across the life span: The Revised Dimensions of Temperament Survey (DOTS-R). *Journal of Adolescent Research, 1*(2), 213-230.

Zigler, E., & Stevenson, M. (1993). *Children in a changing world: Development and social issues*. Pacific Grove, CA: Brooks/Cole.

Zimmerman, R. (1982). Foster care in retrospect. New Orleans, LA: *Tulane Studies in Social Welfare, 14*, 1-125.

Zumwalt, J. G. (1997, December). Nineteen—and alone in the world. *Parade Magazine*, 5-8.

Zwimpfer, D. (1983). Indicators of adoption breakdown. *Social Casework, 64*, 169-177.

# Index